Fragments of the Century

MICHAEL HARRINGTON

A Touchstone Book
Published by Simon and Schuster

A Touchstone Book
Published by Simon and Schuster
A Division of Gulf & Western Corporation
Simon & Schuster Building
Rockefeller Center
1230 Avenue of the Americas
New York, New York 10020

Manufactured in the United States of America

1   2   3   4   5   6   7   8   9   10

Library of Congress Cataloging in Publication Data

Harrington, Michael.
    Fragments of the century.

    (A Touchstone book)
    Autobiographical.
    Reprint of the 1st ed. published by Saturday Review
Press, New York.
    1.   United States—Social conditions—1945-
2.   United States—Politics and government—1945-
3.   Harrington, Michael.   I.   Title.
[HN58.H24   1977]   309.1'73'092   76-53796
ISBN 0-671-22653-3

For my sons,
Alexander and Teddy

Contents

Fragments of the Century

Prologue

This book contains some personal fragments of the twentieth century, some bits of a life in progress which bear the cultural and political markings of these times, some shards.

It is autobiographical, but not an autobiography. I have no desire to write a confession in the manner of Rousseau, nor even just to recount my days up until now. I speak of myself in order to understand better the age in which I live; I want to be intimate and nostalgic about an epoch, not about me. My remembrance of things past is, then, selective: I will not tell you whether I had trouble going to sleep; I have lingered over only those parts of my experience that seem to contain the evidence of history.

I was born on February 24, 1928, in St. Louis, Missouri, the son of a gentle lawyer who fought in France during the First World War and an idealistic mother who is a teacher and educator. My childhood was spent in a happy and secure middle-class home during the Great Depression, and though I vaguely recall breadlines and the shiny union buttons on the caps of truck drivers, it is from afar. I grew up in a pleasant Irish Catholic ghetto, which made the death of God particularly poignant for me.

I left St. Louis to be a poet and blundered upon the end of Bohemia in New York and Paris and other cities. In the years of Cold War repression I joined a minuscule radical movement which helped me to see working people, the poor, and the blacks at a time when sensible, pragmatic thinkers treated them as if they were invisible. As a result, I was an early, if quite modest, participant in the struggles led by Martin Luther King, Jr., in the formation of the New Left in the sixties, and in the campaign against the war in Vietnam.

I should be dejected. The seventies promise to be the neo-fifties, a period of retreat and conservatism and deradicalization. Already some of the best of the comrades with whom I shared the bad old days have turned their backs on our values. Indeed, it might seem that my life and times up until now describe a vicious circle: from the social neglect of Dwight Eisenhower through the hopes awakened by John Kennedy and the Lyndon Johnson of 1964 and 1965, then back again to the social neglect of Richard Nixon.

I should be dejected, but I am not. There is a revolution that proceeds apace at this very moment, even if the President of the United States and the disillusioned intellectual refugees from the Left do not recognize it. It is not that linear progression of confrontations and battles at the barricades dreamed by romantics in the sixties, which the newly sobered thinkers of the seventies now believe was a chimera. It is not a vogue, like long hair or rock music. It is transforming our psyches and spirits and even the way our eyes see, as well as our politics and economics.

This revolution is inevitable—only its outcome is in doubt. So it is that I will end, not on a note of assured triumph, but with a wager on the uncertain, sure to be unprecedented, future.

Above all, I hope that these pages may transmit some of the sights and sounds, the textures, of the history I am living. I have been on terms of some familiarity with the religious, political, and cultural crises of the age. I am, to be sure, like Eliot's Prufrock, only an attendant lord, one that will do to swell a progress, start a scene or two. Still, the century has written on me and perhaps these fragments may evoke, even illuminate, a time and place.

1. A Pious Apostasy

" 'What do I hear?' the old Pope now said, pricking up his ears. 'Oh Zarathustra, you are so pious for you believe with such disbelief. Some God in you drives you to this godlessness. Isn't it your piety itself that no longer permits you to believe in God?' "

Thus Spake Zarathustra

I am a pious apostate, an atheist shocked by the faithlessness of the believers, a fellow traveler of moderate Catholicism who has been out of the Church for more than twenty years.

I also have an intimate knowledge of the tragic papacy of John XXIII. Not that I ever knew that good and holy man. I saw him only once, on a summer's day in 1959 at a mass audience at Castel Gandolfo. While an officious monsignor was translating his remarks, John triumphed over the ceremony of the occasion by taking a large handkerchief out of his cassock with mischievous solemnity and then blowing his nose with a loud peasant honk. I was charmed by that little scene, yet it hardly turned me into an insider.

Still, my knowledge about the rise and tragedy of John's reign is quite personal. From the vantage point of a childhood and adolescence in St. Louis, I can understand what happened when the Pope stepped forward, boldly and innocently, to proclaim a springtime of faith. He told his flock to forget the dogmas for a while and listen to their hearts. They did, and discovered that they could no longer hear the voice of God within themselves. Looking back on that Irish Catholic world into which I was born, I know why—or at least part of the American reason why.

I

At first glance it is preposterous to describe the middle-class Irish Catholic society in St. Louis, Missouri, as a ghetto. But it was, and the deeper reality makes for what my Jesuit teachers called an argument *a fortiori:* if we, without serious memory of British oppression on the old sod or Yankee discrimination on the new, still lived in a pale of our own making, our experience shows how deep-rooted the ghetto tendency in America was. In exploring this point it will also be necessary to destroy some cherished stereotypes, particularly the identification of the Irish-American with the New York and Boston slums. Senator Eugene McCarthy, the ironic poet and ideologist, is as authentically Irish-American as Al Smith (who really wasn't that Irish after all).

In St. Louis we sang about how Irish Eyes are Smiling, not of Roddy McCorley true to the last on the gallows of Antrim Town. If you had told me that the Irish Republic was proclaimed in 1916 by a revolutionary Marxist named James Connolly who stood at the head of the first workers' army in the history of the world, I would have rejected it as a Communist lie. It was only years later, when Irish folk singer friends in a Greenwich Village bar led me to the chronicles of my own heritage, that I had any idea of such facts. True enough, family legend proudly told that my maternal grandfather, Patrick Richard Fitzgibbon, left Ireland only a step ahead of the authorities. But my cousins and I did not partake of that suffering, angry identity eight centuries of British savagery had imposed upon the Irish people. We were Americans.

Or more precisely, we were Midwestern Irish-Americans. In the Northeast the county associations from Killarney and Tipperary still survived, and wizened drinkers boasted on St. Paddy's Day of how they had fought for Irish freedom in the

Dublin General Post Office on that glorious Easter Monday of 1916. (The GPO could never have possibly accommodated the hordes of patriots who later claimed to have been there.) But in St. Louis even those memories had vanished by my generation, and all that remained was a vague, somewhat stagy Irish sentimentality and a cultural nostalgia perpetuated by wakes and tenors. Perhaps that was because the most assimilationist of the immigrants had pushed on from Boston and New York to the heartland. Certainly it was related to the fact that the Midwestern ruling class was not as culturally secure and socially vicious as the Eastern. In any case we were not born wounded.

It was a shock to me when I went as a sixteen-year-old to Holy Cross College in Worcester, Massachusetts, and met some of the Irish whom the very real ghettoes of the Northeast had made militantly paranoid. They were the children and grandchildren of workers who had read signs telling them "No Irish Need Apply." The despised Yankees had brutalized them into a sullen ethnocentrism, which was then democratically turned not simply against Jews and Negroes, but against Italians, Lithuanians, Poles, and other non-Irish Catholics as well. Their memories of persecution—in America, not Ireland— were still raw. Protestants, I learned, were "APAers," a reference to an anti-Catholic fraternal order, the American Protective Association, which had flourished half a century before mainly in the Mid and Far West, but whose fame had been kept alive by hatred in New England.

St. Louis was different. The living Irish Republican tradition of the East Coast cities was missing and social class and national origin were not as intertwined as in New York and Boston. Not that we all had lace curtains. During the Depression one of my uncles carried bags at the railroad station; another was out of work for several years. And I can remember going with my mother down to Father Tim Dempsey's St. Patrick's Church where that venerable priest—a legendary and saintly man who also arbitrated the bloody disputes of the

Irish underworld—presided over a breadline. But Irish did not necessarily mean poor or even working class. My grandfather lived in a big three-story house and grew roses in the back yard; one uncle was a judge, another a corporation attorney; my father was a patent lawyer and my mother a former schoolteacher who received her master's degree in economics from St. Louis University when I was about ten.

Moreover, St. Louis had been founded by French Catholics. The white Anglo-Saxon Protestants were, therefore, somewhat arriviste, and the Catholic Old Cathedral down by the levee had greater status and historical importance than any Episcopalian house of worship. Since we shared a religion with the aristocracy of the city—and a religion that was still hostile to intermarriage, at that—I was welcome at the larger debutante balls as a son of the middle class even though I was only two generations removed from steerage. And we did not necessarily cluster in neighborhoods. On the most important street of my youth there were more Jews than Irish.

The Irishman of the stereotype is the hard-drinking, brawling, embittered product of the New York and Boston slums. But out in the Midwest there was a different, much less frantic ethnic experience, particularly for those of us whose parents had fought their way into the middle class. Studs Lonigan was quite real up in Chicago, and I am sure that an equivalently tough Irish world existed in St. Louis. But it was not dominant, and the talented, or the lucky, could escape from it as their counterparts in the Northeastern cities could not. It was this much more relaxed and less embattled Catholicism that produced an extremely innovating Church in places like St. Louis and Chicago. St. Louis University, in a border city with racist traditions, integrated voluntarily in 1945, and Cardinal Ritter won a CIO award for ending segregation in the churches a few years later. And there was one marvelously liturgical parish where Monsignor Martin Helriegel had taught the schoolchildren and the ordinary parishioners to love, and sing, Gregorian chant.

And yet—the *a fortiori* begins to rumble—even that happy, secure and relatively unresentful world was a ghetto. For, as Freud so well understood, social habits of thought and action can survive centuries after their original function disappears. We did not know British imperialists, Yankee bosses, or Protestant princes first hand, yet they haunted our every waking moment. Above all, our ghettoization had been institutionalized by a Roman Catholic Church which had been engaged in a defensive struggle against the modern world for four hundred years or more. Once the cultural and political walls of our ghetto began to crack and crumble, our theology did too.

Let me be a bit more specific about that ghetto, which has now disappeared with such portentous consequences.

In part the life of my grandfather, Patrick Richard Fitzgibbon, was the familiar stuff of ethnic folklore. He lived in the classic Irish-American world of his immigrant generation, that seamless continuum in which being Irish, Catholic, and Democratic were but aspects of a single reality. He once pulled a rack of right-wing Catholic pamphlets from the wall of the vestibule of St. Rose's Church, remarking that politics had no place in the Church, i.e., that Father Coughlin had no right to attack Franklin Roosevelt. When he was bedridden during the 1944 Presidential campaign and discovered that the priest who was bringing him Communion was going to vote for Thomas Dewey, the Republican candidate, he refused to take the sacrament from the hands of such a heretic until after Roosevelt was reelected. Once, sitting on the porch after Republican neighbors had crossed over into the Democratic primary to vote for my Uncle David, Aunt Grace asked him if he would take a Republican ballot under similar circumstances. He rocked thoughtfully and replied, "Mind your own goddamned business."

Of such material is the plaster statue of the warm-hearted Irishman made. The love of scholarship does not, however, fit quite so neatly into that mold. When I was about eight or nine

I learned to serve mass. I memorized the Latin responses, and in keeping with the altar boy fashion of the time I could recite the Confiteor at absolutely breakneck speed without the least suspicion that I was thereby summoning the hosts of heaven to hear my sins. As I proudly mouthed the prayers for my grandfather, he stopped me and asked me to translate them. When I told him that I had only learned the Latin by rote, he all but dismissed the accomplishment as unworthy of a thinking child. The traditions of the land of saints and scholars had survived among us even if we didn't know its history.

My grandfather, who was a grade school dropout, knew the great speeches on Irish freedom by heart and could, of course, explicate every one of them. He read newspapers from Ireland and the *Manchester Guardian* as well. I was not, like many Jews, brought up in a fervid atmosphere of intellectuality born of religious commitment to the Book and reinforced by an anti-Semitism that made excellence a necessity. We had outlets in law, politics, and medicine that were still very much denied the Jews. But there was an Irish-American intellectualism—a ghetto intellectuality, to be sure—which went deep. The Jesuits were its quintessence and they, like John XXIII, were to become unwitting agents of disbelief.

The Jesuits were no longer the fabled conspirators for Christ of their own myth, priestly Machiavellians who schemed against Catholic monarchs as well as Protestants and who had even run their own bureaucratic collectivist state in Paraguay. That principled atheist Leon Trotsky said of them in that guise, "The Jesuits represented a militant organization, strictly centralized, aggressive and dangerous not only to its enemies but also to allies. In his psychology and methods of action the Jesuit of the 'heroic' period distinguished himself from an average priest as the warrior of the church from its shopkeeper." (Trotsky, Marxologues will note, made his Jesuit something of a Catholic Bolshevik.)

At St. Louis University High School and Holy Cross College the Jesuits' heroic period was long since dead. But something of the spirit of being shock troops of Christ on the perimeters of the Faith still persisted.

The names of my teachers were Kelly and Carey and Dieters and Kennedy and they came from middle-class, mainly Irish, backgrounds. They were, like my grandfather, democrats and, not so uniformly, Democrats. Unlike my grandfather, their intellectual drive had been disciplined by fifteen years of rigorous training that included three years of philosophy and four of theology. If they had become quite American, and not at all "jesuitical" in the conniving, European sense of the term, they had maintained significant links to their own history of four hundred years of militant elitism.

Ignatius of Loyola, a soldier turned saint, had founded the Society on a military model, and it became the cutting edge of the Counter-Reformation. By 1940, when I encountered the Jesuits in St. Louis, they still prided themselves on being able to stand up to the best the opposition had to offer. For the Jesuits, as Franz Mehring, the Marxist historian, has noted, spearheaded the Catholic movement that emerged as the medieval synthesis was disintegrating and which consciously sought to adapt the old values to the new, capitalist society. They were thus the modern critics of the modern world, and in my day in St. Louis they often earned their advanced degrees at the great secular universities. Their temptation to heresy, as their many enemies within the Church were always quick to point out (Pascal most brilliantly), was rationalist. I was being a true son of the Society when at the Catholic Worker I concluded that the doctrine of the Trinity—that God is three persons but a single nature—was not, as orthodoxy taught, a mystery. It was, I thought, a demonstrable proposition to anyone who understood the dialectical commonplace that one is always three.*

I do not, however, make the Jesuits so central to this dis-

---

* I would still defend my heresy, if a bit facetiously and from an atheist point of view. What I then found in Augustine's *De Trinitate* I later discovered in Hegel and Marx.

cussion simply because they played such a role in my own intellectual life. They were historically the vanguard organization of the Irish, who dominated Catholicism in the United States. In the second half of the nineteenth century the English-speaking Irish defeated their German brethren who wanted foreign-language parishes. From that time until the present, the decisive debates within American Catholicism took place among the Irish, and the Jesuits, who had taken a somewhat conservative stand in the original arguments, were the theorizing elite of the clerical stratum that ran the Church. They were largely drawn from the middle class; they staffed the best Catholic colleges and universities; they were the professional intellectuals in the ghetto. When their synthesis came unstuck in the post–John XXIII period, the event was to have a devastating impact upon the middle class whose mentors they were.

At St. Louis University High School (the Catholic Church, Lenny Bruce once said, is the only "the" Church; and with a similar arrogance we always called it "the" high school) we were a remarkable cross section of Catholic America. There were children of aristocrats and/or wealth whose parents felt that a Jesuit education was superior to that of any private school; a fair number of scholarship students from working-class backgrounds; and a majority from middle-class homes. There were no blacks, for the integration struggle was still several years distant in St. Louis. Aside from the fact that we were all of a single faith, there was nothing to set us off from the other high school students in the city.

But we followed a classic curriculum that had its antecedents in the Ratio Studiorum, the traditional Jesuit theory of education formulated in 1559, and it was not typically American. We took four years of Latin and two of Greek and, long before Russian space successes drove American educators to try to give academic excellence a status equal to athletic prowess, there was a deference accorded to intellect. As a freshman on the student newspaper I heard the sports editor discussing—freely, voluntarily, naturally—his sonnets with his friends. Later, when I took an extra course in history rather than suffer through physics, I was assigned to do independent research (I was fifteen): a critique of Jean Jacques Rousseau from the point of view of Jacques Maritain's analysis of the Reformation and the Enlightenment. The very last day of my final year at the high school, Mr. (now Father) Van Roo, a tall, ascetically thin and intense Jesuit scholastic who had shepherded us through Virgil, spent the entire period discussing a popular song, "Wrong, would it be wrong to kiss, seeing we feel like this?" It was, he argued, a typical example of the rampant relativism and hedonism of the culture.

Mr. Van Roo's analysis was a shrewd use of everyday speech and culture for philosophic purposes (for all I know he may have been reading some of the English theorists who had raised that method to the status of a principle). But it was also revealing of an essential aspect of a Jesuit education. Our knowledge was not free floating; it was always consciously related to ethical and religious values. So it was that at St. Louis University High School—and later at Holy Cross College—philosophy and theology were regarded as the sovereigns of the sciences, infinitely superior to physics and mathematics, which only dealt with proximate, not with last, causes.

Actually we and the Jesuits were laboring under a ghetto misapprehension. We thought we were learning the Thomism of the *Summa Theologica*. In reality, as I realized while reading Etienne Gilson some years later, our philosophy derived more from Francisco Suarez, a seventeenth-century Jesuit, than from Thomas. Suarez had given primacy to essence over existence in his reading of the perennial Catholic philosophy. He thus laid the basis for a decadent, rationalist interpretation of the Scholastic tradition, one that was admirably suited to the polemical needs of the Counter-Reformation—or of the embattled Catholic ghetto within Protestant America—because it could be reduced to a convenient catechetical form.

So we learned our "Thomism" in neat syllogisms. Thesis One in Epistemology: That which implicitly asserts which it explicitly denies is theoretically absurd; but universal skepticism implicitly asserts that which it explicitly denies (it is not skeptical about skepticism; it is an assertion of certitude, if only about the ubiquity of doubt); therefore universal skepticism is theoretically absurd. We disposed of the giants of Western philosophy in "scholia," short historic summaries of the errors of our philosophic opponents which followed upon succinct statements of our truth. I remember being particularly impressed by the way Immanuel Kant was destroyed in a few brilliant lines. How, I asked my professor, could a man so patently superficial ever have commanded anyone's attention? After I left college and read Kant for myself, secure in the knowledge that I had already refuted him, I immediately became a Kantian.

It was sex that brought the full weight of that ponderous Jesuit system to bear. Catholicism, as has often been noted, has been run for many centuries by celibates—but not, it should be added, by teetotalers. Therefore, sins of the flesh could be committed in the twinkling of a pornographic thought while a mortal sin of drunkenness required that a man drink himself into animal incomprehension (that simple distinction is, of course, a major clue to the social history of the Irish in America). We discussed sex endlessly and scholastically, and various retreat masters would refine our reflections (one said that an erection was nature's stop sign, an interpretation that seemed to us to be at direct odds with our experience). The crucial question was always the same: Where precisely did one cross the line from venial to mortal lust? Kissing? Soul kissing? Clothed petting or unbuttoned petting? Hours, even days, were spent in theorizing about the tantalizing boundary, not the least because even the most academic discussion about sex is libidinous. What we wrongly took to be the *Summa Theologica* was solemnly applied to what went on in the back seat of a car.

I am being somewhat unfair to my past. There were, to be

sure, ludicrous aspects of those philosophy courses with their rote wisdom. And yet the underlying assumption of all that sterilized categorizing was vibrant. The Jesuits were convinced that ideas have consequences, that philosophy is the record of an ongoing debate over the most important issues before mankind. It was sad that such an essentially passionate attitude toward the life of the mind was buried within stilted theses and scholia. Yet it was unmistakably there.

A preposterous coincidence, routine in these incredible times, might illustrate what I mean. One of my classmates at Saint Louis University High School—he arranged my first date and we and the young ladies went to the movies in his family's chauffeur-driven limousine—was Thomas A. Dooley. After the collapse of the French in Indochina, Tom Dooley, now a navy doctor, played a heroic role ministering to the Catholic refugees fleeing south. Later, he returned to Vietnam as a civilian, working among the people. He died tragically young and his memory is kept alive by people, most of them probably politically and theologically conservative, who venerate him as a sort of anti-Communist Albert Schweitzer. I never saw Tom Dooley after the mid-forties, but it is clear that we had developed profound political differences. And yet, I suspect each of us was motivated, in part at least, by the Jesuit inspiration of our adolescence that insisted so strenuously that a man must live his philosophy.

More to the present point, that Jesuit model of thought, which had been developed in Europe as a response to the Reformation, was admirably suited to the needs of the American Catholic ghetto. It provided the new middle class of Catholic lawyers and doctors with a somewhat sophisticated justification for their faith. If I am understood with some subtlety— for intellectual phenomena are never "reflections" of social reality but always, and only in part, a complex refraction of it —the Jesuit system was the philosophical analogue of the daily experience of a closed, Catholic world.

Indeed that decadent Jesuit Thomism functioned very

much like the vulgar Marxism of the Second International. In Germany and, above all, in Austria (as Joseph Buttinger's *Twilight of Socialism* poignantly evokes) the working-class movement before the rise of Hitler was a countersociety with its own cultural institutions, its cooperatives and theatre groups. It even had its own substitute for religion, a schematized and inevitabilist version of Marx that was as corrupt, and popular, as our reading of St. Thomas.* This gave an "aroma of necessity" to the struggles of the masses (the phrase is Gramsci's) and helped them to resist the blandishments of bourgeois culture. In much the same way, the Jesuits' "Scholastic philosophy" was designed to immunize us against infection from American secularism.

With our Jesuit philosophy we were supposed to be able to journey to the edge of the ghetto, and even to sally forth into the atheist darkness, with a reasoned confidence in our faith. It was, we were taught, only a highly articulate statement of the truths known to the humblest Catholic, and we treasured the legend that Louis Pasteur, great scientist that he was, had said that he envied the faith of Breton fishermen. At Holy Cross a good Jesuit friend and I would often discuss how leading professors at Harvard or Yale—or so our rumor said —were jealous of our integrated philosophy. In our closed system all non-Catholics were the victims of an invincible ignorance, struggling in the gloom for a light we already possessed.

* I have long thought that my Jesuit education predisposed me to the worst and best of Marx's thought. I was first attracted to the catechetical aspects of that great genius and the marvelous, superficial accounts of historic progression of which he was so unfairly made the sponsor. But on a deeper level, the Marxian Renaissance conception of a good society as a place in which every man might rise to intellectual heights was not unlike the Jesuit ideal, not the least because both philosophies, the revolutionary and the counterrevolutionary, were rooted in an aristocratic, classic heritage and disdained the utilitarianism of the bourgeoisie. In his *Prison Notebooks* Antonio Gramsci, who as an Italian Communist was a particularly bitter foe of the Jesuits, records similar feelings including his respect for the teaching of Latin in high school.

Indeed our insistence on the invincible ignorance of the unbelievers marked us as theological liberals by the standards of the day. Father Leonard Feeny, S.J., one of the few Americans imaginative enough to start a minor and ugly schism at that time, was disciplined for consigning all non-Catholics to hell. With greater tolerance, we serenely explained both faith and anti-faith as complementary parts of a unified system. Yet twenty years after I had learned its immortal certitudes that Jesuit synthesis was in a shambles.

It was a June morning in 1971 and the Holy Cross graduation was being held at Fitton Field, the football stadium. The parents sat in the stands, the graduates on the field, and the valedictorian was speaking from a tented podium. Significantly enough, I was there to make the commencement address and receive an honorary doctorate even though most sophisticated Catholics—and, I presumed, the authorities at Holy Cross—knew that I was an apostate. (I was invited to talk to the students; Frank Shakespeare, a Nixon Republican who had presided over the U.S. Information Agency and a classmate of mine, spoke to the alumni the same week. Had they switched audiences, both of us would probably have been booed.) The valedictorian casually told the assembled families and friends that only a minority of those receiving degrees that day were orthodox Catholics. In 1947, when I was the salutatorian, such a statement would, of course, have been untrue; but had it been made, the graduating class would have rioted and removed the offending speaker from the platform. What had happened between those two graduation ceremonies, separated by a mere twenty-four years?

Many things. One of them was that the ghetto walls had begun to crack. That does not mean that the great majority of Catholics, particularly the later immigrants from Southern and Eastern Europe, had changed their way of thinking. But the stratum that had given the Church its American officer corps had gone through momentous transformations. Irish

Catholics, the dominant minority within the Church, had moved into, and upward within, the middle class. In the mid-sixties data from the National Opinion Research Center showed that the Irish were twice as likely to go to college as the average American; in the early seventies the Center found them more integrationist than any other Catholic ethnic group (only the Jews outstripped them in this respect in the population as a whole). So the fathers had become secure enough to become Republicans, and some of the sons to become radicals. In that process 1960 obviously marked a turning point, for the moment that an Irish Catholic Democrat—even if from Harvard—became President, that continuum of politics, religion, and national identity in which my grandfather had lived was no longer a functional necessity for self-defense.

Once that happened, once the social bonds that reinforced Catholic ideology had been loosened, the Jesuits, and the American Church along with them, were the victims of their own ingenuity; my old teachers went sliding down the slippery slope they had prepared as a trap for their enemies.

The slippery slope is the nickname of that rationalist theory that holds that anyone who says A must therefore also say Z. In one current and popular Catholic statement of it, it is argued that anyone who permits the abortion of a defective fetus must accept the euthanasia of the retarded, the aging, or anyone else who does not conform to society's definitions of normality. One of the many problems with this theory is that it does not recognize the complexity of the human soul: the proponents of abortion reform usually also advocate the abolition of capital punishment and are, if anything, more sensitive to the claims of life than their opponents. Ironically, those who become impassioned about the rights of a fetus were often complacent about bombing women and children to death in Vietnam.

The Jesuit version of this doctrine was a sort of Rube Goldberg contraption in which every thesis was intricately wired to every other thesis and each part, no matter how small, was therefore indispensable. So one shoved antagonists down the slippery slope: deny God and there is no basis for morality and Nazi genocide is inevitable; deny Christ, or Mary, and there is no basis for God; reject the Pope, the bishop, the pastor, or any priest to whom you were talking, and you reject Christ, God, morality, etc. That great anti-Jesuit Dostoevsky understood this line of thought brilliantly and had one of his characters cry out, "If there is no God then what significance does my rank of captain have?" Once, however, the possibility of change and error were admitted within such a system— once Pope John opened a window in the Vatican—then the Jesuits went skittering down the slippery slope they had prepared for their adversaries. For if you could question any significant part of their synthesis, as John encouraged people to do, then the whole thing collapsed like a house of cards.

II

I fell down that slippery Jesuit slope long before it became a mass experience. I had decided that it was not only monstrous but a violation of the principle of causality for God to decree the infinite punishment of hell for any finite human act, no matter how terrible it might be. Once I came to that position—which is probably a commonplace among many Catholics in the post–Vatican Council era—the rationalist faith the Jesuits had jerry-built for me came tumbling down around my ears.

But then, after two years of indecisive apostasy, I read myself back into the Church. Both of my mentors in that reconversion were the authors of forbidden books, Blaise Pascal and Sören Kierkegaard. One night while reading the *Pensées* after a long immersion in Kierkegaard, I decided in a most unjesuitical fashion to return to Catholicism. I no longer felt that I could prove my faith, but now I was willing to make a wager, a doubting and even desperate wager, on it: *Credo quia absurdam*. I believe because it is absurd. Through the

French Jansenist and the Danish Protestant, I had rediscovered the existential, and Augustinian, tradition. Early the next morning I went over to Our Lady of Pompeii, an Italo-American church in the South Village, and went to confession to a priest who hardly understood English. That was well enough since it had been an exciting two years away from the prohibitions of Rome. That afternoon I searched out the Catholic Worker.

The Catholic radical movement in the fifties, which had the Worker at its center, turned out to be one more illustration of how deeply the ghetto spirit was embedded in American Catholicism. For it asserted itself not simply in the Irish middle class of St. Louis or among the Jesuits at Holy Cross, but even in an anarchist, pacifist, and Christian communist community.

All I knew of the Catholic Worker when I walked into its House of Hospitality on Chrystie Street just off New York's Skid Row (the Bowery) was that it was as far Left as you could go within the Church. When I entered that ramshackle building I did not even know that the Worker was committed to voluntary poverty or that the "staff" shared rooms, clothes, and food with the alcoholics and drifters who were admitted on a first-come-first-served basis. I asked for a job and a young lady told me, "You can work here, but we can't pay you anything." That sounded fine to me and I stayed for almost two years. There were about fifty people living in the house, and breadlines twice a day. Our ideal was "to see Christ in every man," including the pathetic, shambling, shivering creature who would wander in off the streets with his pants caked with urine and his face scabbed with blood.

Besides engaging in the corporeal works of mercy, we thought of ourselves as lay apostles at the center of a movement for Christian renewal. At mealtime, at the regular Friday night meetings, or at retreats or conferences at the (then) two Catholic Worker farms in New York State, we discussed the new developments in Catholic theology and philosophy. The talk was of Jean Danielou, Henri De Lubac, Yves Congar, Jacques Maritain, Gabriel Marcel, Romano Guardini, and the other, mainly European, thinkers who were, without knowing it, preparing the way for Vatican II. And we debated non-Catholic thinkers in that gentle Catholic household: Marx, Engels, Dostoevsky, Kropotkin, Emma Goldman, and Freud. My first speech in the Worker's Friday series was given one summer evening in the back yard when I shared my reading of Martin Buber's essays on communitarian socialism with an audience divided between the adepts and the somewhat perplexed refugees from the Bowery.

We were, we told ourselves, the leaven that would make the bread rise. We felt a kinship with the new experiments within the Church, particularly in France. And each time the Vatican disciplined the innovators, we suffered in spirit. I remember being tremendously impressed when a French Left Catholic who had come to the States as part of a Marshall Plan productivity mission told us of a French priest who had abandoned the Church and joined the Communist party. "If only he had left the Church for a woman," our French friend said. "That the Vatican could understand." Living in Cardinal Spellman's diocese, where sins of the flesh took precedence over those of the spirit and where it was usually assumed that a priest who became a Marxist did so because of a woman, the European attitude seemed marvelously sophisticated and respectful of intellectual values.

When Dwight Macdonald was working on a profile of Dorothy Day, the Worker's co-founder and presiding spirit, he came to a conference at our farm near Newburgh, New York. After hearing our intense and passionate discussions of theology, he told me that it reminded him of a Trotskyist debate in the thirties, except that the points of reference were Augustine and Aquinas, not Marx and Engels. The whole experience puzzled him, Dorothy Day most of all.

Dorothy is a presence. When she comes into a room even a stranger who had never even heard of her would realize that someone significant had just entered. When I met her in 1951 she was a striking woman in her early fifties with a severe, almost Slavic, and yet very serene face. With her hair braided around her head and the babushka she sometimes wore, she might have been a peasant or, had the Dostoevsky she read so avidly written of women as he did of monks, a mystic in one of his great novels. She had come to New York during the period of radical and Bohemian ferment during the First World War. She worked for a while as a reporter on the *Socialist Call,* was arrested as part of the feminist movement, and became a full-fledged member of the Bohemian revolutionary scene. She had known Mike Gold and Max Eastman and Eugene O'Neill. (O'Neill taught her Frances Thompson's "Hound of Heaven" in a Sixth Avenue speakeasy; years later, as he lay dying, Dorothy wired Cardinal Cushing to ask that he try and see him, which he did.)

Even in the early fifties her friends from the old days, like Alan Tate, Caroline Gordon, and Peggy Cowley were always turning up at the Worker. I was once given a seersucker jacket of Tate's from the common store and even though it was sizes too small I was proud to wear the raiment of an established poet. In those first innocent days when I had just begun to discover the complex world into which I had blundered, Dorothy startled me over coffee one morning when I mentioned one of my then favorite poets, Hart Crane. "Oh that Hart," she said. "I used to have breakfast with him all the time when I was pregnant with Tamar."

Tamar was Dorothy's daughter by a common law marriage that ended in the mid-twenties when she converted to Catholicism. When she joined the Church, she did not forget the radical convictions of her youth. At first, she functioned primarily as a Left-wing journalist, but then, during the worst years of the Great Depression in the early thirties, she teamed up with Peter Maurin, a strange, intense, self-taught Catholic philosopher, and together they launched the Catholic Worker, determined to prove that Catholics could be as militant about the cause of social justice as Communists. In its first period the

Worker was the center for all of the innovative currents within American Catholicism: trade unionism, utopianism, liturgical reform, and interracialism. But Italian-Americans were disturbed by Dorothy's pacifist and political attack on Mussolini's invasion of Ethiopia, and the entire Church—or almost all of it—was scandalized by her refusal to support Franco in Spain. When World War II came and the Worker stuck to its pacifist convictions, with some of its supporters going to federal prison and others to the Civilian Public Service camps set up for conscientious objectors, Dorothy lost most of her mass support.

When I got to know her in 1951, Dorothy was a bitter, principled opponent of the war in Korea, where Cardinal Spellman used to sprinkle holy water on the guns every Christmas. She was also determined to deglamorize her youthful days in the Village. She had seen the tragedy of alcoholism in horrible detail at the Worker and Malcolm Cowley's remark in *Exile's Return* that she used to drink the Italian mobsters under the table had lost its charm. She had become a symbol of Catholic radicalism and commitment, and people whispered behind her back that she would probably be canonized some day. The memories of a Bohemian girlhood were not for her.

Strangely enough, though, Dorothy mistook the triumph of her life in the Church for a failure. From its foundation, the Catholic Worker had inspired almost every one of the Catholic social movements. But for Dorothy, the pacifist-anarchist vision was global and every time someone accepted a portion of her program but rejected its totality she took it as a betrayal. In this attitude she was not so much logical or jesuitical (sustained analysis has never been Dorothy's forte) as existential and, to dare a phrase in the era of women's liberation, quite feminine. In any case, there were very few people who agreed with her on everything but hundreds of thousands who were profoundly influenced by her life.

Above all, Dorothy is a Catholic. That is a point that used to elude many outsiders, particularly in the fifties. There she

was, in the middle of the McCarthy period, an outspoken foe
of the Korean war and a champion of civil disobedience, active in the fight to save the Rosenbergs from death, a defender
of civil liberties for Communists. People like Dwight Macdonald initially assumed that she must be some sort of Quaker in-
filtrator within the Church of Rome. But she spoke of Pope
Pius XII as our "dear, sweet Holy Father" and publicly proclaimed what she had once privately told Archbishop (later
Cardinal) McIntyre when the New York Archdiocese was
thinking of disciplining her for her stand on the Korean war:
that if Cardinal Spellman told her to close down the paper,
she would. For Dorothy, and the rest of us, were Catholics,
however politically radical we might be.

Our religion was sacramental, marked by the outward signs
of its inner grace. In that sense it was the very antithesis of the
Quaker emphasis upon a completely unadorned and unstruc-
tured worship. Every evening we would line up in facing rows
and recite the monastic Compline—those consoling psalms of
the traditional prayers at the end of the day that called upon
the protection of the Almighty for his servants. We made our
retreats in silence and sometimes the food was blessed by
sprinkling water on it from the leaves of a fresh cut branch.
Our complaint was not that Cardinal Spellman was too Catholic but that he was not Catholic enough. We thought that bishops and popes should actually follow the Sermon on the
Mount.

That spirit affected me so profoundly that it almost led me
to the penitentiary. In the late forties I became a conscientious
objector on my own. Ever the son of the Jesuits, I argued that
the atomic bomb was a disproportionate and immoral means
to any end and that it therefore violated the conditions for a
just war as developed by Aquinas, Suarez, and Bellarmine.
When the Korean war broke out, I felt that I had to refuse to
go, but I was alone in my decision; I didn't know another C.O.
It was a time of intense emotion, of isolation, and there were
enormous pressures from my family in St. Louis against my

taking such a position. (I suspect that it must have seemed to them not simply un-American, but worse, Protestant.) After stormy confrontations I volunteered for the Army Medical Reserve with the understanding that I would soon be activated and sent to Korea

Some bureaucrat in the Pentagon thereupon changed my life. He decided that the federal reserves would not be called up, so in January, 1951, I transferred to a New York unit. In February I joined the Worker. On drill nights I felt myself an outcast. I waited until everyone was at dinner and then sneaked out of the house in my uniform, the livery of my compromise. There was constant discussion of how I could be so unprincipled. One gentle pacifist, Hector Black (the last I heard of him, in the mid-sixties, he was living and working in a ghetto in Atlanta), was particularly persuasive.

But it was the army itself that finally turned me into a complete conscientious objector. My unit had been ordered to active duty for summer training in 1951. It was a hospital group based in Brooklyn, and I had explained my ethical position to the completely sympathetic, and mainly Jewish, officers. They had assured me that my noncombatant scruples would be respected, but it turned out they had no control over the matter. As soon as we arrived at Camp Drum higher authority sent me, and all the others who were not veterans, to the infantry. I did not want to seem a fanatic—soldiers can be a tyrannically conformist peer group—and yet, as I read the psalms in my breviary, I was convinced that I had to take a stand. The next morning I asked to see the captain.

It was a ludicrous scene. I was terrified at my own audacity in challenging a gigantic system of authority. I also did not know how to salute, whether to keep my cap on indoors, or anything about military etiquette. I stood there, trembling and filled with the Holy Spirit, while the captain yelled at me that if I were a C.O., why in the goddamned hell had I volunteered for the army? In exasperation he finally said that I didn't have to take a rifle but that I must march with the troops to the first exercise. "What is that," I asked. "Calisthenics," he said. It turned out to be hand grenade practice. That precipitated another crisis and I thought for a while that I was headed for the stockade. Eventually, though, the army threw up its hands and sent me back to the medics.

And yet my emotions were mixed. One day I was walking along the road and an infantry column marched by. For all my conscience, I yearned to be one of them (I understood how Simone Weil, the Jewish radical, could write that her heart had involuntarily quickened when a Nazi band passed along the street). But what maintained and stiffened my will was that almost primitive Christian sense of mission that pervaded the Worker. When I came back to New York I went off to a Benedictine abbey for a three-day private retreat. The days in that place had a simple and flowing sweep; it was like living a Gregorian chant. In the evening when the monks filed out onto the altar for Compline, I was alone in the darkened body of the church. There is a state of being that the religious call interior silence. I lived in it briefly and decided that, no matter what the cost, I would break all connections with the army.

So I told my unit in Brooklyn that I was resigning. The officers were willing to accept that, but the army telexed back, in an official fury, that I could not leave. I turned in my uniform, refused to go to drills, and waited to be arrested. After about a year of dangling, I was turned over to my local draft board rather than to the federal authorities and they gave me full recognition as an objector. Then the technicians at the induction center (C.O's had to take the regular physical) made such an outrageous misreading of my chest X-ray that I was sure there was some coded note on my file to reject this crackpot one way or another. Over my objections, both verbal and written—I wanted to prove that pacifists were not shirkers and I was therefore anxious to do my alternate public service —I was declared physically unfit and my records were stored, as a cheerful clerk told me, "among the guys with no arms and no legs." About two years later the reserve bureaucracy, which did not recognize mavericks or conscience, automatically ground out an honorable discharge when my original term was up. So you might say that I am a veteran.

Years later when I heard the good news of Pope John I assumed that *aggiornamento* of the Church would mean a return to the simple verities and the religious passion of the Worker. I had dinner during Christmas of 1959 with my Uncle Dave and his good friend Father Dismas Clark, the "hoodlum priest" who spent his time with prisoners and men condemned to death. Clark, a most unjesuitical Jesuit, was beside himself with joy at the news that John had gone to Regina Coeli jail in Rome. So was I. Neither of us knew that the process the new Pontiff had set in motion would undermine the entire ghetto, even its radical corner. For we at the Worker, for all our rebellion and jail sentences, were impeccably orthodox.

My own Pascalian wager ended on a bus in December, 1952, when I was going to speak at a communion breakfast in Pennsylvania. By the time I arrived at the church I had decided that I could not go to communion since I no longer believed in the faith, not even by way of an existential leap. I gave a little talk on civil rights and, to my embarrassment on this first day of my definitive apostasy, a woman came up to me and said that I had helped her become a better Christian. Riding back to New York, I was not, as I had anticipated, racked by a Dostoevskian sense of loss. The whole experience was, I am afraid, about as tragic as getting off a streetcar. What I did not know then was that twenty years later, as the Church began to come unstuck, I would become an atheist fellow traveler of moderate Catholicism.

III

At first I thought that John XXIII would be able to initiate a gentle revolution from above within his Church. I remember the hope I felt one December night in 1963 when I was walking through the streets of Rome with John Cogley, an old

friend and a brilliant participant-observer of American Catholicism. It was a poignant time for the two of us, children of
the Irish Catholic Church in the American Midwest. We talked
in the shadow of two deaths.

I was born the year Al Smith lost the Presidency. Throughout my youth I was told that he had been defeated because he
was a Catholic (the truth is much more complicated than that,
as I learned later). John Cogley was a few years older, but a
member of the same generation. Now John F. Kennedy, who
had symbolized the acceptance of the Catholic as American,
had just been murdered. My wife Stephanie and I had heard
that terrible news in Milan. In our shock we had roamed the
city looking for Americans with whom we could share our
grief. The men at the Associated Press office received us as if
we were members of the dead President's family: they gave us
a desk and brought us each new report from the ticker. Yet
they were only Italian, even if magnificently and generously
so. When we finally did hear American voices back at our hotel, they came from some conservative Texas businessmen who
were discussing what kind of rifle sights must have been used
in the killing.

So in the middle of the night we called the Cogleys, who
were spending the year in Rome. During the 1960 campaign
John had worked on the national Kennedy staff and had
helped prepare the candidate for his crucial presentation on
church and state before the ministerial association in Houston. He and his wife were not surprised that we phoned. All
night other Americans, with the same sense of wounded na-
tionality, had been calling. So walking with them through
Rome a few weeks later was like an Irish wake, sad but talkative and clannishly close.

The other death that hovered over us that evening was, like
that antiphon that concludes the Gregorian requiem, "The
Angels lead thee into paradise," joyous. John XXIII had died
earlier in the year but his passing seemed the culmination of
life, not, as with Kennedy, its obscene denial. That after-

noon we had all attended a press conference near St. Peter's to
mark the end of one of the sessions of the Second Vatican
Council. There was a hustle and bustle as the experts, the *pe-
riti,* told of a Church on the eve of epochal fulfillment. And on
that chill, wet December night in Rome it seemed to us that
the window John had opened in the Vatican indeed looked
out upon the springtime. In fact, it allowed people to see
God's funeral.

The breakup of the Catholic ghetto—in the world as well
as in St. Louis and America—had been the proximate cause
of the crisis of Catholicism. But it would not have had such
enormous, and devastating, effect if it had not coincided with
the death agony of God. So what my Irish and Midwestern
experience refracts is the most crucial spiritual process of the
twentieth century.

God began to die a long time ago. In the seventeenth century that most subtle of Christians, Blaise Pascal, had already
understood that the modern world was transforming the very
role and position of divinity. Writing in a time of social and
cultural upheaval, a man of the new science and the old religion, Pascal realized that the only possible God was now *deus
absconditus,* the hidden God. (Lucien Goldmann's *Le Dieu
Caché* is a brilliant analysis of that Pascalian theology and the
spirit of classic French tragedy.) When Pascal wrote that the
"vast silences of the infinite" frightened him, he was not talking of the heavens but of the new space mathematics was defining. Over the centuries his fears were, of course, corroborated. The more man created the world in which he lived, the
less God was necessary, in Dietrich Bonhoeffer's phrase, as a
"working hypothesis."

In the twentieth century it was the Protestants who first became candid about these things. In the writings of that pro-
tean thinker Karl Barth God is utterly transcendent and the
Catholic effort to proceed by way of analogy from the finite
to the infinite is condemned as a blasphemous attempt to lay
hands upon Him. Then in the theology of Tillich and Bult-

mann and Bonhoeffer the process proceeded apace. One admitted an atheistic reality and then tried to baptize it by an act of the religious will. In his famous letters from prison Bonhoeffer was admirably frank:

> The time when people could be told everything by means of words, whether theological or pious, is over, and so is the time of inwardness and conscience—and that means the time of religion in general. We are moving towards a completely religionless time; people as they are now simply cannot be religious any more. Even those who honestly describe themselves as "religious" do not in the least act up to it, and so they presumably mean something quite different by "religious." Our whole nineteen-hundred-year-old Christian preaching and theology rest upon the "religious *a priori*" of mankind. "Christianity" has always been a form —perhaps the true form—of "religion." But if one day it becomes clear that this *a priori* does not exist at all, but was a historically conditioned and transient form of human self-expression, and if therefore man becomes radically religionless—and I think this is already more or less the case . . . what does that mean for Christianity?

Bonhoeffer went on in a brave and doomed attempt to find some basis for faith in such a world, to seek for a "religionless Christianity," a way of speaking of God in a world without religion. However laudable the intention, that is an impossibility. The devastating attack upon the "death of God" theology is so simple and yet so persuasive: it is a patent contradiction in terms.

As a contemporary American Catholic philosopher, Eugene Fontinell, wrestled with the problem, "If one insists that the only worth-while function of creeds, dogmas and sacred scripture is to give knowledge [about God] then I think that the game is over and we are forced from the evidence supplied from historical experience to conclude that they are worthless. But, in my opinion, that is not their function. Rather they must be seen as efforts of the community to articulate its continuing encounter with the 'nameless one.' " And Leslie Dewart, the author of an influential book of the sixties, *The Future of Belief,* holds that it is an anthropomorphic inheritance from Greek philosophy that makes Catholics talk about God as a "being," as "someone" "out there." In Dewart's analysis, it may even be necessary to drop the very name of God (while retaining the Catholic religion) or to devise new ways to speak about God "without naming him at all."

Dewart and Fontinell were at least quite serious in attempting to believe under impossible theological conditions. More timorous people responded—I speak now of a tiny, but quite influential, minority who, if past experience is any guide, are the precursors of the masses—by a shamefaced, hypocritical Catholic atheism. They retain the outward trappings of belief, particularly when they help to legitimate a personal political opinion, but they have abandoned its substance. They make me, as an atheist, a sympathizer of moderate Catholicism, for I find their decision to stay in a church in which they no longer believe to be irreligious—perhaps the only form of genuine blasphemy open to modern man. Like Zarathustra, I am much too pious to believe in that pathetic "God."

Others, more serious than the Catholic atheists, substituted social action for theology. But one need not believe in God, or Christ, or the Church to struggle for the good society. When prelates were blessing reaction in the nineteenth century atheistic socialists were acting in a profoundly "Christian" way. It is a gain that the priest and nun are now to be found so often on the picket line, and the social encyclicals of John XXIII mark a great advance for both religion and the politics of the Left. But the priest, nun, and Pope must, if they remain true to their commitment, insist that there is some supernatural inspiration that brings them to the common struggle with the atheist and the agnostic. Activism can never replace faith even though it can be fecundated by it.

That point was essential to the Catholicism of the Catholic Worker—and, for that matter, the Catholicism of the Catholic

Church since St. Augustine. In a seminal dispute Augustine had argued against the Donatists who believed that a bishop's betrayal of his trust in the face of persecution deprived him of his episcopal powers. Augustine held that an individual's worth—his goodness or badness—had nothing to do with the objective validity of the sacraments he administered. Their grace, he said, depended upon God, not man. On the basis of this distinction we at the Worker recognized in Cardinal Spellman—pro-war, anti–civil libertarian, orthodox in the most narrow and deadly sense of the term—the vicar of Christ. For the ultimate truth of a religion does not rest upon its worldly virtues, or even on how it practices what it preaches, but upon the existence of the God whom it witnesses. The moment a church forgets that central reality it ceases to be a church.

The most serious attempt to face up to this demand has led post-Christian Christians back to Hegel. Hegel taught that man's growing self-consciousness was at the same time the consciousness of God; that human progress marked the emergence of, and was inspired by, the Idea. Fontinell is saying something like that when he focuses upon the "efforts of the community to articulate its continuing encounter with the 'nameless one.' " So are those Catholics who use the popular definition (since Vatican II) of the Church was the "people of God." In Hegel's day, when the religious *a priori* still existed, such a sentiment made sense for there actually was a community of belief. But that has vanished now—or is vanishing—and what the new, Hegelian Christians invoke is not so much God as the common nostalgia caused by his disappearance.

The encounter with the "nameless one" may well provide spiritual sustenance for a small minority of sophisticated intellectuals. It will not, however, sustain a church or provide a basis for a culture. Even if one assumes Fontinell to be right, his position is one more proclamation of the end of Catholicism. And indeed among my own friends perhaps the most tough-minded and religious are quite prepared to accept just such a conclusion: that the Church must disappear so that the faith may live; that the salvation of Christianity lies in a return to a sectarian existence where the believers are few but the doctrine is serious. Alas, even that courageous perspective is doomed. For God is dead.

If John XXIII had not distracted the faithful from the rote accomplishment of liturgies that had lost their meaning, perhaps they would not have noticed that their deity was missing. Then the Roman Church might have survived, serene and hierarchal, for another fifty years or so. John was, however, too religious, too saintly a man to adopt a strategy of evasion. He wanted people to live their God, so he jostled them out of their pious routine, and that is what alerted them to the fact that God does not exist any longer.

An analogy from a marvelously romantic movie I saw many times in my youth, *Lost Horizon,* might illuminate my point. In that filmed version of James Hilton's novel, life in the valley of Shangri-la lasts far beyond normal expectations. A woman, ancient chronologically but still relatively youthful because of the atmosphere of the place, is driven to the limits of her patience by decades of boring contentment and persuades a new arrival, a young man who has fallen in love with her, to help her strike out for the outside world. Hardly has she left the valley than her face turns into the mask of a wrinkled crone. So, too, with the Church. If it had stayed within its ghetto it would have survived for a time. But the moment that John, with that miraculous faith of his, propelled it into inhospitable regions, the end came rushing on.

In saying this I am not for a moment making a brief for Paul VI and his attempt to close the window John opened. The tragic element in John's action was that it was as necessary as it was unwittingly destructive. The historic moment could not long have been deferred; the choice was between a slow death and a desperate attempt at life. The pathetic aspect of Paul's reign is that his attempts to revive the old authoritarianism in dealing with birth control and clerical celibacy are as understandable as they are inherently ineffective.

God is dead; that is the fundamental fact. In St. Louis,

Missouri—and, I suspect, throughout America—Catholics began to become conscious of that epochal fact in part because their ghetto, which was the social reality that reinforced their philosophy, was shattered. And the Jesuits of my youth, with their superficial, mechanistic vision of the slippery slope, were right. Deny any substantial principle of that intricate and defensive faith created by Catholics in the centuries since the Reformation and the entire structure starts to come tumbling down. Open up the windows, break down the walls, let in the air, and you invite tragedy.

The end, to be sure, is not going to come suddenly. It has begun among the priests and the intellectual elite today. In a decade, or perhaps in several, the masses will assimilate the news. That process is not one I greet joyously, for it leaves a void that atheistic humanism, alas, has thus far failed to fill. When one looks back upon why it happened, John XXIII certainly does not appear to have been its cause. He was only the warm and infinitely appealing saint whom history, with Hegelian cunning, summoned at the right moment in time to preside, filled with the Holy Spirit, over the beginning of the end of the Christian era.

2. The Death of Bohemia

In a frenzy of youthful discovery I found the seacoast of Bohemia on the banks of the Mississippi River in the late 1940s. The port of entry was a bar called, obviously enough, Little Bohemia on a side street just above the levee in St. Louis. I had already learned enough modernist lessons so that, to the horror of sober burghers, I used to push Alexander Calder's mobile at the Art Museum to set it dancing. So it was an epiphany to join the painters and the other regulars in the back of the room at Little Bohemia where they talked about art and psychoanalysis and the motherland of Greenwich Village. There was a business and warehouse district outside and, of a summer's evening, the streets seen through the door were always lonely and deserted, perfect setting for beer and romanticism and the lyric violin passage from Falla's "El Amor Brujo" on the jukebox. Sometimes there was a party later on in an apartment painted black that had mattresses instead of furniture and no doors, not even on the bathroom.

I attended that party for about two decades in New York, San Francisco, Paris, Ibiza, and quite a few other places. Now it is over. I had encountered Bohemia in about the one hundred and twentieth year of its existence and on the eve of its death. Bohemia could not survive the passing of its polar opposite and preconditioned, middle-class morality. Free love and all-night drinking and art for art's sake were consequences of a single stern morality: Thou shalt not be bourgeois. But once the bourgeoisie itself became decadent—

33

once businessmen started hanging non-objective art in the boardroom—Bohemia was deprived of the stifling atmosphere without which it could not breathe.

That is why the Counterculture freaks have such a difficult task falling off the margin of the society. They have no Babbitt to tell them who they are not; they lack that solemn sense of anti-values that was at the center of Bohemian irreverence. For Bohemia, even though it dressed with "aggressive political untidiness" (the phrase is Christopher Isherwood's), was always a conservative place. It appeared in France in the 1830s during the middle-class monarchy of Louis-Philippe when bankers ruled for the first time in their own name. Baudelaire wrote of those years when as riches came to appear as the final goal of the individual, beauty and charity disappeared and debauchery was the only decent alternative. So the original Bohemians (the French thought that all gypsies came from Bohemia and that artists were becoming gypsylike) protested outlandishly in the name of artistic tradition against a boorish ruling class. That is why Baudelaire, as he smoked hashish, thought of himself as an aristocrat, a dandy in an age of upstarts. Never has immorality been so moralistic.

From Baudelaire's time until a few years ago there were all kinds of Bohemias: of aristocrats, workers, American Negroes, frauds, geniuses, dilettantes on swinging tours of poverty, and many more. Bohemia was generally Left-wing in France and sometimes Right-wing in Germany; it was a bitter necessity for the outcast artists of late-nineteenth-century Paris and a lark for Mabel Dodge as she featured Wobblies like Big Bill Haywood and anarchists like Emma Goldman in her Lower Fifth Avenue salon before World War I. At the University of Chicago in 1948 there was even a graduate student Bohemia, spread out through a decaying interracial neighborhood with appropriately seedy rooms for rent (it has since been urban-renewed into academic gentility). There were book stores like the Red Door that sold the littlest of little magazines, and campus organizations would raise funds by showing obscure Surrealist film classics or documentaries on the Bolshevik Revolution. There were, of course, bars, those perpetual town meeting houses of any Bohemia, where blacks and whites drank together a generation ahead of the fashion and sang about the Spanish Civil War rather than happy college days. One couple I knew kept the complete works of Trollope in the bathroom for browsing and the husband regularly broke into stream-of-consciousness monologues about the most intimate details of his marriage while his wife listened serenely.

Everyone I knew at Chicago had a poem or play or novel in the works and one history student was carefully and falsely documenting his life so that if he ever became famous he would drive his biographers mad. Lindy, the first girl whom I dated there, was typical of the place. She lived with relatives and after listening to romantic music—Sibelius' "Swan of Tuonela" was a favorite—typed her novels in the bathroom in the middle of the night. Her books were primarily about people at the university, dealt candidly with their sex lives, and sometimes used real names, a fact that enlivened meetings of the Creative Writing Club where manuscripts were read. It also brought a letter from a New York editor who rejected her novel but invited her to dinner. When we agreed, with some unpleasantness, to stop seeing each other, she threatened to write a novel about me.

Several years later I learned that Lindy had killed herself. But at the time that dark denouement, and the ambiguities that were to afflict the rest of us, were not yet apparent. We practiced the established rites of nonconformity found in the academic underground in places like Antioch, Sarah Lawrence, Bard, Black Mountain, Reed, and Bennington. The night most of the master's candidates in English literature stood on mailboxes along Fifty-fifth Street could thus be explained as a not particularly imaginative exercise in collegiate Dada. But what made Chicago unique was that all this was done under the patronage of Aristotle and Aquinas.

Robert Hutchins, the guiding genius of the university, abolished intercollegiate football in the thirties and, with one stroke, appealed to that tiny minority that saw college not as a four-year beer bust or a middle-class trade school, but as a Left Bank of the mind where ideas, like the poems and paintings of Bohemia, were their own excuse for being. Hutchins then added insult to injury by sponsoring an Aristotelian-Thomist revival in the middle of the Depression, when most fashionable thinkers were turning toward a superficial Marxism. There were, to be sure, some people at Chicago who were studying law and even business administration. And by an incredible irony the Manhattan Project conducted the first controlled nuclear fission in the history of mankind at Stagg Field; the end of intercollegiate football had facilitated the creation of the atom bomb. Yet the dominant mood at the university was Aristotelian-Thomist Bohemian, for there was an iconoclastic respect for standards and a contempt for middle-class utilitarianism.

One December evening in 1949, while on my way home to cram for a crucial exam the next day, I bought a copy of Joseph Conrad's *Victory,* a book that had nothing to do with the test or any other course of mine. When I got to my room I decided to read a few pages of the novel before I got down to the serious business of studying. At four in the morning I finished Conrad's poignant account of how a man cannot hide himself from life and love. That epitomized the spirit of Chicago in those days: there were even some students who waited for months to go to the registrar's to find out their grades on the gounds that a professor's opinion of their work was an irrelevance. And there was a rage to talk, to discuss, to articulate, that surged through bars and drugstores and love affairs.

We were, to be sure, pampered rebels. Some of us received allowances from home that provided us with the material security to disdain the middle class. But what made us something more than just privileged and posturing youths having a fling on the edge of society was that we really were serious, and even passionate, about ideas for their own sake. It was that commitment that linked us to the tormented and starving geniuses of the School of Paris. It also made our bizarre Aristotelian-Thomist Bohemia part of a major cultural movement in the America of the thirties and forties.

There was no basis for a Right-wing Bohemia in this country because there was no feudal past for the opponents of middle-class morality to identify with. Instead there was the spiritual domination of white, small-town, Protestant America, the rule not of a bourgeoisie, which was bad enough, but of a booboisie (Mencken's word), which was worse. So in the years before World War I the political and cultural revolutionaries were comrades. In Greenwich Village there was a promiscuous confraternity of dissidence: of free love and free verse, socialism and anarchism, John Reed's radical journalism and Eugene O'Neill's realistic theatre, of painters from the Ashcan School and muckrakers, of Max Eastman's *Masses* with its anti-capitalist cartoons and Margaret Young's *Little Review* with its imagist poems and Ezra Pound's latest European discovery.

But by the thirties all that had changed. The Stalinization of Communism had poisoned the political as well as the literary Left. Indeed, it turned out that Babbitt and Stalin had quite similar views on the arts: they wanted symphonies that could be whistled and paintings that told stories with morals. They only differed as to what nonartistic values art should serve, the one favoring Midwestern boosterism, the other Russian totalitarianism. It was a group of intellectuals around *Partisan Review* who, in keeping with Bohemian tradition, rose up against the new philistines of the Left in the name of high standards. They simultaneously defended Marxism in politics and nonrepresentationalism in the arts; they admired T. S. Eliot, the self-proclaimed classicist, royalist, and Anglo-Catholic, and Leon Trotsky, the organizer of the October Revolution.

Some years later, in 1952, I got a glimpse of the twilight of that *Partisan Review* world at a party at Dwight Macdonald's apartment in an old brownstone on the eastern fringe of the Village. There was intense literary-political talk but the feature of the evening was a tiny opera company under the direction of Noah Greenberg—once the leader of a Trotskyist faction in the seamen's union, later the founder of the Pro Musica, a group that specializes in Renaissance music—which performed Purcell's "Dido and Aeneas" in the living room. This synthesis, in which the lions of Marxism and the lambs of high culture lay down together, was breaking up even as I observed it at that party. (For instance, Macdonald, who had edited the anarcho-pacifist magazine *Politics,* was now writing for *The New Yorker.*) But it had dominated the best of American intellectual life in the thirties and forties and it was one reason why the Bohemian style and Aristotelian-Thomist content at Chicago were not so contradictory after all.

In the late forties Chicago was, as always, the second city. New York was the center of Bohemia. I arrived one fall afternoon in 1949, put down my bags, and went out to find Greenwich Village.

I did not know it then but only a year before Albert Parry, who had lived and chronicled the Village in the twenties and thirties, had returned for a visit and reported that it had disappeared. Such a report is in keeping with a venerable tradition. As early as 1865 a Frenchman was proclaiming that "the joyous Bohemia of the 1830s is no longer possible today." The Village, which only became a Bohemian center in the years before World War I, was, Henry Miller has written, finished by the 1920s (when Parry found it going full blast). "There is nothing," Miller wrote, "but dives and joints, nothing but pederasts, Lesbians, pimps, tarts, fakes and phonies of all description." "Everything," he concluded, "is cheap, tawdry, vulgar and phony." And in the thirties Malcolm Cowley argued that Greenwich Village had ended because women were smoking cigarettes in the Bronx and drinking gin and cocktails in Omaha.

They were all wrong. The Village did not die until after I got there. I do not thus insist on the exact decade of death out of some cultural necrophilia nor am I simply indulging the nostalgia of an aging ex-Bohemian trying to immortalize his own youth as part of a culminating moment in a history of more than one hundred and twenty-five years. There are two reasons why I am so adamant. First of all, I really did find a Bohemia of talent, and sometimes genius, in the New York of the late forties and fifties. Secondly, and much more significantly, it is of great importance to understand that the Counterculture of the sixties and seventies is not a continuation of the Bohemian tradition but a radical departure from it.

At first glance that seems preposterous. Thackeray's description of the Paris Bohemia of the mid-nineteenth century seems to have been written to describe the East Village or Telegraph Avenue in Berkeley today: "Some young men of genius have ringlets hanging over their shoulders. . . . As for beards, there is no end to them; all my friends the artists have beards under all sorts of caps—Chinese caps, Mandarin caps, Greek skullcaps, English jockey caps, Middle Age caps . . . Spanish nets and striped worsted night caps. Fancy all the jackets you have seen." But this similarity is only on the surface, for the Counterculture is the expression of massive changes in class structure and the role of the arts in society that killed Bohemia. And my attempt to be precise in dating the moment of death is not an act of pedantry but part of an effort to locate a momentous turning point in contemporary culture.

That first evening in 1949 I was not looking for historical trends. I wandered in and out of a few bars around Sheridan Square and then drifted into a place called Café Bohemia on Barrow Street. It was in a lesbian phase (the police and organized crime, which jointly supervised such things in the Village, rarely allowed a homosexual haunt to run for more than a few years) and, like all straight young men from the Middle West, I found that fascinating. I got into a conversation with an attractive young woman, but then her girl friend ap-

peared, angry with my heterosexual poaching. "You don't belong here, buddy," she said. "You're a San Remo type." The
next night I went to the Remo and found out that she was
right.

The San Remo was an Italian restaurant at the uneasy intersection of Greenwich Village and Little Italy with bad,
yellowed paintings over the bar and the Entr'Acte from Wolf-
Ferrari's "Jewels of the Madonna" on the jukebox. In 1949
it was the united front of the Village. There were a few old
Bohemians, like Maxwell Bodenheim, the poet and novelist
who dated back to the pre-World War I ferment in Chicago and
was now a shouting, mumbling, drunken, hollow-eyed memory of himself (Bodenheim and his last wife, Ruth, were to be
murdered by a psychotic a few years later). There were seamen on the beach, the most important single contingent from
working-class Bohemia. Some of them had fought in Spain;
one had been a leading Communist in the National Maritime
Union but he broke with the party and was later expelled
from the union. They all combined two seemingly antagonistic life-styles: the militant and the vagabond.

At that time most of the radical seamen were being driven
out of their jobs by the loyalty program and had plenty of
time to drink and reminisce about Spain in the Remo. Among
the other regulars there were heterosexuals on the make; homosexuals who preferred erotic integration to the exclusively
gay bars then on Eighth Street; Communists, socialists, and
Trotskyists; potheads; writers of the older generation like
James Agee, and innovators of the future like Allen Ginsberg,
and Julian Beck and Judith Malina, who were to found the
Living Theatre. Only one really important element in the Village was missing: the painters, like de Kooning, Klein, and
Pollock, who at that moment were taking over the artistic
leadership of the world from Paris, drank at the Cedar over
on University Place along with some of the Black Mountain
poets.

The Remo was, of course, interracial, as far as that was

possible in the late forties. One night after I had been in resi-
dence for about a year I brought the fiancée of a friend of
mine in St. Louis to see the "real" Village in the San Remo.
As we walked into the bar I could feel her stiffen. It was not
because there were obvious homosexuals, both male and fe-
male, or because some of the girls were barefoot or there was
a hum of four-letter words. Oblivious of the exotic flora and
fauna around her, she asked with some agitation, "Are those
two white girls over there on a date with those Negroes they're
sitting with?"

There were only a few remittance men among us, so the
strategies for survival varied: over the years I worked doing
articles for the *Columbia Encyclopedia,* as a writer trainee for
Life, as a soda jerk hiring out by the day, a machine operator
in a shop owned by socialist friends where the bosses and the
workers discussed the Russian Revolution at lunch break, as a
functionary in a civil liberties organization, and as a free-
lance writer-researcher for a foundation. When one was forced
into the workday world there was always the anticipation of
the joys of socialized Bohemianism to come: unemployment
insurance. I called my twenty-six weeks on the dole my
Thomas E. Dewey Fellowship in honor of the Governor and
spent it studying the Italian Renaissance. Later on one Village
friend made some money on the side by appearing on the quiz
show *The Sixty-four Thousand Dollar Question,* and proved
something about middle-class morality by being the only participant to quit when he found out that it was rigged. And
there were crews of Village jocks, alcoholics, and repatriated
expatriates who provided the most raffish moving van service
in the world.

The object was to avoid the routine of nine-to-five, to find a
space in which to think, to write, perhaps just to dribble away
a life. In the afternoons the sweet smell of pot perfumed the
balcony air of the Loew's Sheridan, perhaps the only commercial movie house in New York where a passing reference to
Leon Trotsky could provoke a small ovation. Sometimes the

conversations literally lasted until dawn. Every night at the Remo, Tony, who ran the tiny after-hours joint in the rear of a luncheonette around the corner, came in for his ice and we sometimes followed him back at four in the morning. On Third Street there was another speakeasy, a marvelous demi-monde of mobsters, call girls, and transvestites. They charged $1.25 for a beer, the standard extortion in the Mafia bars of the period, so we used to sneak in a last bottle from the Remo under our coats and drink it while watching the customers, the best floor show in the Village.

I remember one party with over a hundred people in a huge loft, all naked. It was in honor of Winny, a striking black woman who, legend had it, had once indulged her penchant for public disrobing by boarding a Sixth Avenue bus in the nude. She had, of course, stripped to receive birthday greetings and it seemed to her guests that it was the gentlemanly and ladylike thing to follow her example. So it was that when the police arrived to check out a noise complaint they found a milling mass of drinking, chatting, naked people. In one of the most extreme demonstrations of official aplomb I have ever witnessed they did not once refer to that extraordinary fact. But as they left one officer winked.

At that party one could meet a good portion of the Bohemian cadre in New York. For the Village—and I stress now one of the crucial differences between Bohemia and the Counterculture of the sixties and seventies—was small and organized on a human scale. Take a not untypical chain of circumstances. Through friends at the Remo (whom I still see from time to time, more than twenty years later) I met a young woman, Barbara Bank. She invited me to a party at Norman Mailer's huge loft over on First Avenue where, only two years out of St. Louis and goggle-eyed, I talked with writers and painters and gallery owners and even saw Marlon Brando. Mailer—and I mean no harm to his image as an *enfant terrible*—is one of the nicest men I have ever known, with a marvelous memory for names of nobodies from St.

Louis. In the world he dominated I became friends with Dan Wolf and Ed Fancher, who were to found *The Village Voice;* met Susan Sontag, who was teaching philosophy then, and the playwright Maria Irene Fornés and the poet Denise Levertov; and glimpsed visiting celebrities like Alberto Moravia and William Styron across the room at crowded parties.

We were a handful of voluntary exiles from a middle class which itself was still fairly small. But then in the sixties three major trends intersected: the post-World War II baby boom began to come of age; there was a relative affluence which gave the new armies of the young more economic independence than any generation in human history; and there was the near collapse of almost every institution of social control, including the church, the family, and, for a significant number, the discipline of the labor market—it was no longer true that he who does not work shall not eat. As a result, the freaks of the sixties and seventies came in hordes and rebelled in confusion against liberal permissiveness. The clothes, the hostility to middle-class values, were very much like those of Bohemia. But they were a mass movement on an uncharted social frontier; we, who preceded them by only ten or twenty years, had been a self-appointed savior remnant within the citadel of traditional banality.

So Christopher Jencks was wrong when he wrote that "Instead of one Greenwich Village in New York, populated by a handful of rebels from traditional homes, America developed scores of campus villages populated by young people whose values were shaped by the ideals espoused by their liberal parents." That is to miss one of the most crucial and Hegelian truths about contemporary culture: that increases in quantity eventually mean a change in quality, that a Bohemia that enrolls a good portion of a generation is no longer a Bohemia.

My point, for reasons utterly beyond my control, is elitist. It could not, alas, be otherwise. When the great majority of people were kept in the cultural darkness and the rulers were tasteless makers of money, the enclaves of art had to be the refuges of an outcast minority of aesthetic artistocrats even when some of them were starving. One of the virtues of that cruel necessity was that the Bohemian scale was intimate. To recognize, and even celebrate, that fact is not to apologize for the outrageous maldistribution of economic, and therefore spiritual, resources that gave rise to it. A love of Renaissance painting and sculpture hardly makes one an accomplice of the Borgias.

So it was good that, on a warm Sunday afternoon in the early fifties when the folk singers were performing over by the fountain, I would know half of the people in Washington Square Park on sight. (In 1961 we even took on the police in the "Folk Song Riots" to defend the right to sing.) The Village was large enough to have a sense of community, of society, and small enough for everyone to remain an individual. It is something else again when hundreds of thousands of young people gather at a Woodstock Festival to listen to highly paid superstars in commercialized and collectivized rites of libera-tion. That does not mean that I want to go back to the old in-justices where the many were hungry and the few could be sensitive. I fought for the social programs that freed those young people to go to Woodstock and I do not think our struggles went halfway far enough. But still, in preparing the way for something utterly unprecedented, a mass Counter-culture, they destroyed the possibility of Bohemia.

Do I romanticize that sheltered little nonconformist world of my youth? Here is William Gaddis' bitter description of the San Remo in *The Recognitions:* "And by now they were at the door of the Viareggia [the Remo's pen name in the novel], a small Italian bar of nepotistic honesty before it was discovered by the exotics. Neighborhood people still came in vanquished numbers and mostly in the afternoon, before the two small dining rooms and the bar were taken over by the educated classes, an ill-dressed, under-fed, over-drunken group of squatters with minds so highly developed that they were excused from good manners, tastes so refined in one direction that they were excused from having none in any other, emotions so cultivated that the only aberration was normality, all afloat here on sodden pools of depravity, calculated only to manifest the pricelessness of what they were throwing away, the three sexes in two colors, a group of people mentally and physically the wrong size."

Mary McCarthy was not quite so unflattering. She toured the Village for the *New York Post* in the winter of 1950 and found the Remo to be an American Café de Flore (the Flore was the café in St.-Germain-des-Prés where Sartre and Beauvoir held existentialist court right after World War II). But still she did not find much substance in the Village but only a place "where young people throng for a few years before settling down to 'real life,' where taxis full of tourists pursue the pleasure principle outside the ordinary time, where bands of teenage nihilists, outside of everything, from nowhere, rove the streets like a potential mob, and where certain disabled veterans of life, art and politics exercise mutual charity and philosophize all night long, as though already translated into the next world."

Gaddis and McCarthy were partly right and utterly wrong, having failed to understand one of the most crucial single truths about Bohemia. There were certainly "over-drunken squatters" around the Village then (though "sodden pools of depravity" is a bit melodramatic). And there were "disabled veterans of life, art and politics." But they were obvious and inevitable. Throughout the history of Bohemia the poseurs, the failures, and the frauds have always overwhelmingly outnumbered the serious artists. Théophile Gautier, that quintessential literary man of the age of Baudelaire, had identified one of the Remo types almost a century before Gaddis and McCarthy noticed him: "In admiring beauty, he forgot to express it, and whatever he felt deeply, he believed that he had given form."

Indeed it is a cruel truth of the history of all art and literature that most would-be poets, writers, and painters fail. The man or woman of real talent is rare, the born genius rarer still. For every book that survives the merciless judgment of time, there are nine hundred and ninety-nine rotting unread in libraries and nine thousand and ninety-nine that were never written in the first place. It is thus an insight of no particular value to say that most of the conversations at the Remo were, at best, cultured superficialities, and usually not even that good. It could not have been otherwise.

And yet—and here again the contrast with the Counterculture is marked—our phoniness had high standards. We postured about the first rate, about Proust and Joyce and Kafka, the later Beethoven quartets and Balanchine choreography, Marx and Lenin. So there was always the possibility that the sophisticated inanities could become serious and substantial, that one would hear or say a truth or even be incited to create. The proof is in the production. Over the years the people I knew in the Village worked to considerable effect. I think, for example, of the writers and performers I knew when I went to the White Horse, the Remo's successor, every night for more than ten years.

At first glance the saga of the Horse in those days confirms the worst fears of Gaddis and McCarthy. It was a party that lasted longer than a decade. In the early fifties it was the haunt of Irish longshoremen, Catholic liberals and radicals, socialists and Communists. Norman Mailer used to hold Sunday afternoons there for a varied assortment of writers like Vance Bourjaily, Calder Willingham, and William Styron. A little later on Dylan Thomas began telling audiences that he drank there and every English major in the Northeast corridor began to make a pilgrimage to the White Horse. Still later on it became a rollicking hangout for folk singers.

It was a party in the sense that on any given night, or week, or month, you knew you would see the same people. In the middle of that public bar, even when it was jammed on a post–Dylan Thomas weekend, there was an invisible space that the regulars inhabited like a London club. Pretty girls could enter it rather easily, men much less so, and the faces changed slowly. We had our tabs, our phone messages, even our mail, and 1961 was not that different from 1951. So the Horse fulfilled a classic Bohemian function; it was, to borrow from a French writer, "a kind of organization of disorganization."

The women were sexually liberated in the twenties and thirties sense of the word: they recognized their own erotic needs and slept with men whom they loved, or just liked. If a couple left the Horse together at closing time it was taken as probable that they would share a bed; if they drank together two nights in a row they achieved the social status of—to use the period's favorite cliché—a relationship. In the early fifties you would sometimes meet a Wilhelm Reichian in search of the ultimate orgasm—though it often seemed to me that the Reichian girls were trying to shout down their own tightness and timidity with incantations to the uncontrollable rhythms of life. But for all the casual intimacy of those days the scene was not depraved or sluttish and it actually produced a fair number of marriages. Now, of course, our daring experimentation is the sexual orthodoxy of college students.

For some that ten-year party was a moral disaster, an amusing waste of life. (Our own legend had it, with some truth I suspect, that one group moved from their table in the front room of the Horse to the South of France without interrupting their conversation and musical beds.) For others it was, just as Mary McCarthy said, an episode, a prelude to entering the world of "real life." For instance, I used to drink in the White Horse with Bernard Cornfeld, then a socialist, later the ill-fated financial genius of Investors Overseas Services; and Daniel Patrick Moynihan would drop by in the fifties when he was on Averell Harriman's staff to listen to Irish songs and talk politics. But there were also a significant number for whom the Horse was a place to relax after serious work. I think of just a few of them, some regulars, some occasionals, all part of the scene: there were writers like Mailer, James Baldwin, Jules Feiffer, Dan Wakefield, and Richard Fariña; musicians and performers like the Clancy Brothers and Tommy Makem, Bob Dylan, Caroline Hester, David Amram; poets like Joel Oppenheimer and Delmore Schwartz.

I know my own case best. I was in the Horse every night for more than ten years. As the people of Königsberg were said to set their clocks by Immanuel Kant's walks, you would see me, punctually dissolute, appear on week nights at midnight and on weekends at one o'clock. At two in the morning you could usually observe me engaged in an intense conversation of no great importance and at a distance I must have seemed one of Gaddis' squatters. But if I slept until eleven or noon every day, I worked for twelve hours after I got up, reading, writing, or doing socialist organizing. The late night was a gregarious, potentially erotic release from a disciplined existence. The world of nine-to-five was a routine; of twelve-to-twelve a choice.

There were obviously a good number of people in the Village following the same kind of internal schedule on the inside of a seemingly discombobulated life. In addition to those I've already mentioned there were Dan Wolf and Ed Fancher, who created a new style of journalism at *The Village Voice;* José Quintero, Ellen Stewart, and Theodore Mann, who were part of the Off-Broadway theatre renaissance; and the painters one would see around the Cedar—Pollock, de Kooning, Klein, Rivers—who helped make New York the art center of the world.

And there was Dylan Thomas. The White Horse was his home away from home when he was in New York, and from the point of view of the regulars, the fame and crowds he brought to it were calamitous. Old Ernie, the owner, even stopped giving out the chess sets. Anyone with a vision of the poet divinely drunk upon the midnight might ponder Thomas' final evenings at the Horse. He was a slobbering, incomprehensible man slumped over the table and surrounded by a retinue of sycophants and young girls who wanted to go to bed with immortality. ("These little maggots," he had written in a denunciation of his own Bohemianism in 1934, "are my companions for most of the time.") That last night at the Horse he was half carried out and taken to the Chelsea Hotel where he began to die the death he had been so long preparing for himself. Old Ernie took up a collection for Thomas' widow, and one longshoreman gave and another didn't. "Who's that for?" said the one who didn't contribute. "Oh," his friend answered, "some drunk who used to hang around here just died."

But the non-Bohemian world was not always as indifferent, or even tolerant, as those longshoremen. Malcolm Cowley was right in the thirties to notice that the traditional American mores were being subverted and to argue that the destruction of middle-class morality would mark the end of Bohemia. He was, however, a generation premature. In the late forties and the fifties the basic institutions of American righteousness— belief in God, family, and the holy destiny of this nation— were still intact. Old Ernie asked me one night if we couldn't sing more of the radical songs in German and French rather than English so the other patrons wouldn't understand the words. It was less amusing on another night when a group of us sat singing labor songs in a working-class bar around the corner from the Horse. Eventually management phoned the police to protect our exit from a back door. We had persuaded the trade union regulars there not of our solidarity with them, but that we were Communists.

And on a number of occasions during the McCarthy years Irish working-class kids from the neighborhood made fist-swinging, chair-throwing raids on the Horse. They used to scream that we were Commies and faggots, the latter epithet expressing their fury that we were always in the company of good-looking and liberated women while they drank in the patriotic virility of all-male groups. Jimmy Baldwin suffered most from this hostility. One night Baldwin, Dick Bagley, the cameraman who made *On the Bowery* and a regular at the

White Horse, and two girls were drinking at the Paddock, a bar up the street. Some of the working-class patrons were furious to see a black man sitting next to a white woman and they jumped Baldwin and Bagley.

Some years later, in Paris in the winter of 1963, Baldwin and some friends and I were talking of the black movement in the States and he went back in horrified reminiscence to that night in the Paddock. He remembered how, as a man tried to kick him in the genitals, he squeezed himself into a ball in the dirt under the bar. It was, he said, a terrible confirmation of his knowledge that he would never be safe in white America, that someone was always lying in wait. In Jane Jacobs' account of the neighborhood in *The Death and Life of Great American Cities* (she lived a few doors down from the Horse) all these tensions are omitted and the street life of the place is praised for making it safe. She apparently did not realize that the friendly tavern across from her, The Ideal, was nicknamed The Ordeal by the White Horse regulars who used to go there when Ernie closed early. It was the scene of tense confrontations between Bohemia and square America.

But then, somewhere around the early sixties, America lost that faith in its own philistine righteousness and Bohemia began to die. One of the beginnings of that end, I now realize, was the night a gawky kid named Bob Dylan showed up at the Horse in a floppy hat.

Robert Shelton, a regular and then the folk music critic of *The New York Times,* had been among the very first to recognize Dylan's talent. Once, quite late after the Horse closed, we all went over to McGowan's on Greenwich Avenue and, at Shelton's urging, Dylan gave an impromptu concert. I heard the future and I didn't like it. Dylan's singing had a diffidence, a studied artlessness, which was, I suspect, one of the reasons for his impact upon his generation. But it was lost on me, at least at first. (Later, standing before the State House in Montgomery on the last day of Martin Luther King, Jr.'s Selma March and listening to "Blowin' in the Wind" speak for that vast multitude, I learned with a shiver to appreciate his genius.)

Indeed, Dylan's singing was like the speechmaking in Students for a Democratic Society during the early years. At the time I privately called it the stutter style. It assumed that any show of logic or rhetorical skill was prima facie proof of hypocrisy and dishonesty, the mark of the manipulator. The sincere man was therefore supposed to be confused and half-articulate and anguished in his self-revelation. By that standard the fact that Dylan did not have a good voice in any conventional sense of the word was one of his highest recommendations.

To be sure Dylan, particularly in the first period of his fame, looked back to Woody Guthrie and the tradition of the political vagabond. That impulse was very much alive in the Village when he arrived. I remember one Sunday afternoon in 1961 over at Sheridan Square when Guthrie's friends and admirers—Freddy Hellerman and Lee Hays from the Weavers, Oscar Brand, Will Geer, and Logan English and many others—gathered around him. He sat, slumped and emaciated and dying, while they sang him a farewell in the words of his own songs. Dylan had, of course, absorbed that Guthrie spirit and it infused his early work and even his life-style. But even then his calculated indifference was a portent of the sixties rather than an echo of Guthrie's passionate thirties. It was no accident that so many of his contemporaries mistook him for a major poet. Modernism, which had always had its links with Bohemia, was proud of the demands it made upon its tiny public. Now, however, popular songs were to be regarded as high poetry, much as ecstasy was thought to be rolled up in a pill or a joint.

Perhaps Allen Ginsberg was even more symptomatic of that change than Dylan. He had been around the Remo when I arrived in 1949, but I did not meet him until 1964 when he and Peter Orlovsky and another friend came to our apartment to see my wife who was then on the staff of the *Voice*. They had just been picketing in the snow in front of the Women's House of Detention as part of their campaign to legalize marijuana. I was working on a book review of a study of cannabis and, after having hung his socks on the radiator to dry, Ginsberg sat there and cited court decisions, official inquiries, and academic analyses, with the authority of a scholar and the enthusiasm of a militant.

For Ginsberg has deep roots in American tradition. He traces himself back, of course, to Walt Whitman and he has obvious affinities with the Bohemia of personal exploration typified by Henry Miller. But his penchant for organization and detail—he functioned as a sort of international address book and courier for the Beat Generation—was part of his radical political background. So in one aspect Ginsberg is a literary-political rebel on the model of the pre-World War I Villager, an innovator in art, social attitudes, and life-style. The young who turned him into a guru tended to ignore his traditionalism and critical standards. They imitated only the flamboyant and mad poet chanting mantras or casually incanting a description of homosexual orgasm before a large crowd.

This one-sided reading of Ginsberg was part of a new sensibility that Irving Howe has brilliantly defined: "It is impatient with literary structure, complexity and coherence, only yesterday the catchwords of our criticism. It wants instead works of literature—though literature may be the wrong word—that will be as absolute as the sun, as unarguable as orgasm and as delicious as a lollipop."

Without getting too McLuhanesque about the point, I wonder if the mass Counterculture may not be a reflection of the very hyped and videotaped world it professes to despise. As early as 1960 Ned Polsky, the sociologist of deviance, discovered that the Beats around the Village had a quality that set them off from all previous generations of Bohemia: they did not read. More recently, Theodore Roszak, the theorist of the Counterculture, has rejected all of the mainstream assumptions of the West since the scientific revolution of the seventeenth century. Roszak's emphasis is upon personal experience, mysticism, drugs. The intricacies of literature and symbolism have as little place in that universe as they do in the instantaneous world of the media.

As Don McNeill, the brilliant participant-observer of the Counterculture who died tragically at twenty-three, wrote of the East Village: "The transient rut is not a creative way. It is a fertilizing, procreative experience for a few. It is an interim for a few. For more, it is a long road down, laced with drugs, especially amphetamines. Many dig the descent; oblivion can be seductive. There is a fascination in being strung out for days on amphetamine, a fascination in Rolling Stone echoes, a fascination in the communal chaos of the Lower East Side, as far removed from Westchester as is India. If you wade in too deep, you may learn that the East Side undertow is no myth."

Bohemia died in that undertow. Walking around the East Village in the summer of 1966 was like attending a huge Halloween party. The streets were alive with frontiersmen and guerrillas and painters from the 1830s. There were bearded homosexuals aggressively holding hands, girls with long, straight hair walking barefoot on filthy sidewalks to prove their organic oneness with nature, and teen-agers panhandling or sitting and staring blankly, strung out on drugs. Gangs of Puerto Ricans and blacks sometimes clashed with the flower children and the brutal law of the drug pushers was already in evidence. The aging Russians and Ukrainians whose lives had once centered around Tompkins Square Park were bewildered by all these comings and goings and terrified by the "love" the young offered them (it was, to paraphrase a remark of Paul Goodman's, love spoken through clenched teeth and the flowers they sometimes pressed upon the old people might as well have been bricks).

Now all that is gone. Within five years the myth died because it never had very deep roots. There are fewer runaways and no one in that East Side jungle with its ubiquitous junkie rip-offs believes in love anymore. Roszak had talked of the proclamation of "a new heaven and a new earth" but Woodstock turned into Altamont in a matter of months and the community was witness not to love but to a murder. Bohemia had its madness, and even its killings, but it was based upon solid cultural foundations and lasted more than a century. But before its epitaph can be complete the Bohemian death must be seen in the city of the Bohemian birth—Paris.

I

I first went to Paris in 1959 during a sunny summer when the bright awnings on the apartment buildings along the Seine were like Impressionist brush strokes. I came back one gray morning in early January, 1963. It was my pilgrimage to the origins of Bohemia, a search for that magic city in which Hemingway's generation had so enjoyed itself being lost. I did not find it, of course. That was not simply because it is impossible to relive someone else's past, which is true enough. It was also because the world of writers and artists had been transformed in France as well as in America and for many of the same reasons.

Still there were remnants of that mythic Paris and I found them quickly because Bohemia was international. I had known for some time that there was a national underground within the United States. It existed in obvious places like the Village, San Francisco's North Beach, and the Venice section of Los Angeles; but I had also discovered it on houseboats in Seattle, in a town above an Indian village near Albuquerque, and in a German-American beer garden in Austin, Texas. Now it turned out that the network was transatlantic. Let me give just one series of preposterous interconnections that were not at all untypical.

Early in January in Paris I ran into George Hahn. He had served as a model for A. E. Kugelman, the hip hero of "Saloon Society," Bill Manville's column in *The Village Voice,* and had been known to buy drinks for the entire White Horse.

Through him I met his cousin, Otto Hahn, the French art critic for *L'Express,* and through Otto various French artists and intellectuals, including one who explained the tragicomic genius of Jerry Lewis to me at a party. When Stephanie Gervis came over in March—we were married at the city hall of the 13th arrondissement in May—George lent us his apartment in Ibiza. A Paris friend from the Bohemia on the Ile St. Louis who was also an old Ibiza hand met us on the quai. He introduced us to the dissolute colony of artists, drifters, and con men—one of them was called "Wanted John"—who partied year round at cheap Spanish prices. A few days later at a *vernissage* at a farmhouse on this island in the Mediterranean I looked up and there stood an old acquaintance from New York, Morsette Watts, perhaps the most swinging black militant to be expelled from a Negro college for participating in the first sit-in of 1960.

But all was not amusing coincidence. My room was a Bohemian cliché in a ten-franc-a-night hotel on the Left Bank with the toilet one flight up and the shower, which had to be reserved at a price, two flights down. In imagination, it was a marvelously appropriate place to work on a new book on decadence in Western civilization. The romance, however, did not survive the first day. The winter was bitter cold, the worst, the papers said, since the great freeze of 1871. I would sit on the radiator with my feet on the wash basin and read *Remembrance of Things Past* by the light of the only bright bulb in that dreary room. Or else I would warm my bottom in the hot water of the bidet while wearing a sweater.

It was Joseph Barry who saved me from the lonely desolation of that winter. He was the Paris correspondent for the *New York Post* and still saw the city through legendary glasses even though he had lived its reality for years. Joe took me to a party at Don Fink's house on the Rue Hypolite Maindron. The evening was in honor of the American painter Alice Baber, who was then married to Paul Jenkins, among the best known of the American artists in Paris. The two living floors and the studio at the top of the house were filled with painters, writers, people from *Paris Review,* and the like. It was like coming home. I left late that night, more than a little drunk, and the city was covered with snow, as if it were posing for a painting of itself. The next morning I woke with a hangover and the streets were filled with slush.

The party at Don's was in continuous session at La Coupole, that year's Parisian equivalant of the Horse. It was not a bar but a section of a bar: the tables in the rear on the left-hand side of that cavernous room. Social status was defined by tablecloths: the bourgeois customers ate off linen; we had paper. A group of painters, writers, and international floaters would assemble there practically every evening for the traditional rites of talk, drink, and sexual scouting. And it was there that one of my oldest prejudices was reinforced: that painters are the best people in Bohemia.

Actors and performers are often occupationally stagy; writers seem to be a random sample of mankind; but painters, for some reason, have always struck me as particularly outgoing and generous. Don Fink, the only man in La Coupole who could drink as many *sérieux* of beer as I (the jumbo size was called a *formidable*) is an excellent example. A veteran who lost an eye in the Second World War, he has been living and painting in Paris since the early fifties. He speaks a reckless French composed mainly of infinitives which somehow communicates to Parisians who could not understand my bookish subjunctives. His painting, like his French, was an act of living, not of theory. In that period he was creating delicate abstractions in an almost Japanese mood.

Perhaps the warmth and directness I found among painters like Don is related to the tactile immediacy of their sensibility. They are concerned with the connotations and evocativeness of form and color rather than with the denotations of words. And artists are more like a community than writers, not the least because they must go in person to see each other's work. As a result, they exchanged paintings. On Don Fink's walls you could see canvases by most of his friends. Indeed, that generosity even extended to outsiders like myself. I remember my delighted surprise when after three amiable weeks of living next to Alexander Calder in the Loire Valley in 1966 that utterly likable bear of a genius asked Stephanie and me to take any one of his most recent gouaches.

Don and the people I met through him had the Bohemian style: the casual dress, irregular hours, and contempt for middle-class virtues. And yet there was another side to their world. Don's studio was in his house where he and his wife were raising two children. He attended the regular poker sessions at James Jones' magnificent apartment on the Ile St. Louis and played tennis at the courts on Boulevard Arago. In the summer of 1963 when Americans in Paris marched to the Embassy to present a petition in solidarity with the civil rights March on Washington, the demonstration was conducted according to protocol and by invitation. The order of the line of march was determined by celebrity status: James Jones and Jimmy Baldwin were in the lead.

And that winter at La Coupole one of the topics of discussion was Vincent Price's trip to Paris to buy paintings for some big department store. There were certified geniuses among the regulars, like César, who first made his mark by compressing a Honda into a sculpture and is now listed in the Petit Larousse as a master, yet at times the talk among my friends sounded like the chatter at a convention of small businessmen. This mood was not simply confined to the expatriates. I found that out when I was doing an article for an old White Horse friend, Chester Krone. Chester had become the editor of a small stable of girlie magazines and needed copy to fill up the pages between the pictures of naked women. He was an exceedingly literate man and he knew of my poverty. So he suggested assignments, like interviewing Nicole Saint Phalle, which were a major source of my income that year.

Although Nicky Saint Phalle was part American and had studied in New York, she belonged to one of the most avant-

garde of the French artistic tendencies. Her friend Tinguely
was the inventor of sculptures that blew themselves up. Saint
Phalle's own specialty at that time was to pin sacks of paint
over a canvas and then to break them by firing a gun at them.
This was in keeping with the desire of artists over the last
half-century or more to scandalize the middle class with more
and more outrageous definitions of art. But César and
Tinguely and Saint Phalle were praised and purchased, not
exiled. The bourgeoisie, and even the American booboisie,
had sold out by buying in.

There were, to be sure, painters' worlds much less established and secure than the one I found through Joe Barry and
Don Fink. The artists I met over on the Ile St. Louis were
younger, poorer, and more French than those in the back of
La Coupole. Moreover, 1963 turned out to be a year of
transition even for the successful painters in Paris and in the
years that followed the money did not flow in quite as lav-
ishly. But the dollars and cents are not the real criterion of the
transformation that has taken place. Of all the people who
once lived in Bohemia, the painters are still the most finan-
cially precarious and in New York today they survive by
teaching. But whatever the difficulties, they are no longer on
that lonely margin of society.

In the process of that transition Bohemia conquered and
killed itself. Two incidents, one from Paris, the other from
New York, might serve as a final epitaph.

One day Joe Barry took me to have tea with Alice B. Toklas. That lonely survivor of the heroic period of twentieth-
century modernism was losing her sight and had to have people read to her. Joe was one of the chief organizers of that
effort, recruiting volunteers from the regulars at La Coupole.
In her apartment the walls were bare. But you could see the
faded spots that marked the places where the incomparable
paintings she and Gertrude Stein had bought, often for a
song, had been hung. Stein had willed them to Toklas for her
lifetime and then to her own heirs. But Stein's heirs were not

about to allow an old lady to keep such a treasure in an un-guarded apartment and got permission to take them away. Those works, which once had been the personal witness of hungry creators who sold them to the few people who under-stood their aesthetic value, had now become commodities to be placed under guard. All that remained of the legendary past in which Toklas had lived were two chairs embroidered according to a design by Pablo Picasso.

Back in New York in 1970 my wife and I went to *The Village Voice* Christmas party. Once those annual get-togethers were held in Ed Fancher's railroad flat on Christopher Street and had been family celebrations. But now the *Voice* had be-come a successful national institution. Its friends and employ-ees needed the vast space of Howard Moody's Judson Memo-rial Church for their revels. As our cab crossed Bleecker Street toward Washington Square we passed the corner where the Remo had stood. It had become a Howard Johnson's.

3. We Happy Few

A plenum of the National Committee of the Young Socialist League was held in September, 1954, at our headquarters, 114 West Fourteenth Street in New York.

Outside, Fourteenth Street was, like the Lower East Side, in transition from Jewish to Puerto Rican working class and teeming with bargain hunters at the cut-rate stores. Three blocks to the east was Union Square, long a historic assembly point for radicals, now the haunt of a handful of aging garment workers who still engaged in vociferous debate and of drifters from the Bowery. A few doors from us was the headquarters of the Salvation Army, once the Left wing of English Methodism, now an almost conventional church whose lassies, with their pinched and bland faces, sometimes marched past our window. Our meeting hall was a shabby loft with benches and unmatched folding chairs that had been salvaged from a number of defunct organizations. We sat around a table littered with mimeographed documents and sodden coffee containers and argued with great passion through a two-day agenda.

This was the first meeting of the YSL Committee since our founding convention in February of 1954. At that time the Young People's Socialist League, which had left the Socialist party because of the latter's refusal to denounce the war in Korea, had combined forces with the Socialist Youth League, the youth affiliate of the Independent Socialist League. Now we were confronted with two major issues. A minority tendency had been organized and had submitted a resolution en-

We Happy Few 61

titled "Tasks of the September Plenum" which accused the majority of backing off from the struggle for revolutionary power and demanded that our cadres be rearmed from the arsenal of Marxism.

There was also a discussion of the correct socialist policy in Indochina, which went on well into the night and attracted an audience of older comrades from the ISL. What, precisely, should we say to the workers in Saigon and Hanoi? Should we advise them to create a new movement which would fight both the French colonialists and the Stalinists within the Viet Minh? Or should they enter into the Viet Minh and contest with Ho Chi Minh for leadership? There were appropriate quotations from Marx and Lenin on the national question and Trotsky on the Chinese Revolution. We then decided by a majority that the Indochinese proletariat should organize independently.

At the time these deliberations took place our newly unified socialist youth movement had eighty-three members in the United States of America.

We might have seemed simply the *reductio ad absurdum* of the catastrophe history had visited upon Marx's Eleventh Thesis on Feuerbach: "The philosophers," our mentor had written, "have only *interpreted* the world in various ways; now the time has come to *change* the world." The abyss had opened up under that theory in August, 1914, when the socialist workers of Europe joined bourgeois armies and proceeded to slaughter one another in what was probably the most senseless carnage in human history. From that day forward how could one pretend that Marx was right in asserting a unity of theory and practice? The working class, which was supposed to have no fatherland, had turned out to be patriotic even unto death.

From that moment on the Marxian synthesis was subjected to blow after blow: the Russian Revolution degenerated into Stalinist totalitarianism; fascism triumphed in Italy, Germany, and Spain; and when the victorious Labour majority of 1945 marched into Parliament singing "The Red Flag," the Tories responded not with armed counterrevolution, but with a rendition of "For He's a Jolly Good Fellow" in honor of the defeated Winston Churchill.

So we sat in our drab loft on Fourteenth Street, a remnant of the not so glorious but quite dead past, and our Marxist sophistication stood in inverse ratio to any possibility of changing the world. It would be simple enough to explore the humor of that contrast through a dozen anecdotes. Only that would obscure the real, and rather astounding, truth: that theories of considerable importance were being conserved and even deepened in apparently silly little debates; and that the ideas generated there would influence the mass movements of the 1960s.

At a time when the "American celebrants," as C. Wright Mills used to call them, were announcing the end of the working class, the disappearance of poverty, and the recognition of intellect by a once philistine capitalist society, we rightly asserted the contrary. When the ideologists of the Cold War were analyzing a Stalinist system of such monolithic implacability that no internal resistance was possible, we awaited—and anticipated—the East German general strike of 1953, the Polish and Hungarian Octobers of 1956, the Czechoslovakian "springtime" of 1968, and the Polish strikes of 1970–1971. And when it seemed that the outlawing of segregation in public education would nonviolently emancipate the Negroes, we argued that a much more profound struggle against economic and social racism would be required.

We were, God knows, hardly infallible. We were often definitely and decisively wrong. We had said that there was no real difference between Eisenhower and Stevenson in 1952 and 1956 and, later, between Kennedy and Nixon in 1960. We expected that American trade unionists would dramatically and cleanly break with the Democratic party and create their own labor party. And we sometimes conjured up an international Third Camp, neither capitalist nor Communist, which was the child of our wish rather than of reality. Yet, on balance, I would argue that our Marxism—our bookish, ineffective, impractical Marxism—permitted us to make a valuable contribution to the forces engaged in changing American society.

Indeed, our isolation may have been an advantage. Little sects, Marx had once remarked, are only justified in times when there is no mass working-class movement of the Left, but under such circumstances they play a necessary role. The media were not looking over our shoulder as they were with the New Left of the sixties. We could, therefore, commit our stupidities in private and painfully work out our ideas without being required to defend them instantly before a television camera. Since we were so short on practice we had nothing else to do but become long on theory.

That theory, to be sure, did not relate to reality as Marx had defined it. But it did relate to the unprecedented reality we were forced to discover. I stress this point because I am writing in the early seventies, at a time when another period of political and cultural conservatism may be beginning. In showing the relevance of socialist ideas developed during the reactionary McCarthy era, perhaps I may help prepare some for the difficult and even lonely struggles that are to come.

Finally, there is a personal message in this account of radicalism in the fifties which also has social implications. It was as a socialist, and because I was a socialist, that I fell in love with America. In saying that I am not indulging in romantic nostalgia about youthful days on the road but rather underlining a crucial political truth. If the Left wants to change this country because it hates it, then the people will never listen to the Left and the people will be right. To be a socialist—to be a Marxist—is to make an act of faith, of love even, toward this land. It is to sense the seed beneath the snow; to see, beneath the veneer of corruption and meanness and the commercialization of human relationships, men and women capable of controlling their own destinies. To be a radical is, in the best and only decent sense of the word, patriotic.

I

I became a socialist in 1948, the last year of the thirties.

Political decades do not, of course, obey calendars and in Harry Truman's "give 'em hell" campaign of 1948, which opened at an auto workers' meeting in Cadillac Square, Detroit, the spirit of Franklin Roosevelt and the issues of the thirties were still abroad in the land. But no sooner was Truman elected than the fifties began (politically speaking, the decade of the forties did not exist). The Cold War and its attendant theme of domestic anti-Communism dominated American life; and the nation began to turn toward both Eisenhower and Joe McCarthy. So I came of age at the very last moment when the philosophical preoccupations of the Great Depression were still primary, and at the very first moment of a sharp shift to the Right.

Actually, I had first rebelled against my family's Irish Catholic New Dealism by becoming a Taft conservative. The fact is not quite as bizarre as it might seem since the Robert A. Taft whom I admired was, to my imagination at least, a radical. He was a civil libertarian who had defended the right of Communists to teach in public schools, an opponent of the big businessmen of the Northeast, an Adam Smith anarchist. At least so I thought. Then at Yale Law School, which I attended in 1947–1948, there were nine months of ideological debates during which I manfully defended my Taft position even as I was privately being persuaded by the opposition. The professors were mainly liberals and my classmates, most of them returned veterans, were left liberals, Henry Wallacites, socialists, and Communists. The day I left law school I switched from Taft Republicanism to democratic socialism without even bothering to tarry a while in the liberal camp in between.

Ironically, Jesuit anti-socialism also had a hand in my conversion. At Holy Cross I had been taught that socialism was immoral because it denied the right of every family to that private property which was necessary to raise children in Christian decency. At Yale I realized that it was capitalism, not socialism, that denied that right.

At first, my change of conviction hardly mattered. I was really more interested in writing poetry than in the class struggle (after five years of working at it every day I published five poems in *Poetry Chicago* and then was forced to admit that I had no talent, or at least no genius). So there was a distinctly aesthetic and elitist dimension to my Leftism. In my mind, and in the articles of the little magazines I read, the artistic innovations of the School of Paris, sexual freedom, and socialism were all part of the same philosophy. Capitalism was not so much cruel and exploitative as crass and vulgar: the bourgeois was hated as a boor rather than as a thief. Thus I thought it only mildly embarrassing to go to a large debutante party at a country club in St. Louis and sit in front of a swimming pool filled with flowers and drink some rich father's whiskey while trying to convince a friend that capitalism was a rotten system.

I was also under the spell of the fight to create an independent Israel. I was Irish enough to accept without question the truth of Zionist attacks on British imperialism, and the holocaust of the European Jews seemed to me the most monstrous evil since time began. I read with sympathy Arthur Koestler's apology for the terrorist wing of Zionism and I learned the melody of the "Hatikvah" from a record and the words from the *Fireside Book of Folk Songs*. To this day I am one of the few people I know who can sing that Jewish anthem in English.

I emphasize the profundities, limitations, inconsistencies— and occasional silliness—of my original socialist commitment for a reason. There are pop sociologists and bitter Leftists who note the affluent background of so many of the young radicals of the sixties and relate that fact to certain elitist aspects of their politics. Of course. And yet that is hardly an exhaustive description of the contradictory, sloppy processes of

hearts and minds; and it is certainly not a prediction of future
behavior. All of our youthful impulses can be reduced to ra-
tionalizations of class position or psychic need, but that does
not tell us what they will become in adult life.

In my case, my convictions began to become deadly serious
one day in the fall of 1949. I needed money so I could stake
myself to go to New York and write poetry. Without any idealistic thought on my part, and through the political influence
of a cousin and ward leader, I was given a job in the Pupil
Welfare Department of the St. Louis Public Schools. I was
assigned to the Madison School, located in an Arkansas
sharecropper district down near the river, not far from a
"Hooverville," one of those colonies of driftwood and tincan
shacks that had survived from the Depression. One rainy day
I went into an old, decaying building. The cooking smells
and the stench from the broken, stopped-up toilets and the
murmurous cranky sound of the people were a revelation. It
was my moment on the road to Damascus. Suddenly the abstract and statistical and aesthetic outrages I had reacted to
at Yale and Chicago became real and personal and insistent.
A few hours later, riding the Grand Avenue streetcar, I realized that somehow I must spend the rest of my life trying to
obliterate that kind of house and to work with the people
who lived there.

When I arrived in New York in the fall of 1949 I was still
vague about exactly what I was going to do and the drive to
write poetry was important to me. As I was running out of
money that winter, I took a job as a writer-trainee at *Life*
magazine. The personnel director, Jim Crider, was prophetic.
He told me that he had been against hiring me but had been
overruled by the editors. I asked him why he didn't want me
on the staff. "Because," Crider replied, "you are not our kind
of person." He was right. Six months later I quit and in less
than a year I was at the Catholic Worker.

II

The Worker was part of the lay apostolate within the Catholic Church. It was also a participant in the radical movement in New York.

In early 1951, when I first encountered the organized Left, it was a sorry vestige of its thirties self. The more exotic sects —Trotskyist slivers that had broken with Trotskyist splinters over the precise moment at which Russia ceased to be socialist —had ceased to exist. The Communists were being persecuted by the government and infiltrated by the FBI, and were themselves engaging in an internal witch-hunt against both white and male chauvinists. The Socialist party of Norman Thomas could still tap a reservoir of good will, primarily because of Thomas' presence, but it was only the merest shadow of the organization that had polled almost a million votes in the Presidential race of 1932. There were various anarchist grouplets, one of them led by a comrade who after fighting in Spain for the Loyalists was nearly executed by the Russian secret police, which was settling scores with Left anti-Stalinists. When he debarked in the United States he received a hero's welcome: he was told that he had been elected to the Central Committees of both organizations into which his old group had split. There was a remnant of the Industrial Workers of the World, the famed Wobblies, irreverently presided over by Sam Weiner, a painter and one of the few genuine workers in the movement. The Socialist Workers party represented "orthodox" Trotskyism, and the Independent Socialist League and Max Shachtman were in transition from unorthodox Trotskyism to democratic socialism.

Every once in a while one got a hint of that sense of radical community that had once flourished in America. The first socialist organization I joined, the Young People's Socialist League, used to hold cheap weekend campouts on Fire Island. The young rebels would bring their sleeping bags and chip in five dollars a head for a weekend's supply of food and beer.

The first time out, a group of people stopped several hundred yards from us and took off their clothes. They were, we learned later, members of the Nature Friends of America, a group that had social democratic links in Europe and at least some pro-Communist tendencies in the United States. Some of us walked over toward the nude campers and as we neared the women drew their clothes around themselves. "Do you belong to any group in New York?" they asked. We explained that we were socialists and the women immediately dropped their coverings. We were accepted as comrades rather than voyeurs.

In the main, though, the transition from the St. Louis middle class to New York radicalism was more serious than Fire Island excursions (though it should be emphasized that there was not a little joy and camaraderie even when the police were looking over our shoulders).

On the first anniversary of the Korean war in June, 1951, I was sent to represent the Catholic Worker at an anti-war march and the participants gathered beforehand in a meadow in Central Park. There I met Bayard Rustin, a tall, intense Negro with more than a touch of a British accent, who asked coolly if we were going to get arrested. I was still a well-mannered middle-class youth from St. Louis, and I listened with frightened fascination while my new friends argued the pros and cons of defying the police if we were ordered to move on. I was enormously relieved when it was decided that revolutionary strategy on that day did not require a confrontation with the forces of order.

We marched single file through Times Square, a motley little band startling the tourists with signs proclaiming that the Korean war was evil. (I saw myself shuffling along in that pathetic little parade and I thought I looked like one of those cartoon figures with a placard announcing the end of the world.) We finally set up shop on Seventh Avenue and Fortieth Street for about an hour of street speaking. Just after I had finished my indictment of the war, Dave Dellinger began to talk and a man came screaming through the curious crowd, yelling that we were a bunch of Commies. He grabbed a picket sign, tore off the cardboard, and rushed toward the speakers' stand brandishing the stick like a club. Bayard calmly offered him a second picket sign, which succeeded in bewildering him, and he dropped both sticks. But he kept howling that Dellinger was a traitor.

Dellinger replied that we were pacifists, not Communists. Then, said the man, come down here so I can hit you and see if you really will turn the other cheek. Dellinger left the stand and walked over to reason with our disturbed critic. The latter planted himself carefully and punched Dellinger in the jaw, knocking him to the ground. Some girls leapt in front of the man so that he couldn't kick Dellinger while he was down on the pavement. By this time the fellow was hopelessly confused and began to admit that perhaps we were not Communists after all. Meanwhile, Bayard had mounted the speakers' stand and was making a running commentary on the scene, pointing out that it proved the enormous power of nonviolence.

Not all our demonstrations were that eventful, but the danger of violence in those fervid McCarthyite years was omnipresent. Later on, when I had acquired a little time and rank in the movement, I was usually assigned to be the picket captain because I was Irish. The police would aggressively demand our leader. I would step forward, and they would ask my name. There was usually a stunned silence when I answered and then some remark like, "Michael, my boy, what are you doing with *these* people?" One time we were picketing the British and Irish Railways office in Rockefeller Center. After the regular conversation with the puzzled sergeant, he asked me, "But Michael, how can you march against the Irish Railways?" "That," I told him, "is the North of Irish Railways." The law gave us most friendly protection the rest of that day.

Aside from marching, we would discuss. Endlessly. Besides Rustin and Dellinger and Norman Thomas, I met people like Paul Goodman, Dwight Macdonald, and A. J. Muste. Some-

times we would come together—all fifty or seventy-five of us
—at the Labor Temple on Fourteenth Street and celebrate
May Day or pledge our solidarity with some distant struggle,
like a strike in Spain. At one point I became the secretary of
the Committee to Defend Franco's Labor Victims—restitu-
tion, I hoped, for having joined as a boy in the prayers of
thanksgiving offered at St. Rose's Church when the fascists
crossed the Ebro River—and I met the exiles.

They were a sad, aging, terribly appealing group of men
who lived on remembered loves and hatreds. They were, of
course, utterly committed to the fight against Franco, and accounts of our little meetings and picket lines were sometimes
printed in illegal newspapers distributed in Spain. The exiles
also kept up all the animosities that had split the anti-fascist
camp: the various socialist and anarchist tendencies had not
forgotten a single difference from fifteen or more years before.
From time to time tragedy struck. One of our supporters was
a warm, scholarly Dominican named Jesus de Galindas. He
was kidnapped in New York and murdered by Trujillo in
1954. And there were other exiles. My friend Carola Weingar-
ten, with whom I worked at the Workers Defense League, was
the daughter of a leading German Communist who had been
expelled from the party by the Stalinists. Carola had fled Germany the day the Nazis took power, and after spending time
in France, finally made her way to New York. She was party-
less, bitterly critical of the social democrats, a sworn enemy of
the Communists, but still resolutely dedicated to her Marxist
ideals. In talking with her, the disputes of the European Left
became personal and emotional to me. To this day if I come
across the name of some forgotten revolutionary of whom
Carola spoke, it is like reading about a dead friend.

It was not just the foreigners who were exiles; so were those
of us born in America. Our homeland was the Left. In the era
of Debs and the Wobblies and in the thirties it had existed in
the United States. Now it had disappeared, except for our tat-
tered little remnant. Some of my comrades were still working

in the factories and pursuing union politics, particularly in the Auto Workers Union, but by the end of the fifties most of them would either have joined the paid union staff or left the shop for better jobs. For the most part, though, we were college-educated rebels who had been drawn to the movement by its theories rather than by its leadership of workers. As internal exiles in our own country we behaved like exiles everywhere: we met, talked endlessly, and divided over seemingly abstruse questions of revolutionary doctrine.

Yet it turned out that we were arguing about reality, certainly more so than the American celebrants in the academy and the press. Consider the Young Socialist League (YSL) which began with those eighty-three members and after four years of effort and sacrifice ended—quite proudly, I might add—with about two hundred and fifty.

Most of the grouplets were nicknamed for their leader. There were Cannonites, Cochranites, Musteites, Sweezyites, Browderites, Gatesites, and once I even met a Bordigist (a follower of Amadeo Bordiga, the leader of the ultra-Lefts in the Italian Communist party of the twenties). We were Shachtmanites.

Max Shachtman joined the Left wing of the Socialist party shortly after the Russian Revolution because the American Communists, with whom he really wanted to make contact, were so far underground that he could only reach them by first participating in a split from the social democrats. In the twenties he wrote for the *Daily Worker* and rose to be a member of the Communist Party Central Committee, the body that expelled him in 1928. In that year James P. Cannon, a very "American" Communist from a Midwestern and trade unionist background, had grudgingly gone to Moscow for the Sixth World Congress of the Communist International. While in Moscow, he accidentally obtained a translation of Trotsky's critique of the Draft Program of the International and it convinced him. When he returned to the United States Cannon persuaded Shachtman and a few other Communist comrades that Trotsky was right and American Trotskyism was born.

Those were bitter, difficult days. The Communists turned on their schismatic comrades with fury and violence. When Shachtman traveled with Trotsky from Prinkipo to France in 1933 he was, like all of the leader's close associates, armed in anticipation of an assassination attempt by the Stalinists. (Shachtman, a born if somewhat prolix story teller, added amusing details to that footnote to history: Because his passport was issued in Chicago it was reported in the French press that the Russian revolutionary had hired "un gangster" to protect him; and, at the behest of Trotsky's wife, Natalia Sedova, he strolled the deck of their ship with an automatic in the waistband of his white ducks so that the secret police would know that the Trotskyists were prepared.) All those fearful precautions were anything but romantic: Trotsky's son died under mysterious circumstances in a Paris hospital, a number of his secretaries and guards were murdered, and Cannon's secretary in New York turned out to be a Stalinist plant; eventually Stalin reached halfway around the world and stuck a pickaxe into Trotsky's skull.

So it was that when Max gave a speech, which sometimes lasted for about three hours, his presentation of socialist theory was usually suffused with personal emotion and experience. In 1956 during the upheaval in Poland I heard him speak to an audience primarily composed of students. None of us, not even those who had been working with Shachtman for some years, knew the names of the Polish Communists reviled, and sometimes murdered, by Stalin when he purged the party in Poland in the thirties. Yet as Max recited their names, sometimes with just an identifying tag—"a trade unionist, a working-class militant"—it was like hearing the roll call of revolutionary martyrs who were bone of our bone, flesh of our flesh.

Indeed, one of the most distinctive aspects of learning Marxist theory and history in the radical movement rather than in the classroom was that the process was existential. When we debated the decision of the Bolsheviks to put down the uprising at Kronstadt in 1921, it was not an issue of the dead past. Each one of us was asking himself what he would have done under the circumstances. As a result, the disagreements over events that had taken place thirty years earlier often took on the intensity of a debate over future policy. Those who supported the suppression of the revolt at Kronstadt were charged with authoritarian and dictatorial tendencies, and they responded by accusing their opponents of softheadedness and sentimentality.

For Max Shachtman the climactic debate took place in 1938 and 1939 and it pitted him against his own hero, Trotsky. It was a remarkable act of psychological courage for the American disciple, who had never led more than a handful of people and was now only the second in command of a small American sect, to challenge the Marxism of the chairman of the Petersburg Soviet in 1905, the leader of the Military Revolutionary Committee which had seized power in Petrograd in 1917, the co-worker of Lenin, and the organizer of the Red Army. But Shachtman did. In the process he plumbed the democratic essence of Marxism.

The point in issue was the class nature of the Soviet Union. For all his bitter hatred of Stalin, Trotsky defended Russia as a progressive society. It was, he said, a degenerated workers' state. The nationalized property and planning, he argued, were in the objective interests of the proletariat, and indeed of mankind, and struck a blow against capitalism. The totalitarian dictatorship was the means by which a bureaucratic caste had usurped the power that rightly belonged to the working class, but even so, that caste protected and extended the public ownership of the means of production, which was the defining feature of the society. Therefore, Trotsky concluded, Marxists should defend the Soviet Union against any external aggressor and must even understand that the Russian invaders of Finland were doing the virtuous work of history; but at the same time, the true Bolshevik-Leninists should seek to transform the Stalinist system internally.

Shachtman developed a theory of bureaucratic collectivism

in opposition to Trotsky.* The state in Russia, Shachtman said, did indeed own the means of production but that did not make it progressive. Where the state owns the means of production, he argued, the crucial question becomes: Who owns the state? There is only one way for the people to own the state —through political democracy and the consequent right to change the policies and personnel of the state. The Soviet bureaucracy, he therefore held, was not a caste temporarily ruling in the name of the workers; it was a new class, the first exemplar of a new form of society that was both anti-capitalist and anti-socialist.

Shachtman's ideas did not, to be sure, emerge out of thin air. In the twenties there had been Russian Left Communists who had argued that Russia was becoming "state capitalist" and that theory was further developed by their co-thinkers outside of Russia—most notably the "Council Communists," particularly in Holland—in the thirties. Christian Rakovsky, an old Bolshevik who joined the Trotskyist opposition, capitulated to Stalin in 1934, and was then once again purged, made some remarks about a new class in the late twenties. This notion, Anton Ciliga has reported, had its adherents in the political concentration camps in Russia in those years. In France in the thirties Lucien Laurat, a Marxist colleague of Léon Blum, had written on Russian Communism as a new form of class society. Later on, long after Shachtman had independently developed his point of view, that most conscientious and courageous of Yugoslavian revolutionaries, Milovan Djilas, published his famous study *The New Class*. However, it was Shachtman who worked out the basic theory of bureaucratic collectivism in the most rigorously Marxist fashion.

---

* I compress a complex history, since Shachtman did not complete his elaboration of the theory until after Trotsky was assassinated; and I omit some of the people who played a role in this process, most notably Joseph Carter, but also James Burnham, who was briefly a co-thinker of Shachtman and whose *Managerial Revolution* popularizes, and trivializes, some of their common ideas.

There are many implications to this theory. The one that concerns me most here has to do with democracy. Shachtman had understood the crucial Marxist truth of the twentieth and the twenty-first centuries: that democracy is not an element of the "superstructure" in a modern technological society, but is the only way that the "base" can exercise social control over that superstructure. Private ownership of the means of production has been the defining aspect of bourgeois society; bureaucratic and totalitarian ownership is the essence of Communist class society; truly democratic ownership and control is the ideal of socialist society.

Given such an analysis, then, the political demand for democratic freedom under Communism was the stuff of social revolution. Once such a program would be put into practice —as the Poles and Hungarians attempted to do in 1956 and the Czechoslovakians in 1968—it was not simply that the old Stalinist bureaucrats would be swept out of office. The people would now vote on basic economic decisions and they would hardly continue to expand heavy industry at the expense of popular consumption or concede class privileges—villas, vacations, the best schools—to the bureaucracy. Thus the very allocation of resources in the society would be transformed.

This theory, as it turns out, does not simply apply to Russia. In the absence of a capitalist road to modernization in the Third World, the totalitarian accumulation of capital pioneered by Stalin seems to offer a way to industrialize incipient elites throughout Asia, Africa, and Latin America. Indeed it became possible for an anti-Communist regime, like that of Gaafar al-Numeiry in the Sudan in the early seventies, to jail or execute Communists while following the very policies his victims had advocated. And the advanced capitalist countries, with the integration of the corporations and the state, might be moving toward yet another form of bureaucratic collectivism. These extensions of Shachtman's theories have led me to a basic proposition: that the future is not going to be a choice between capitalism, Communism, and socialism, but between bureaucratic collectivism, advantageous to both executives and commissars, and democratic collectivism, i.e., socialism.

We explored some of these ideas in our socialist loft on Fourteenth Street and engaged in seemingly Talmudic exegeses of the holy writ according to Karl Marx. I submitted some articles to our mimeographed discussion bulletin (circulation: 150) in which I argued that Russia was not imperialist, which would indicate the presence of capitalist drives, but only expansionist. Since both I and my critics in the YSL were united by an implacable hostility to actual Soviet policy, that argument would probably have struck an outsider as an enormous quibble over nonexistent differences. On another occasion I spent about six months writing four different versions of a pamphlet on the Khrushchev thaw in the Soviet union, and when I had finally satisfied the committee that all of my analyses were sufficiently refined and dialectical, the material was so dated we could not publish it. Yet our determination to be precise and Marxist in these matters was not as mandarin as it might at first seem, for it led us to some very practical insights.

In the early fifties a good many American intellectuals, including some who had once defended the Soviet Union as Communists or orthodox Trotskyists, had stood their idealism on its head. Where the Soviet reality had once been seen as utterly harmonious, it was now viewed as a monolithic evil, a seamless system of repression in which there was no real possibility of internal resistance since all voluntary associations— unions, churches, cultural centers, even the family—were under the control of the state. That, for instance, was the thrust of a most influential book of the period, Hannah Arendt's *The Origins of Totalitarianism*.* This thesis provided a rationale for supporting America in the Cold War since it held that the only possibility of freedom for the peoples under Communism depended on anti-Communist military power.

* Arendt later modified her views, but not her analysis, particularly after the revolutionary events of 1956 inside the Communist world.

We insisted that the class struggle persisted even within the Soviet bloc. For a corollary of our view that the Communist bureaucracy constituted an incipient ruling class was that the Communist workers, peasants, and intellectuals had a class interest opposed to that of their masters. In June, 1953, the work quotas were raised on construction projects in East Berlin. When the workers resisted, the offending order was rescinded, and this victory set in motion a tumultuous general strike that spread throughout East Germany. In Poland in 1956 a ferment begun by students and intellectuals associated with the paper *Po Postu* became the focus of national discontent and the workers occupied the factories to demonstrate their hostility to the Russians. Again in 1956, in Budapest, the proletarians of "Red Csepel," the working-class district, responded to the appeal of the students of the Petoffi Circle and actually, if only briefly, overthrew the Communist regime.

In Czechoslovakia in 1968 there was another surge toward democratic socialism, and in the winter of 1970–1971 the Polish workers again took to the streets. At the same time there were signs of resistance within Russia itself among intellectuals like Solzhenitsyn, Sinyavsky, and Daniel. In short, our seemingly sectarian and pedantic insistence upon analyzing the Communist experience in Marxian terms had allowed us to anticipate a series of world-shaking events and to escape that fascination with the cobra's eye of Stalinism that had led so many liberals and ex-radicals into the Cold War camp.

III

Since we were such determined, but unhysterical, anti-Communists, our very existence contradicts two of the myths of the McCarthy period. On the Left, among younger academics and radicals, there are those who say that there was no resistance to the witch-hunters, that all the liberals and radicals caved in. On the Right, there are those who still think that McCarthyism struck exclusively at Communists, their friends, and dupes. In fact, we were principled anti-Communists, we fought the persecution of Communists at every step, and we were hounded by the authorities for our pains.

Sidney Hook's *Heresy Yes, Conspiracy No* was the bible for those liberals and socialists who refused to stand up for Communist rights. Ironically the book was dedicated to Norman Thomas, who agreed with Hook for a fairly brief period but soon became once more one of the most adamant defenders of liberty in the land. The Communists, Hook argued, were not heretics whose unpopular ideas were protected under the First Amendment. They were conspirators, not simply against a democratic government, but against intellectual freedom itself. Therefore, in the name of the American tradition, Communists were not to be accorded those protections that were designed to safeguard the free exchange of ideas they were working so hard to subvert.

We replied—and I was one of our main spokesmen on this issue, polemicizing against Hook in *Commonweal, Dissent, The New International,* and *Anvil*—that competence should be the only criterion for determining the right to teach. If a Communist, or a liberal, or a conservative, or a fascist, turned the classroom into a soapbox for political agitation, or if he discriminated against students who disagreed with his views, or engaged in any other form of incompetent academic conduct, he should be sacked for cause after a due process determination by his peers. But if his politics were vile, including advocacy of detestable and even treasonable ideas, but his teaching met rational standards, then he must not be fired.

This position put us into sharp opposition with a good part of the liberal and ex-radical community. In particular, we fought against the American Committee for Cultural Freedom, and I wrote a long article in *Dissent* denouncing their capitulation to Cold War repressiveness. It is not true, therefore, to suggest, as Christopher Lasch does in *The Agony of the American Left,* that the entire anti-Communist Left followed the lead of Cultural Freedom people like Irving Kristol.

Dissent, which was particularly tough on this issue, had the support of intellectuals and writers like Paul Goodman, C. Wright Mills, Meyer Schapiro, and Erich Fromm. James Wechsler at the *New York Post* kept up a steady fire against the witch-hunters; so did thousands of liberals and socialists in organizations like the American Civil Liberties Union and Americans for Democratic Action. The anti-Communist Left was split, no doubt about it; but there were two sides to the split. It is thus impossible to assert that anti-Communism inevitably meant adaptation to McCarthyism.

The Communists whose civil liberties we defended detested us. My first contact with them occurred during the Rosenberg case when I was the organizer of the Catholic Worker effort to win clemency for the condemned couple. We issued a statement deploring the Rosenbergs' impending execution on two grounds: the political circumstances of the trial and the ugly mood of the country; and our principled opposition to capital punishment at all times and places. The *Daily Worker* picked up our declaration, and it was widely circulated by the Rosenberg Committee, only they deleted our comments on capital punishment, particularly, I am sure, because they were specifically applied to the Soviet Union as well as to the United States.

Indeed when two members of the YSL were up for expulsion from Students for Democratic Action (SDA), then the youth arm of Americans for Democratic Action (ADA), there was an incredible alliance. We had gained something of a hearing in SDA, primarily because of our principled defense of the rights of Communists. Some of the ADAers were disturbed, however, because they felt we were inciting the youth to carry the battle into the adult organization. So the more conservative wing of SDA, at the behest of those elders, moved to expel two SDAers who also belonged to the Young Socialist League. There was a donnybrook of a convention at Sarah Lawrence College and our members won the right to stay in the group. However, in the accompanying wheeling and dealing a representative of the Communist youth made a bloc with some of the SDA Right-wingers against the Trotskyist disrupters, i.e., against the defenders of Communist rights. Such were the wages of virtue.

We did not, moreover, contemplate McCarthyism simply from the outside. The FBI took a lively interest in the YSL. Their concern was absurd on the face of it, yet deeply symptomatic of a major trend in American life. Our maximum strength before we united with the Young People's Socialist League in 1958 was 250 members. We could not, I used to say, overthrow the Fourteenth Street subway stop on the Seventh Avenue line. Yet the federal police lavished the kind of attention on us that would have been appropriate to a mass armed revolutionary movement.

The FBI was most likely to approach our people in one of two situations. Those who had just joined, or were thinking about joining, were often accosted; and the discontented who were about to quit received special notice. The latter fact convinced us that we were either bugged or infiltrated. How else explain that the morning after a meeting at which a leader of a minority faction was defeated in the course of a nasty debate two agents were waiting at his door to find out if he wanted to cooperate with the Bureau? Indeed, the FBI almost always drove our disillusioned members back to us: one visit from them was usually enough to reconvert a waverer to the need to rejoin our struggle against McCarthyism.

I was not only our civil liberties expert but also functioned as a sort of security chief. I used to instruct the members on their rights when approached by the FBI—the best procedure was to refuse to cooperate at all; or, at least, to demand that questions be put in writing or be asked in the presence of a third party, something the Bureau would never do—and they were told to report to me if they were questioned. On one occasion I heard a rumor that one of our trusted people was working with the Bureau and to this day I do not know whether it was true or false. What I do know is that that kind of suspicion and paranoia can poison an organization, and one wonders therefore whether the rumor was planted by the FBI itself.

I myself was never stopped by the Bureau but I did encounter them when I was on the staff of the Workers Defense League and I got fairly detailed accounts of their attempted conversations with YSLers. They seemed to me to be, with an occasional exception, unsophisticated McCarthyites who believed that a handful of atheistic Bolsheviks had overthrown Christianity in Russia and might do it here. But how, then, could they cope with our passionate anti-Stalinism?

They did so, I think, in a way that reveals something about American society in those years. When the Cold War broke out, the United States was the dominant economic and military power in the world. Its imperialism had either been internal —the hegemony of the industrial states over the South in particular—or had taken the form of anti-colonialism, of demanding an "open door" in a China already divided up into Western spheres of influence. Therefore America in that period was burdened with an excessive innocence. It did not understand that it profited from the workings of the world market so as to exact a tribute from the poor lands. (For some time now the prices of the industrial goods of the big powers have been going up and those for the raw materials of the Third World have been going down. An "equal" exchange between such economic unequals means that the starving sell cheap and the affluent sell dear.) To the United States, therefore, the anti-Yankee feeling or neo-Leninism spreading throughout Asia, Africa, and Latin America was inexplicable and ungrateful. This country could not make a historical and social analysis of the appeal of revolution, and of Communism, in various parts of the globe, for that would have involved a recognition of the objective validity of at least some of the anti-American charges. As a result, the Cold War ideology became more and more conspiratorial: conditions throughout the world were basically acceptable and improving, but subtle and diabolic Communist agitators had somehow misled people into opposition to Washington and worse. Even sophisticates like Sidney Hook came to place more and more stress on the conspiracy theme. In fact, as the most believable testimony of people who were party members at the time shows, the American Communists were never even close to being a "clear and present danger." They were a bewildered, confused, infiltrated group, and if their leaders convicted under the Smith Act did manage to elude the FBI with some ease, it was only because the Bureau was nowhere near as effective as J. Edgar Hoover claimed it was.

If this analysis is right, then the FBI's ridiculous waste of time in investigating the YSL makes sense. We were small—but aren't all conspiracies? We were anti-Communists—but we were also Marxists, and in the crunch wouldn't we support the other side?

Perhaps the summary example of the absurdity of the government's harassment of us took place in October, 1957. We had scheduled a meeting in solidarity with the Hungarian Revolution of one year before. The featured speaker was to be a Hungarian refugee, a member of the Petoffi Circle, which initiated the uprising, and a leading participant in that rebellion against Communist totalitarianism. He called me a few days before the scheduled meeting, his voice shaking with emotion. Government agents had told him that if he appeared at our meeting, his legal status in the United States would be jeopardized. I wonder if it ever occurred to the FBI why a supposedly subversive organization like ours wanted to memorialize the Hungarian Revolution in the first place.

Our problems were not, however, confined to an occasional overture from the FBI. The YSL was fraternally related to the Independent Socialist League (ISL), an organization with a membership about as menacing as our own. One day in 1947 the ISL (or, more precisely, its predecessor organization, the Workers party) learned that it had been placed upon the Attorney General's List of Subversive Organizations. There had been no hearing, no statement of charges, no warning. From that moment on, the ISL's members and friends were subjected to serious harassment: they were fired from jobs as security risks, given less than honorable discharges from the army after having served in it honorably, refused work, and so on. The legal action against this outrage was begun at once but the first hearing did not take place until the mid-fifties, which meant that all accused of association with the ISL were subjected to extra-legal, economic, and political persecution for years without any constitutional basis for the government's action.

When in the mid-fifties Joseph Rauh, the ADA leader, lawyer, and civil libertarian, defended the ISL before a hearing examiner, it turned out the government could only prove the ISL was a socialist organization, a fact it proclaimed every day of its existence. Rauh also represented Shachtman in a suit to get a passport denied him because, as an ISLer, he was considered subversive. In June, 1955, the United States Court of Appeals ruled—eight years after the original listing of the ISL—that Shachtman had been denied his rights under the Due Process Clause of the Constitution since there had been no hearing and no charges when the ISL was listed. At this point Washington became fearful that the ISL case against the List itself might provoke the Warren Court into declaring the whole program unconstitutional. So a letter was dispatched to the ISL from the Department of Justice in 1957, saying that the government had just realized that it did not have a basis for declaring the organization subversive. A mere ten years of harassment and persecution resulted from this "oversight."

I got a bit of revenge on the government for all this one day on Governors Island. One of our members—a hostile leader of a minority about to split—was being denied his right to be drafted on the grounds that he was a subversive. We hardly wanted our people to be forced into the army, but we didn't want them kept out on anti-libertarian grounds either. I appeared as an expert witness before a board of three colonels which was hearing the protest. Everyone was more or less dozing as they questioned me about the speakers at our meetings. "Do you, Mr. Harrington, support the overthrow of the United States Government by force and violence under any conditions?" droned one officer. "Yes sir," I replied, and suddenly the three colonels stopped napping. The senior officer insisted on taking over the questioning and he asked what circumstances would lead me to approve of overthrowing the government. "Were America Communist or fascist, colonel, I would not be a loyal citizen." They glowered at me and went back to sleep.

It sounds amusing now. It wasn't then. A YSLer, Shelly Abrams, died in an accident in California. The police found our material in his apartment and turned it over to the California Un-American Activities Committee, which was run by a vicious McCarthyite named Tenney. His committee's report that year would have been hilarious were it not backed by such sinister power. The YSL was described as the conspiratorial architect of a worldwide united front between the Communists and the socialists. (What Willy Brandt, Hugh Gaitskell, and Tage Erlander would have thought if they knew that our tiny little group was making deals on their behalf with the Russians is hard to imagine.) At one point, the report quoted a letter from the business manager of *Labor Action,* our newspaper, to Abrams, telling him that his bundle order had been increased. That meant that the most onerous and unpopular duty of the membership, distributing the paper, had been made even more burdensome for Shelly. The report solemnly declared this was evidence that Abrams was steadily climbing upward in the hierarchy of the YSL.

The Abrams story broke when I was in California as John Cogley's assistant in the Fund for the Republic study of blacklisting in the movies, television, and theatre. The effort to drive all alleged Communists out of the entertainment industry had begun with the 1947 hearings of the House Un-

American Activities Committee on party influence in Hollywood (which produced the persecution of "the Hollywood
Ten"). Then, with the Korean war and the related rise of Joe
McCarthy in 1950, the vigilantes went to work with a venge-
ance. The theatre, which had a small and educated audience,
stood fast, but Madison Avenue and the film studios capitulated in haste. The advertising agencies and the giant corporations they represented wanted one hundred percent acceptance
for their products; they could be intimidated by four or five
letters from McCarthyites attacking them for using an accused
actor or actress on a show. In Hollywood the production
chiefs, led by Dore Schary, had originally wanted to fight
blacklisting in 1947. They were summoned to a meeting at the
Waldorf in New York. The financiers who bankrolled their
films told them to be civil libertarians with their own money
but not with the bank's, and they were sent back to the Coast
to announce a purge. With Stalinist delicacy the money men
insisted that Schary be the man to announce the policy change
in public.

For more than a year Cogley and I interviewed people on
all sides, listening and not arguing even when a McCarthyite
or a Stalinist said something that outraged us. We talked to
Madison Avenue "security" people who would assure us that
they were liberals, deny that a blacklist existed, ask for ano-
nymity, close the door, and then show us the list. In Hollywood Kim Hunter, an actress even the Rightists admitted had
not been a Communist, still could not work because she refused to repudiate votes she had cast in her union that happened to coincide with the Communist position. Hunter, and
others who wanted to work, were supposed to write an abject
letter denouncing their sins, real or imaginary. The letter was
then approved by some leading McCarthyite—George Sokol-
sky, the Hearst columnist, was particularly active in this area
—and could be used to stop an American Legion boycott or
picket line.

Talking to so many people who hated one another was an

emotionally exhausting experience. The executives who enforced the blacklist were, for the most part, frightened liberals. Most, but not all, of the Communists pretended to be mere liberals and anyone who mentioned their masquerade was charged with "red-baiting." There were lies and hypocrisy all around, and though Cogley and I unambiguously defended the victims, including the Stalinists among them, they did not always charm us. There was, however, one humorous moment. In doing some library research I had discovered that Dalton Trumbo, the blacklisted screenwriter, had boasted under his own byline in the *Daily Worker* that the party had kept anti-Communist content out of the movies. In my interview with him I rephrased his own statement and asked him if it was true. He denied it, and I let the matter drop. (Our policy was never to dispute an interviewee's statement, only to record it.) Half an hour later he suddenly looked at me, laughed, and said, "You son of a bitch, you read the article!" He then explained that it still wasn't true, that it was a rationalization for the Hollywood party's inactivity designed to mollify party critics in New York.

While I was in Hollywood on this assignment for the Fund for the Republic, in New York Frederick Woltman, the Pulitzer Prize–winning Communist expert of the *World Telegram,* ran a front-page article on me entitled "Find Marxist at Fund for Republic." Woltman unmasked my authorship—under my own name—of a lengthy discussion of Marxist aesthetics, a clear danger to the society. It seemed then that the witch-hunt was closing in. Fulton Lewis, Jr., had been broadcasting nightly denunciations of the Fund and we assumed that he would pick up on the Woltman story or follow up on the Tenney Committee report. I talked with Robert Hutchins, the president of the Fund, about the fact that I would probably soon become a major argument in the case made for depriving the organization of its tax exempt status.

In a remarkable display of courage (which refutes the notion that all liberals caved in before the McCarthyites), Hutchins dismissed my offer to resign. He asked me to prepare a statement on why the Fund had hired me and said that if a public comment were necessary, he would simply sign and issue it. At this point a quirk of Rightist infighting kept me from becoming a *cause célèbre*. Woltman had written some articles denouncing Joe McCarthy from an anti-Communist point of view, and Fulton Lewis and his friends never forgave him for that impertinence. Therefore, even though I was excellent material for a smear—would the man in the street ever understand that it was precisely my Marxism that made me an anti-Communist?—Lewis never mentioned my presence at the Fund.

However, when Cogley was called to testify before the House Un-American Activities Committee I did get proper notice. The committee and its supporters did not like Cogley's report on the blacklist. So they subpoenaed him for a day of hostile grilling and then permitted his enemies to consume a leisurely week in filling the record with uncontested innuendo about the Fund project. When asked why he had hired me, Cogley made use of a background paper I had given him that listed my articles on Communism. One of the reasons, he told the committee, was my expertise on Communism as evidenced by my article on how the Stalinists had tried to manipulate the issue of anti-Semitism in the Rosenberg case. That seemed to confuse the committee members, but later on that week they had a staff member inaccurately testify under oath that I would back the Soviet Union in a war with the United States. Someone had probably told him that I was a Trotskyist and he had simply imputed Trotsky's position to me without realizing that I belonged to a group that had decisively and publicly rejected it.

Such incidents show that the anti-Communist Left was not at all as cowardly as some of the recent interpretations of the fifties suggest. A good number of us fought against both Stalinism and American repression and for the same democratic reasons. The thesis that any and all anti-Communism is an ally of reaction is not simply wrong in theory; my friends and I proved it was wrong in practice.

IV

Perhaps the strangest effect of those years in the radical movement in the fifties was that they led to my love affair with America.

Being an itinerant socialist agitator meant that I saw a great deal of the country. When I could get a plane ticket from the Fund in order to do some work for it, I would leapfrog from New York to Los Angeles, speaking to socialist groups on the way. More often than not I traveled by bus or hitched rides. One November I hitchhiked from New York to Oberlin, Ohio, and back for one speech (the man who invited me to the campus was the college chaplain, Harvey Cox, who later made a name for himself as the author of *The Secular City*). But the truly climactic, and most emotional, journey for me took place during the fall of 1958.

The Independent Socialist League had voted to dissolve itself and its members had joined the Socialist party of Norman Thomas. The YSL had merged with the SP's youth arm, the Young People's Socialist League (the YPSL—or, as it is known in radical and labor history, the Yipsel). I was thirty at the time, a mere stripling by the standards of European youth leaders, but I was already being called "America's oldest young socialist," so it was decided that I would have only one more year of membership in the Yipsel. As part of that plan, I set out across the country in September of 1958. The voyage was a personal and political epiphany.

That autumn the sixties were beginning to stir within the fifties and our tiny socialist movement was emerging from its sectarian isolation. The McCarthyites were in retreat, although we were disturbed that the most effective foe of the witch-hunt was the Supreme Court, an appointive institution that acted from on high. Martin Luther King, Jr., had ap-

peared in Montgomery, Alabama, in 1955 and the first black
mass movement in the South since the days of Booker T. Washington had coalesced around him. This was to be a particularly fateful fact for us socialists for it meant that we had the
opportunity to become part of a vibrant development and
found, *mirabile dictu,* that the theories we had been debating
in that Fourteenth Street loft actually referred to reality.

In 1958 the student movement began to revive, too. That
summer I had gone to the congress of the National Students
Association where, through my friendship with Curtis Gans, I
had attached myself to the University of North Carolina delegation. I was present when the caucus of Southern delegates
discussed their integrationist motions in soft drawls and voted
to back them on the floor of the plenary session. And, thanks
to the National Association of Manufacturers and other conservative business forces, 1958 was also a year of liberal-labor
resurgence. "Right-to-work" laws were on the ballot in a number of states, including Ohio, California, Colorado, and Washington. They had provoked the most militant trade union
political mobilization in years, and the "Class of '58" in Congress was the most liberal since the New Deal.

Although I did not clearly understand it at the time, my
tour, which began the end of September and lasted almost
until December, took place under the most favorable of auspices. Moreover, that Talmudic Marxism I had learned in New
York had kept my eyes focused upon poverty and the continuing existence of a working class in America. It was because of
my politics that I was able to see the country through which I
traveled.

I proceeded toward a golden Midwestern fall by way of
Washington, D.C., Antioch College in Yellow Springs, Ohio
("My literary meeting," I wrote back to the national office,
"was attended by 250 students, one-third of the college, and
constituted a clear fire hazard"), and then Chicago. The University of Chicago, where I had taken my master's in English
literature, was one of our strong areas, so I used it as my base,

staying with Fred and Debbie Meier and making forays into
Wisconsin and Indiana as well as working the Chicago area.
Lake Michigan, it seemed to me, was never bluer.

From Chicago, I flew to Denver where I borrowed a car
from one of the comrades. As you drive to Boulder, you come
to a rise in the road and suddenly the Great Plains end and
the first escarpment of the Rockies rises out of the land. After
Denver came Albuquerque (I wrote to New York, "The DC 7
banks and drops. . . . A vast panorama of desert and mesa
opens to view, spotted with yellow [the turning aspens] and
hazed red [the subsoil]"). I stayed in Placitas, a little
Spanish-American village some twenty miles from the city
with a view of the mountains and desert.

Next, I flew to California. ("The Point," I wrote of a then
favorite bar, "is still there in Malibu. It perches over the Pacific and the waves come right up to the porch on which you
sit and drink.") At Berkeley, the new student political party,
Slate, which was the first harbinger of the tumult of the sixties, was coming into existence. Then I went to Portland and
Seattle and Vancouver, British Columbia. With our man in Seattle, Arlon Tussing, I drove through the Cascade Mountains
to Walla Walla and Chesney, Washington, for speeches. I described that experience in an article in *Commonweal:* "At
the truckers' stop in the Cascade Mountains where breakfast
is ten strips of bacon, four eggs and a pile of home fries, the
coffee cups [which were much bigger than in the East] are
one of the forms defining a history and a way of living."

From Seattle I came back to more meetings in San Francisco, returned to Denver and Chicago, and hitchhiked in the
snow from the Cleveland airport to Oberlin College. It had
been early fall when I had arrived in Ohio; it was winter on
my return. I had an almost unbearable sense of the immensity,
the beauty and variety of the United States of America. My
country was not as homogenized and stupefied as the critics of
mass culture suggested. In Cleveland there was the black comrade who took me to a ghetto bar. When it seemed some of the

customers were going to protest violently against our interracial group, he wryly asked, "Would you take me to a white
place like this?" In Los Angeles there was Kate, the Auto
Workers Union activist, who had arrived at many of the same
conclusions as I, but through work and organizing rather than
books. In Seattle the Counterculture of the sixties was emerging; friends kept the marijuana in a sugar bowl which was
placed in the center of the kitchen table after dinner, like a
box of cigars. In Stockton, California, a wind-burned migrant
at the union hall shocked me by telling me how much he
loved his job as a fruit picker.

The experience was the final, existential proof of a basic
Marxist proposition I had been struggling to formulate for
some time: If you consider your country capable of socialism,
you must love it and trust it deeply. You must sense the dignity and the humanity of the people that survive and even
grow despite the injustices of the system. You must be—if
the word be purged of every bit of jingoism—a patriot, for
you hold to the astounding conviction that your land and its
people can become socialist.

The year 1958 was more than a personal revelation for me,
it was a fateful turning point.

We socialists, true to one of the most ancient traditions of
American radicalism, had bravely and stupidly held that there
was no "real" difference between the major parties and we regarded the official leadership of the unions as timid bureaucrats who dammed and diverted the energy of the rank and
file. To our credit, we never adopted the extreme form of this
illusion, the thesis that liberalism represents the main enemy
in America since its reforms retard the revolution. Even at
our most sectarian we made blocs with nonsocialist liberals in
defense of civil liberties, in support of the black struggle, and
for other causes we believed in. But we always drew a line between ourselves and our allies in an election year. We would
not vote for "bourgeois" candidates even though we would
work with them the rest of the time.

Then in 1958 I saw the unions fighting against "right-to-work" laws from inside the Democratic party. "California," I wrote the national office, "is in a ferment. The bosses have politicalized the labor movement better than eighteen million pieces of socialist literature could. In San Francisco the unions registered 80,000 new voters; in Los Angeles, well in excess of that! The labor contribution to the campaign against right-to-work is in excess of half a million bucks. Goddamn, it will be great when it comes, that old labor party, and maybe it's not as far away as we think. Nineteen fifty-eight may be the year when the bourgeoisie began to organize a labor party with a right-to-work campaign."

Within a few years I extended those perceptions and saw that the labor party was already in existence, although because of the perversities of American history and political structure it was concealed *within* the Democratic party. In any case, the actual experience of American politics, not theory, had begun to change my mind. And yet—and this was the tremendous contribution the democratic socialist movement of the fifties made to me—it was our theory that helped us look for the experience that would transform it. While the American celebrants were writing their eulogies to the new ideologyless, classless utopia America had become, we were talking with workers, blacks, students, and the poor.

When I returned from that trip Anatole Shub, then an editor at *Commentary,* took me out to lunch and suggested that I write an article on poverty in America. As I talked to him, and later as I worked on the essay, I realized that I had spent at least seven years doing research. My time at the Catholic Worker and my tours across America had given me a visual, tactile, personal sense of what poverty meant. I was, to be sure, always the middle-class stranger but I had never been, thank God, an objective academician, but always a comrade in the struggle.

I wrote the article for *Commentary* and it was published in 1959. The piece led to my book, *The Other America,* and to a fundamental transformation of my life. That book belonged to the movement, which contributed so much more to me than I to it. If my hitchhiking and speaking tours seem dedicated actions, my recompense was both immediate and enormous. American radicalism gave me eyes to see with.

I do not for a moment suggest that any small group that holds fast to a vision will necessarily make contact with, and even help change, social reality. I have known people who selflessly committed their lives, their personal happiness, their families, to causes and programs that were not worthy of the sacrifice. I do suggest, even if it sounds arrogant, that despite all the errors we made in our isolated, sectarian microcosm, the theories we debated were much more nearly about the real world than many of the prestigious ideas then taught in the best universities. Above all, we were enriched by that most basic of Marxian truths: that all pre-socialist societies are composed of conflicting classes and must be analyzed in terms of their dynamic. Because we tenaciously insisted on that proposition we did not join in the glorification, or obsessive fear, of a Communism without internal contradictions. We waited for the workers and peasants and intellectuals to perceive that their needs collided with the interests of the totalitarian ruling class. They did; they have not ceased doing so.

In the United States we applied the very same notion to an economy and a society that, the American celebrants told us, had solved all basic problems. For all of our mistakes and stupidities, we saw that there were still workers and poor people and we insisted that their needs would become a point of departure for struggle in this country no less than in the Soviet Union. Most important of all, we maintained that there was a seed beneath the snow of the fifties. And there was.

4. The Rise and Fall of the Beloved Community

The most vital social movement of my generation was the freedom struggle of American blacks.

The movement did more than challenge the political, economic, and psychic outrages this nation had so long and so cruelly visited upon Negroes. That self-transformation of millions of black lives was, of course, its essence. But it also had a profound impact upon white America.

The civil rights struggle forced the country to see the shacks and tenements and rotting houses in which Negroes lived. It simultaneously opened the eyes of the nation to a poverty that, though it is unconscionably and discriminatorily black, is, in reality, chiefly white. Indeed, there are poor whites in the South, half-crazed and fanatic in their hatred of the Negro, who benefited enormously from the sacrifices of Martin Luther King, Jr. It was because of the dedication of blacks that Americans in the sixties began to notice those people whom the aristocratic racists of the South called "white trash" and to whom they gave racial "superiority" rather than a livable income.

The labor movement was affected, too. As blacks succeeded in the sixties in striking down the statutory system of Jim Crow in the South, they discovered that the economic structure of the society—in the North, East, South, and West—worked to keep them in an inferior place more effectively than local ordinances that made them ride in the rear of the bus. So the civil rights movement became a powerful force for economic, as well as racial, justice: the great March on Washington of August, 1963, was dedicated to securing jobs as well as freedom because the two were inseparable. The best elements in the trade union movement responded by committing the AFL-CIO to wide-ranging proposals for planned social investments. Significantly, when A. Philip Randolph published a comprehensive program in 1966, it was entitled "A Freedom Budget for All Americans," not "A Freedom Budget for Black Americans."

Negroes were also a major religious force in this period. Ecumenicism flourished on the picket lines and the spirit of the struggle moved among thousands of priests, rabbis, ministers, and nuns. On the college campus the revival of student activism in the sixties was, in considerable measure, inspired by a black crusade that numbered not a few functional illiterates in its ranks. One could go on and on, but the main point is quite clear: black America did more for white America than for itself, giving the entire nation a renewed sense of its own conscience.

So the civil rights movement was the most important social catalyst in the United States since the industrial unionism of the 1930s. It was also an intense emotional experience, sometimes joyous, sometimes bitter, and I propose to look at the reality of those years from that subjective vantage point.

Objectively, the movement was an extraordinary success. It did not dismantle the economic and social infrastructure of American racism. But in a span of about ten years it destroyed a system of statutory Jim Crow that had endured for almost three-quarters of a century. And yet, the beloved community which that struggle called into being—that incredible confraternity of black and white, religious and atheists, even of rich and poor—has vanished. I attempt to evoke it here for two different reasons. It was part of the greatest missed opportunity in American history, of an era of good feeling that the nation senselessly and ignobly dissipated. That tragic error must be carefully described lest it should happen again.

Secondly, in that transitory, and perhaps doomed, movement of interracial solidarity, there was a revelation of the American—perhaps of the human—potential. I describe it so that it might happen again.

I

I first became involved in the civil rights movement for the wrong reasons.

In 1954, when the Supreme Court finally struck down the "separate but equal" doctrine which had rationalized segregated education, we gathered around the committee table in our shabby little socialist loft on Fourteenth Street. None of us was a conscious racist, all of us had spoken and picketed for Negro rights, but none of us had any real contact with the black community. We were initially moved, not because we had any living relationship with the human suffering and dignity in the black ghetto of our own city, but because we sensed the emergence of a new Social Force in American life. Our analysis was simplistic and inaccurate but it pointed us toward some important truths.

The National Association for the Advancement of Colored People (NAACP), we said with some haughtiness and considerable ignorance, was only the expression of the Negro middle class. That was an arrogant, silly way to describe the only black mass organization of the time. But when, with that rash confidence that a little Marxist learning imparts to youth, we said that A. Philip Randolph, with his vision of an alliance of black and white working people, was a crucial figure in American Negro history, we stumbled into an important reality. In this confused mood we decided to go out and join, not the Negroes of America, but their Social Force.

I overstress my point. My comrades and I had, after all, worked closely, and sometimes in very personal relationships, with blacks like Bayard Rustin, Jim Farmer, and William Worthy. In those days, it should be remembered, interracialism was not taken casually by many people, even in the North.

The bar in which Jimmy Baldwin was assaulted by racists was the place where Bayard and I and other members of the Executive Committee of the War Resisters League used to drink after meetings. The radical movement—and Bohemia—were among the very few places where it was natural for blacks and whites to treat one another like human beings.

We were not, then, completely in the grip of *noblesse oblige* when we set out in search of the Negro masses, but we were certainly vague about the average black, who was hardly to be found in our tiny and exceptional little world. That meant that, rather than teaching Negroes the right political line, which was our initial intention, we were to be instructed by them and only gradually—and to this very day, imperfectly —to root out of our Left-wing souls any unconscious and patronizing sense of superiority. Some may seize upon these confessions to demonstrate that Leftists are often neurotically, or badly, motivated. Of course. So is everyone else. Even though there was something condescending and manipulative in our first impulse to join the struggle, we did join and the experience transformed us. Our flawed decision had excellent consequences, certainly for us, and perhaps even for black people.

We had determined, then, to meet this new Social Force which happened to be the suffering humanity of Negro America. I went to talk to Herb Hill, the Labor Secretary of the NAACP. Hill had originally entered the fight against racism as a socialist doing "mass work" in the NAACP. But in the course of organizing militant demonstrations against police brutality in Harlem, Hill's basic loyalty began to shift from his socialist organization to the NAACP itself, and eventually he became a staff member of the NAACP. Indeed his identification with the cause was so strong that he sometimes passed as a Negro. Dark-haired and swarthy, his knowledge of black argot was so impressive that he sometimes confused even Negroes about his racial identity.

In any case, Hill had had practical, living experience with the black struggle and he was one of the first people to begin to educate me out of my sophisticated Marxist ignorance. The NAACP, he pointed out, was a mass organization, and in some areas, like Detroit, workers comprised a good portion of its membership. The charge that it was middle class (the National Association for the Advancement of Certain People, the taunt went), Hill argued, was based on a fundamental misunderstanding of the position of the black middle class. It was the doctor, lawyer, insurance man, or funeral director who had enough money and enough confidence to want to challenge the Jim Crow laws. The sharecropper didn't travel in interstate commerce or try to go to good—and segregated—restaurants. Therefore, Hill said, the men and women who had been most militant and courageous in the struggle—and who had sometimes been murdered because of their convictions— were usually middle class.

At Hill's urging, I found myself attending meetings of the Manhattan branch of the NAACP in 1954. He told me that as a white man I would immediately be suspected of being a Communist and that I should be subdued. The meetings were indeed middle class; lawyers and ministers played the leading roles, and women, good churchgoers with their proper hats and gloves, formed a substantial part of the rank and file. We began with a hymn, James Weldon Johnson's "Negro national anthem" "Lift Every Voice and Sing," and we spent most of our time discussing petty organizational details and the membership drive. It was hard to hear the winds of history whistling through those prim discussions.

Yet journeying into the ghetto I had made contact— tenuous, ambiguous contact, to be sure—with black reality, even if only as a well-meaning socialist tourist. The Social Force began to show its human face to me.

II

I had first met Bayard Rustin in the pacifist and radical movements. Now, as a new stage in the black struggle began, I started to work with him on civil rights projects.

Bayard was born in West Chester, Pennsylvania, a town where, he recalled, "Negroes had few rights, where they could not walk safely through the streets." He was raised in a fatherless home by struggling grandparents, and then discovered as a teen-ager that the woman he thought was his sister was really his mother. After college, Bayard came to New York and eked out a living singing folk and Negro songs with Josh White and Leadbelly (had he so chosen, Bayard could have had a significant career as a singer). During those years he was attracted by the vigorous Communist campaign on behalf of the Scottsboro Boys and joined the Young Communist League. In 1941, when the Communists suddenly switched from their pseudo-pacifist line at the time the Nazis invaded the Soviet Union, Bayard broke with them and returned to his youthful Quakerism.

At that point he also began to organize under the direction of one of the most important black men in the history of America, A. Philip Randolph. A tall, courtly figure whose gentle and old-fashioned demeanor conceals an iron will and a restless, probing mind, Randolph had first come to the front of the struggle after World War I. He had fought the elitist notions then held by W. E. B. Du Bois—that the "talented tenth" of the Negro middle class would save the race—and the extremely powerful nationalist appeal of Marcus Garvey. As a socialist, Randolph stressed the need for a mass movement that would unite black and white workers on the basis of common economic interest. Out of that spirit he had helped build the Brotherhood of Sleeping Car Porters in the twenties, and in the thirties had been a leading force in the establishment of the National Negro Congress, an organization with union and other affiliates that tried to reach blacks untouched by the NAACP.

As World War II approached and war production boomed, Randolph created the March on Washington Movement. In effect, he threatened a huge, and ongoing, black demonstration in the nation's capital at the very moment when the government was describing itself as the arsenal of democracy in the battle with fascism. Such a dramatic revelation of American racism was intolerable from Franklin Roosevelt's point of view. He sent his wife Eleanor to try to convince Randolph to call off the march, but the Negro leader was adamant. Finally, the President was forced to issue an executive order mandating fair employment practices in the war industry.

Bayard Rustin was the youth organizer of the March on Washington Movement. He had learned from Randolph the theory and practice of building mass movements that combined the demand for racial justice with an insistence upon economic gains. His other decisive experience, which became the basis of his relationship with Martin Luther King, Jr., was his conversion to Gandhian nonviolent struggle.

Bayard spent three years in Lewisburg Penitentiary during World War II because of his pacifist convictions. Even inside the walls he and his pacifist comrades waged a constant campaign against Jim Crow and for prisoners' rights and they initiated some important reforms of the federal prison system. After the war Bayard became active in building American support for Indian independence and eventually went to India to work with the Gandhians there. In 1947 he was back in the United States, applying Indian lessons to the American reality by taking the first "freedom ride," a journey of reconciliation through the South that defied segregation laws and led Bayard into confrontations with hostile mobs as well as put him on a North Carolina chain gang for twenty-two days.

For all the richness of his youthful experience, Bayard was as isolated as any other radical when I met him in 1951. He was the disciple of A. J. Muste, the gaunt, aging dean of American pacifism who made his radical proposals in a measured, almost stately, manner and who, though Dutch born, could have posed for an American gothic. Muste, who had been involved in union struggles, was a founder of Brookwood Labor College in the twenties and became a revolutionary Marxist in the thirties. Then he broke with Leon Trotsky and went back to his religious pacifism.

Dave Dellinger was another prominent member of that pacifist world of the early fifties. He had been one of the first men to refuse induction under the 1941 draft act and had served his time in federal prison.

There were many others—Igal Roodenko, a pacifist anarchist who became a printer, the ebullient Ralph De Gia from the War Resisters League, and David McReynolds among them —but Muste, Dellinger, and Rustin were not only the best known but are also of great symbolic importance in any political chronicle of the Left in those years. In a sense, the story of the rise and fall of the beloved community is an account of how these three men drifted apart and how Rustin and Dellinger now, in the early seventies, are at antipodes after beginning their journey from a common point of departure. In the early fifties these later disagreements were unimaginable. We had the comradeship and closeness that political irrelevance had imposed on us. At some of the parties at Bayard's apartment he would play his harpsichord and sing Elizabethan songs or Negro spirituals. We were, like other radicals, the happy few.

Then in 1955 Rosa Parks refused to observe the Jim Crow law on a bus in Montgomery, Alabama, and a young minister, Martin Luther King, Jr., emerged to lead the struggle she had started. Bayard received a call from King to come South and help and suddenly his ideas about nonviolent battle were marvelously relevant.

King, Bayard rightly said at the time, represented a major turning point in the Negro movement. Booker T. Washington had built a mass base in the South after the Civil War and had succeeded in winning some gains in return for counseling blacks to adapt to the racist reality of the region. As part of that arrangement, paternalistic whites helped educate some Negroes so that they could better fulfill their inferior, but necessary, function in the economy. Shortly after the turn of the century Du Bois and the Niagara Movement created the National Association for the Advancement of Colored People.

The struggle became more militant, but it traveled North and concentrated on the "talented tenth," the Negro elite.

In the period before and after World War I the nationalism of Marcus Garvey was also Northern-based, for a mood of angry separatism flourished among blacks who had fled from the Jim Crow South to the emancipated cities of the North, only to discover that the nonstatutory racism there was every bit as oppressive as the segregation laws back home. This was when A. Philip Randolph appeared with his vision of a democratic and social movement for racial justice.

With King, Bayard said, the struggle had once more returned to the South and involved the masses. The movement was based not upon the "talented tenth" or even upon the unions, but upon the black church, the only institution Southern racists had permitted Negroes to hold in their own name. That permissiveness had made good Jim Crow sense, since black religiosity had for years functioned as a substitute for resistance, preaching Christian resignation in the face of brutality. Now King was utterly transforming that passive faith. He had discovered, Bayard continued, that the old religion had a radical potential, for it had prepared people to suffer for their beliefs. From it, therefore, King would be able to build a mass movement committed to tactical nonviolence in the South.

Even in those early years there was an ambiguous aspect to this tactic which was to figure in some of the conflicts that developed later on. In King's movement—and in Bayard's analysis of it—civil disobedience was justified because the minority of activists in a given Southern city or state could appeal to the United States courts on the basis that the laws they were defying were unconstitutional and therefore illegal. The movement was trying to force the issue into the federal arena because black rights could not possibly be won in a tolerable amount of time by going through the racist courts and legislatures of the Old Confederacy. Thus the philosophy was profoundly democratic, and based on a respect for law, although it encouraged noncooperation with local authorities and ordinances.

And yet there were aspects of this approach that could be used by a minority seeking to impose its will on the majority. In the late fifties, for instance, Bayard used to speak of "social dislocation"—a disruption of normal social life that would force society to adopt certain policies because the cost of not doing so would be too high. Bayard formulated that strategy in terms of the Southern mass movement led by King, and the Northern mass movement that was to be created. But when it was taken over by confrontationists in the late sixties, it became a way of rationalizing the elitist actions of nonviolent—and later, violent—shock troops.

In the mid-fifties, though, life was still relatively simple. Bayard saw his function as helping King to develop nonviolent tactics in the South and building mass support for him in the North, a perspective in which both the Gandhian and Randolph philosophies were synthesized.

So it was that we found ourselves working on huge rallies in Madison Square Garden and elsewhere. Under Bayard's direction, and usually operating as an ad hoc committee, we tried to reach out to the unions, the churches, the middle-class liberals and radicals, and win their political and financial support for King. Those of us, like myself, who were new to mass movements began to learn some of the unedifying details of the infighting that surrounds any great cause. I interviewed Roy Wilkins shortly after King had emerged as a leader and Wilkins was surprisingly open and explicit about his fears of a charismatic leader who was not responsible to a stable organization (this was years before the creation of the Southern Christian Leadership Conference). At one of the Garden rallies I met Adam Clayton Powell for the first time. Powell concluded his speech that evening with a passionate peroration, "March with me to Washington, children! March! March! March!" A cynical friend whispered, "Adam won't even go with them as far as the Hudson River."

Most of the mobilizations on which I worked with Bayard were headquartered either at the offices of the Brotherhood of Sleeping Car Porters or at the Negro Labor Committee, both on 125th Street. Sometimes I would feel apprehensive on my way to the subway at night, though usually I was secure in my righteous innocence. One evening in the late fifties we held a rally in the street in front of the Hotel Theresa, then a hub of ghetto life. A. Philip Randolph, Bayard, and others spoke, and a group of us white socialists passed through the crowd collecting money. Our interracial meeting seemed huge and located in the mainstream; the motley group of nationalists across the street were, we thought, a sectarian irrelevance. Afterward a group of us were walking to the subway, still wearing our armbands. We were filled with the spirit of solidarity and struggle until a voice came out of a clump of black people: "Why don't you Jewish Communists go back where you belong?" That hostility, though we did not know it, was a serious portent.

In 1957 Bayard organized the Prayer Pilgrimage for Freedom. It was designed in support of King, but it was also inspired by Randolph. We called all the organizations, rallied our troops, and the buses left from New York before dawn. When we got to the Lincoln Memorial in Washington, thousands of people had already assembled, many of them poor Negroes who had come up from the South. This time the winds of history were indeed whistling; the Social Force was becoming flesh and blood.

It was the first time I heard King. The program was, like every civil rights demonstration I have ever attended, too long. Every faction had to be given the right to make a speech. Then King stepped forward and began to talk in that extraordinarily mellifluous, utterly southern voice of his. He was an orator in the black Baptist mode, the last survivor of a great American rhetorical tradition. He spoke of love and distinguished between eros, chairos, and agape. Not too many of those poverty-stricken blacks understood the Greek words, or the theological distinctions they expressed, yet King was communicating with them on a level deeper than speech. As he concluded on that soft day in May he said quietly, "Give us the ballot," and then told of all the things that could be done with the vote. He repeated with growing intensity "Give us the ballot" until he had summoned up a vision of a new birth of justice in America, and with the last "Give us the ballot" grown and grizzled men standing on the steps of the Memorial had tears streaming down their faces.

The Pilgrimage marked a new beginning for Bayard and the rest of us. We had assembled an informal working group in which two young socialists, Rachelle Horowitz and Tom Kahn, played increasingly important roles. We were beginning to recruit some new youth, and in 1958, when those of us who belonged to the Young Socialist League joined the Socialist party and its youth affiliate, the Young People's Socialist League, there was an upsurge of activity. In Chicago Norman Hill, an intense and brilliant black socialist, was working full time; in New York it was possible to assemble a working party for a new project in just a few days.

In October, 1958, we thought we might bring a few thousand students to Washington on a Youth March for Integrated Schools. More than 10,000 came, a stunning success by the standards of the previous peace marches in which we had all participated. The second Youth March for Integrated Schools was held the next year and this time 30,000 took part in the demonstration, including the graduates from Central High School in Little Rock, Arkansas, the scene of one of the tensest confrontations over integration in the fifties. Our numbers were now so impressive that a delegation gained admission to Dwight Eisenhower's White House.

But we were taken in by our own Leftist stagecraft and romantically believed we were much stronger than we really were. As the buses rolled toward Washington, the ride was usually dominated by the small group of socialists and a larger, but still tiny, delegation of "red diaper babies." (The latter were the children of Communists who took their political lead from their parents.) After 1956, when Khrushchev spoke out about some of Stalin's crimes and then sent Soviet tanks to suppress the Hungarian Revolution, the American Communists were demoralized, and the red diaper babies found themselves sitting next to democratic socialists, or even Trotskyists, who had once been anathema.

Whatever our attitudes toward the Soviet Union or China, we all knew the same songs, so the buses would reverberate to "This Land Is Your Land," the national anthem of the Left, and the ballads of the Spanish Civil War. Snugly secure in the little world of the New York Left and rolling toward Washington in support of a truly just cause, we looked out of the windows, particularly in the Negro sections of the cities through which we passed, and dreamed that this truly was our land, that we were spokesmen for the people. It was true only in the most tenuous and impersonal sense: though the black people along the way were blissfully unaware of who we were, our marches were, in fact, part of the vanguard of the movement they would create in the sixties. But our sense of oneness with the masses was also dangerously delusional. We had nominated ourselves as leaders on the grounds that our ideas were right. Later, when flesh and blood people, and not a Social Force, insisted on choosing their own spokesmen, we learned, sometimes painfully, that politics is not a folk song.

And yet, even in the late fifties we were reaching out. One of the young blacks who came to work on the Youth March was named Bob Moses. Later, in the early sixties, he went into the backwoods of Mississippi as a member of SNCC (Student Nonviolent Coordinating Committee), and braving the murderous hostility of the whites and acting on the values of his philosopher-hero, Albert Camus, helped begin a new social movement that culminated in the enfranchisement of hundreds of thousands of Southern Negroes. And there was Eleanor Holmes at Antioch College who, working with our socialist club there, helped bring busloads of people to Washington. She went on to graduate from Yale Law School, work for the American Civil Liberties Union, and, as Eleanor Holmes Norton, become the Human Rights Commissioner of New York City under the Lindsay Administration.

In those days when the beloved community was assembling there was an innocence, a freshness, an enthusiasm to our militancy. The tiny radical nucleus to which I belonged, the handful of rebel youth from the unrebellious generation of the fifties, had never known a mass movement. Suddenly we were out of the lofts and on the streets looking down the mall in Washington at 30,000 people in the line of march. We were, moreover, the carriers of a special and extremely important idea in the civil rights movement: that beyond the struggle against Jim Crow statutes awaited an even more bitter battle against the entrenched economic and social system underlying racism.

In 1960 there was a quantum leap.

When King had come under legal attack in Alabama Bayard had organized the Committee to Defend Martin Luther King, Jr. So when the black student sit-ins at segregated public facilities began in the winter of 1960 we did not have to create a new, ad hoc organization. When I returned to New York from a two-month nationwide socialist tour that spring, the office on 125th Street was humming, and people were raising funds, organizing rallies, greeting Negro students expelled from colleges in the South. I was sent to the National Students Association meeting on the sit-ins in Washington as one of King's representatives. It was not then considered preposterous for a white radical to be a spokesman for a black leader.

There was another important meeting that spring, which was portentous for the future: a conference of students at the University of Michigan in Ann Arbor called to discuss ways of supporting the new movement. Jim Farmer was there and so was Norman Hill. Perhaps even more significant was the fact that the founding fathers—if one can refer to college students in their twenties that way—of Students for a Democratic Society were also present, Tom Hayden and Al Haber among them. The conference was one of the first explicit points of convergence between the new student movement of the sixties and what was to be called the black revolution.

As that marvelously hectic spring drew to a close we began

to plan for the political conventions of the summer. King and Randolph formed a March on the Conventions Movement for Freedom Now, which was organized by Bayard and later joined by Roy Wilkins. The objective was to create mass demonstrations at the Democratic and Republican conventions to win support for the sit-ins and to demand the enforcement of the Fourteenth Amendment to the Constitution (which provided for a reduction in the Congressional representation of those states that denied citizens the right to vote). I was sent to the Democratic convention in Los Angeles to work with Clarence Jones (now the publisher of Harlem's *Amsterdam News*) and the local leaders of the Brotherhood of Sleeping Car Porters. Norm Hill and Joan Suall were given the job of organizing the protest demonstrations for the Chicago convention of the Republican party.

III

I arrived in Los Angeles filled with a romantic image of myself. In my imagination, I had finally made contact with those socialists and trade unionists who had, at the bidding of the movement, gone out among the masses. That euphoric mood lasted less than twenty-four hours, for within a day I discovered that the black community was not exactly in a state of militant motion. Negroes, just like about everyone else in Los Angeles, were spread out over a huge geographic area, and they lived in rotting, but individual, houses, not in great tenements. The resultant isolation and anomie could be overcome—as the Watts riot was to prove in a violent, negative way in 1965—but in 1960 the city's black community was quieter than most.

The rival factions in Los Angeles were, however, anything but quiet. There was a group loyal to Roy Wilkins which had just lost out in a branch election in the NAACP but still had the ear of the national office; the new leadership of the NAACP; California Communists; competing political figures;

and the leaders of various political and theological factions in the black church. In part, this intense infighting was just one more demonstration of the oversimplicity of the nationalist theory that makes every member of a race or ethnic group a brother or a sister. Social reality is much more antagonistic than that, even among oppressed people. This general proposition was perhaps even more true for Negroes in America than for whites. The racism of the society excluded—still excludes—many, many Negroes from the "normal" (in the bourgeois competitive sense of the word) channels of upward mobility. Sports and entertainment opened up fairly early for those blacks who had exceptional skills, particularly prize-fighting (the sociology of that sport is so obvious: the champion always comes from the lowest group on the social ladder, the one that literally has to fight to survive). But if you couldn't box like Joe Louis or play like Louis Armstrong, what avenues of ambition were open? Very few. Therefore the frustrations of repressed talent were often expressed in the sharp conflicts for leadership in black organizations.

At the first meeting to plan the Los Angeles demonstrations the Communists and their sympathizers red-baited me. My socialism was an open and avowed fact; their Communism was a secret. They attacked me by saying that people should not bring outside ideologies into the community. That assault failed, not least because I had the assistance of an old friend, Max Mont, the secretary of the Jewish Labor Committee in Los Angeles, a long-time socialist who had a great deal of experience with the political labyrinth in Southern California. Ironically, after their initial attack the Communists became some of our most reliable supporters on tactical questions since we shared a conception of a mass movement even though we were bitterly opposed to one another in our most basic ideas of the good society.

For some six weeks I toiled seven days a week trying to find support in the Los Angeles black community for a mass march. I worked with Clarence Jones and out of the office of the Brotherhood of Sleeping Car Porters on Central Avenue. The experience gave me some intimation of how a black must feel when he ventures into the white-dominated world. Normally, I was the only white on the street in the neighborhood. When I walked down the block, or went to a restaurant to get a cup of coffee, I was the stranger people turned to examine (I could have been a cop, a bill collector, or some other agent of hostile authority). Prey to a constant, nagging uneasiness, I began to understand at least the surface of Jimmy Baldwin's comment that a Negro in America must always be on guard, must never relax.

Eventually I became so discouraged with the prospects for the march that I called Bayard in New York and told him that we should call it off. He replied, "My good friend, there is going to be a march. I know there is going to be at least one person on it. You." So Clarence Jones and I kept phoning and meeting with people—Gus Hawkins, later a Congressman, the influential minister Maurice Dawkins, and literally dozens of preachers, trade unionists, and community leaders. There were deep suspicions of outsiders and radicals. When I flew to Oakland to solicit support from the ministerial association, the first thing they demanded was an assurance that the demonstration would not be Communist.

There were also difficulties with the Los Angeles Police Department. The LAPD was under the command of Chief Parker, a tough cop of the old school with a terrible reputation in black and Chicano communities. When I went to request a parade permit about four weeks before the demonstration, I was told that we had missed some legal deadline and could not get it. A confrontation that was hypocritical on both sides followed. The high-ranking officer of the LAPD talked as if his main concern was the civil rights movement. There would be, he said, a lot of Southern delegates in town, and if we staged a mass protest at the convention site on the eve of its opening it would be regarded as provocative and might lead to violence, which would damage the cause of black freedom.

I was about as disingenuous as the police official, speaking as if my main concern were the honor of the department, the good name of the city, and law and order. I told the officer that he was quite right: there could be violence. Think what it would mean to the Los Angeles police, I argued, if we were denied a permit, marched, and violence broke out in front of the television cameras of the world. We stood eyeball to eyeball for almost a month, repeating our phony arguments to each other with a great show of candor. The day before the march the police capitulated and even agreed to give us an escort so we would not have to obey the traffic lights.

The great day came and passed without incident. We had agreed to coordinate our demonstration with the rally for Presidential candidates sponsored by the NAACP, thereby removing one source of friction. The real breakthrough, though, came without our knowing it. Through all those interminable meetings we had actually won the support of several important Negro ministers; on the Sunday of the march entire congregations came to join us when their services ended. Martin King and Roy Wilkins led about 5,000 people down the street, a considerably larger crowd than we had expected.

We arrived in front of the Sports Arena and were met by Paul Butler, the national chairman of the Democratic party. He told us that the convention platform would contain a strong civil rights plank and King and Wilkins made brief statements. It was, I thought, a dramatic pre-convention moment, focusing on one of the most important issues to be debated at Los Angeles and bringing together men of national stature. It hardly received a line in the press or a picture on television. But—and this is symbolic of the priorities of the mass media —a casual unorganized stunt that we had figured out during the last week of preparations for the march received significant publicity.

We decided that we would end the march with a vigil on Sunday afternoon which would continue, twenty-four hours a day, until the passage of an acceptable civil rights plank. We recruited volunteers unsystematically, primarily from among the young people who had been attracted to the big demonstration. We had managed to organize several busloads of students from Berkeley—most of them veterans of the fight against the House Un-American Activities Committee that spring—and a good number of them stayed at our makeshift camp in front of the Arena. Then there were the unexpected contingents, like the car of Cornell undergraduates who arrived one day announcing that they had heard we needed help and had driven across the country to give it.

I was the head picket captain and as the hours rolled on— we ceremoniously changed the total on a sign every hour—a kind of shipboard camaraderie developed. The few hours each day during which we could sleep seemed unreal; the endless marching, chanting, and singing were our reality. On several occasions Right-wing toughs menaced us, but we had numerical superiority plus some rather competent looking Negro street kids. The other political demonstrators came and went, but almost everyone was careful to indicate their solidarity with us. Some of the Stevenson for President people became convinced that I could persuade Martin Luther King to come out for their man, and the phone booths, which we appropriated as our communications center, jangled with their calls.

Sometimes at night a car would pull up and Negroes who had heard of our vigil on the radio would bring us cakes and food, and again I thought that we had really made contact with the black masses. I was at least partly wrong, as I should have known on the day of the march itself. At the NAACP rally after our demonstration Adam Powell gave a blistering anti-white speech. There I was, filled with the holiness of the cause and tired from the weeks of hard organizing, listening to Powell's intense and brilliant demagoguery touch off hatreds that had been so brutally instilled in the minds of his listeners. Indeed, if I had had the perceptiveness to rise above my own exhilaration that day I would have understood a sad truth about myself and the movement.

In the best of us who came into the black struggle from the outside there still lingered the racist effects of our position as whites. We had rooted out the obvious prejudices and even some of the subtler ones. Yet we unconsciously assumed that Negroes wanted to be white. We were the norm, they were the deviation, and therefore they had to integrate "up" to our level. I was fiercely dedicated to the movement and had volunteered most of my time to it that year. And yet there remained an element of *noblesse oblige* in my attitude. I still had not learned to see the faces of individual black men and women. For the most part I was relating generously, bounteously, patronizingly to a Social Force and therefore I could not come to grips with the deep, quite explicable, anger that I sometimes encountered in its members.

The full knowledge of those paradoxes was years away that summer in Los Angeles. Mainly there was the growing sense of the beloved community. Our round-the-clock vigil, like the college fad of swallowing goldfish in the thirties, had caught the eye of the media. There I was, a white, in charge of a picket line for black freedom, and no one thought it strange. Since I am fair-skinned I wore a Los Angeles Dodgers baseball cap to protect my face from the sun, carefully removing it every time a television camera pointed my way. On the day the convention passed the civil rights plank—which was, as Paul Butler had promised, quite enlightened for those times —someone stuck a microphone in my face and asked me what I thought of the decision. I did not realize that a distant camera was carrying my face to the nation, which must have been momentarily bewildered to see a young white in a baseball cap speaking in the name of Martin Luther King, Jr., and complaining that the Democrats had not gone far enough.

It was in Los Angeles during that period that I also got to know King. We picked him up at the airport several days before the march and drove him to his hotel. I was astounded, and a little humbled, to realize that he was younger than I. It was hard to realize that this friendly, slow-talking, and very

Southern man of thirty-one years of age was, as I understood even then, one of the greatest Americans of the century. I marveled that he had the emotional strength and maturity to keep his equilibrium given the fantastic pressures to which he was subjected. When King arrived in Los Angeles important men and women were on the phone morning, noon, and night imploring us to get him to this or that party. We sometimes joked that we would make up our deficit by auctioning a night with Martin Luther King, Jr., to society people. King himself was like the eye of a storm, calm and self-possessed while a tempest whirled around him.

The representatives of John F. Kennedy, King told me, were the only people from a Presidential camp who had contacted him before the convention. He had had breakfast with them and was told that if Kennedy was nominated and elected, they wanted him to draw up the kind of civil rights program he thought should be put into effect. King was deeply impressed by these overtures, and we discussed whether he should come out for Kennedy. I was against it. In part, my reasons were stupid and sectarian, having to do with a lingering inability to advise anyone to back a "bourgeois" candidate. In part, they were based on a serious political analysis. The election, we knew, was going to be close and King had to keep his lines open to Nixon since he might occupy the White House. Therefore, I thought he should avoid a public commitment. I have no way of knowing whether or not my advice influenced King's thinking; I do know that he was privately in favor of Kennedy even prior to the convention.

When I discussed political philosophy with King I ran into another problem: he too nearly agreed with me. King was philosophic by temperament and not a mere activist. In our conversations in Los Angeles, and in later talks, it seemed clear to me that he understood the need for a thoroughgoing democratization of the economy and the political structure of society. He understood that full civil rights for an exploited and hungry mass of black Americans constituted only a first step in the transformation of the intolerable conditions under which they lived. He therefore struck me as having a socialist orientation, and I had the feeling that had I—or someone closer to King like Bayard—pushed that point he would have agreed.

But Martin King, I thought then—and think now in retrospect—had enough obstacles in his way not to add another. Had there been a mass socialist movement that could have given his immediate struggles real support, then one might have urged him to declare himself in favor of a socialist transformation of American society. No such movement existed, so I very carefully refrained from taking some of the ideas we discussed to their logical conclusion. But still it was a revelation to me that this warm and luminous man of the South had, in the course of a much more profound political and intellectual journey than mine, come to a view of America and the world that I largely shared. In Los Angeles, though, our attention was primarily focused on the political battles of that Presidential year.

We all felt that we had succeeded at the convention. The Democratic platform was more liberal on the issue of civil rights than anyone had imagined it might be and there had been a more noticeable black presence than at any previous convention in American politics. Bayard, however, was a temporary victim of factional infighting at the very moment of this modest triumph he helped create. Adam Powell, who had become disturbed at Bayard's growing power as King's man in New York, made a number of threats to force his removal. Some of us thought this might be part of a deal (Powell had thrown in with Eisenhower in 1956, possibly to head off some pending Justice Department action), but whatever the motivation, the attack carried.

Even though Bayard was defeated in that quarrel, we still had a sense of the beloved community that fall. I went down to Atlanta for the second SNCC meeting, which was held at Morehouse and Spellman colleges. I stayed with a Negro family in a very middle-class black ghetto—as the center of the Negro insurance industry, Atlanta has one of the most affluent black elites in the country—and my roommate was Amzie Moore, one of those incredibly courageous heroes of the NAACP in Mississippi. At the conference we discussed the tactics of nonviolence and there was much linking of arms and singing of "We Shall Overcome." After one session I went with King and Ralph Abernathy over to King's house for fried chicken; and one morning we heard, though it was never verified, that a car of Klansmen had roared through the campus the night before.

On election day we held a march in New York which was coordinated with similar efforts by SNCC throughout the South. In an act of extraordinary stupidity I had decided not to vote for Kennedy on the grounds that there was no "real" difference between him and Nixon in the area of civil rights. Fred Shuttlesworth, who was then King's chief lieutenant in Birmingham and who had been bombed and beaten and threatened but had never lost his incredible ebullience, was flabbergasted when he found out that none of his socialist friends in New York were voting for Kennedy. He agreed with our criticisms of Kennedy for not going nearly far enough but he was too seriously involved in the struggle to think for a minute that it made "no difference" whether John Kennedy or Richard Nixon was President of the United States. He was right.

IV

In 1961 and 1962 the civil rights movement grew with incredible rapidity. It was the conscience of the United States of America.

Bayard became the mentor for the first generation of SNCC leaders: Marion Berry, Chuck McDew, James Bevel, and Dianne Nash among them. At CORE a new leadership headed by Jim Farmer had taken over at the time of the sit-ins, and their Freedom Rides were to pose a major challenge to Jim Crow in interstate commerce. A. Philip Randolph established the Negro American Labor Council (NALC) in order to forward his vision of having black trade unionists play a unique and dynamic role in the creation of an interracial mass movement. Bayard had been pushed somewhat to the sidelines and was spending most of his time working against nuclear testing in Africa, but his ideas were rapidly gaining in influence.

For our socialist cadre it was a time of fund raising, picketing, and proselytizing for our distinctive view of a civil rights movement which would be as concerned with economic and social racism as with discriminatory laws. Tom Kahn was attending Howard University and as a result we made contact with a new group of militants. Tom had helped to organize a remarkable lecture series: Bayard debated Malcolm X, Norman Thomas took on Herman Kahn, and I was matched against Fulton Lewis III, who championed the work of the House Un-American Activities Committee.

As a result, new recruits joined our socialist youth organization, including some of the most important militants of the second generation of SNCC leadership—Stokely Carmichael, Cortland Cox, and Ed Brown (Brown's brother, Rap, was later to succeed Stokely as head of SNCC). One night over at Warren Morse's house in Washington I wound up sitting on the stairs, drinking beer and trying to explain to these young black activists why our various struggles would have to converge someday in the battle for socialism itself.

In 1961 and 1962, then, blacks and whites could still learn from one another without embarrassment and in friendship. Some years later Stokely was to refer deprecatingly to those days when he was involved with white socialists, yet that later bitterness should not obscure the genuine camaraderie that existed among us. There was a Socialist party convention in Washington in 1962, and one spokesman for our faction in the civil rights debate was Bob Martinson, a Freedom Rider who had done time in the penitentiary at Parchman, Mississippi. Stokely, who had been in the next cell and had talked a lot with Bob, sat with our friends in the audience and applauded his presentation with enthusiasm.

My own—and first—arrest was not at all as trying as a stay in Parchman Prison. It had been set in motion by a visit I made to Austin, Texas. The liberals and radicals there were more open and unafraid than in any other part of the country, because in Texas anyone who even advocated moderate reform would be attacked as a red revolutionary Bolshevik. I stayed in Austin on several occasions with Ronnie Dugger, the gentle, fervid, and brilliant editor of the *Texas Observer,* and spent time with the paper's staff (including Willie Morris whose *North Toward Home* contains a moving evocation of the place in this period), students from the university, and liberal legislators. The latter group flabbergasted me. It was a revelation to be drinking bourbon at one in the morning and talking at Dugger's to a member of the legislature who was drawling, "Why, I just never knew what you're telling me about Karl Marx, you hear." One lawmaker even insisted that I sing the "Red Flag" with him in the middle of Schultz's beer garden.

In Austin I met some students who were picketing a segregated movie theatre. The manager said that the Jim Crow policy was not locally made but was handed down from the parent company, ABC Paramount, in New York. We didn't know whether that was true or just a dodge, but we decided to apply some pressure in Manhattan. Leonard Goldenson, the head of ABC Paramount, was about to receive some brotherhood award or another, so we decided that a visit from civil rights pickets and a sit-in might discomfit him enough to make him move on the issue. Back in New York I went for a stint on the picket line so unprepared for an arrest that I brought a date along with me. Suddenly it was decided that we had to make a dramatic move and the next thing I knew I was waving goodbye to my young lady friend and being escorted by the police to the paddy wagon and then singing "We Shall Overcome" as we rode through the city streets.

The New York police in those days were relatively polite with civil rights demonstrators (who knew what political connections we might have?). Even though I was thus not particularly fearful when I was locked into a tiny detention cell for the night, the effect was devastating. I was penned up in a cage. I had a metal shelf to try to sleep on, and the night was filled with the screams of a group of transvestites who were exuberantly baiting and/or soliciting the guards. The next day when I was taken down to the tank at the courtroom, I was rumpled and unshaven and not very influential looking. But the guards were shrewd sociologists. My manner, my grammar, and other signs of a middle-class background put them on the alert. To my chagrin, they deferred to me while they cursed and railed at the Negroes and Puerto Ricans who were my fellow prisoners.

V

By the end of 1962 I felt that I was becoming a socialist jukebox. For years I had crisscrossed the country, speaking, organizing, listening. I could answer most of the questions socialists are usually asked in my sleep—and sometimes nearly did. There was, it seemed to me, a very real danger that I would turn into a hack and I felt that my greatest and most militant contribution to the movement would be to get away to think and write seriously. That was when I took off for a year in Europe.

I came back to New York on December 23, 1963. I called Bayard right away to find out where the action was and to reenlist. I did not realize that the beloved community was about to fall apart.

At first it seemed that the movement was proceeding as before, only more massively and with even greater hopes for victory. There was a school boycott in New York, supported by the teachers' union and organized by Bayard. Within less than four years, however, the very forces that had united in that effort for better schools would be locked in the bitter conflict of the New York teachers' strike of 1968. It was the previous closeness that made some of the later disputes so violent. Albert Shanker, the leader of the United Federation of Teachers in New York and the great villain of the community control militants in the strike of 1968, had called me into his office in 1967 to suggest that I write some favorable articles on community control. To this day Shanker carries the check that Martin Luther King, Jr., sent to his bail fund when he was arrested for teacher union activity.

I anticipate the ironies that were to come. In 1964 my friends and I were becoming more active in CORE, which had transformed itself from a small nucleus of Gandhians into a mass organization. Norman Hill had left his job as organizer of the Chicago Socialist party to become one of the CORE leaders. So I found myself at conferences in places like Baltimore and New Orleans. It was also through CORE that I managed to get arrested again, along with Bayard, Jim Farmer, and a number of other friends and comrades, on the opening day of the New York World's Fair. Significantly, we staged our protest, in part at least, to provide a militant alternative to the ultraradicals who wanted to block the New York highways in a "stall-in."

The notion of tying up the roads had actually started with East Harlem CORE, another group with which we had contact. It was composed of tough young men who prided themselves on being "street niggers" rather than Negroes. Through the League for Industrial Democracy we had set up a training program for them and, in addition to debating and discussing social history, they occasionally tried to hustle some of the speakers for organizing money. After Ralph Helstein, then the president of the Packinghouse Workers, talked, they asked him for financial support and he shrewdly replied, "Sign up some dues payers, I don't care how many, and then the union will match whatever you collect." That, as I remember, was the end of the matter.

Such incidents made it impossible to think of the East Harlem group as a Social Force. They were so restlessly individual, so angry in contrast to the Negro students in jackets and ties who had led the first sit-ins in 1960. When I spoke to East Harlem CORE one night in the basement of a Harlem church, a whiskey bottle was passed around while I was making my analysis of poverty in America and the audience grew progressively less attentive to my description of its own miseries. And yet, were it not for the disintegrations, I think we could have deepened our relationships with these self-proclaimed "street niggers." As it was, they gained a certain notoriety when they sat down on one of the New York bridges at rush hour and caused a huge traffic jam in order to dramatize the plight of their neighborhood.

In spite of all the problems, our work in East Harlem made us hopeful. So did the prospects of the Freedom Summer in Mississippi. The idea for that project had mainly originated with Allard Lowenstein, who was later to achieve political celebrity as the organizer of the Dump Johnson Movement of 1967–1968. (Al and I had met in the fifties when I spoke at his alma mater, the University of North Carolina at Chapel Hill.) He had gone to Mississippi in the fall of 1963 to work with Aaron Henry, an embattled leader of the NAACP, on the Freedom Ballot. The idea was to demonstrate that the disenfranchised blacks of that state were so anxious to vote that they would do so in an unofficial election. During that period Norman Thomas, a good friend of Al's, came down to speak in Mississippi and, at almost eighty years of age, was chased by nightriding cars on country roads.

Al had also enlisted a number of Ivy League students in that project and in 1964 he convinced Bob Moses, then the effective leader of SNCC, to endorse the Freedom Summer. There was opposition to the idea within SNCC based on a suspicion of collegiate carpetbaggers, but Moses' approval carried enormous moral authority and the plans were approved. In New York we met at a union hall to discuss the educational program for the Freedom Summer. Staughton Lynd, who was soon to be one of our most bitter critics within the peace movement, was there and quite friendly. Symptomatic of those times was the fact that Lynd, a white, was given a top educational job in the project.

There was another spin-off from the Freedom Ballot of 1963 and the summer project of 1964 which also derived from our convention marches in 1960. Early in 1964 we had begun to discuss mounting a challenge to the racists at the Democratic convention scheduled for Atlantic City. I went out to the West Coast to contact some prominent Democrats (who turned out to be lukewarm); Rachelle Horowitz prepared a memo on precinct organization in Mississippi; and Joe Rauh took over the preparation of a legal brief with help from Eleanor Holmes Norton. To all appearances our happy family was once more working harmoniously together.

But stresses and strains were already beginning to show. The movement was now national in character and embraced tens of thousands of activists. There were SNCC militants who wanted the challenge strictly controlled by people in Mississippi. There were a number of different reasons for their attitude: some were influenced by the ideology of community control, which was making headway in the Left; others felt that they could maximize their own power base in Mississippi by staking out exclusive rights to defend the rights of the poor blacks there; and a handful of Communist and Maoist ideologues saw a possibility to minimize the authority of the national civil rights organizations, which were hostile to them. There were, in short, good and bad, sincere and insincere, motives at work. And the militants of SNCC were also moving away from Martin Luther King, whom they privately referred to as "De Lawd."

About six months later I heard King describe those days to his New York advisory committee, which I had joined. His point of view might have seemed arrogant to an outsider but I thought then—and still think—it represented a sober assessment of the situation. "They have no real contact with the masses," he said of the SNCC organizers in Mississippi. "So when they started this project, they asked me to come down and I went and spoke at the churches and brought out the people for them and made it possible for them to organize." That, however, was a difficult truth for young militants to recognize, since it emphasized their continuing dependence upon King. Indeed, their secret knowledge of that reality may have been why they were so determined not to acknowledge it.

The split over the Mississippi challenge at the Democratic convention was the first sign of the breakup of the beloved community. None of us, even in our wildest hopes, thought that it would be possible to do anything more at Atlantic City than unseat the racist regulars from Mississippi. But then Joe Rauh prepared such a brilliant case, and Fanny Hamer made such a magnificent presentation, that there seemed no limit to the possibilities. A compromise was offered that would have unseated the regulars and brought two honorary delegates from the Mississippi Freedom Democratic party to the convention floor. The SNCC militants, urged on by Congresswoman Edith Green, wanted to make a fight over the issue and attempt to seat their entire delegation; others advised King to accept the deal on the grounds that it represented a great victory and was, in any case, the limit of what could be achieved.

It was in these discussions that Bayard was accused of selling out and the first, and extremely nasty, rift over lesser evilism in politics took place. From the Supreme Court decision against segregation in public education in 1954 until the March on Washington in 1963, the movement was essentially an exercise in protest. Then in 1963 and 1964 the very success of that effort at the moral education of the American people—including the President and the Congress—suddenly required that political choices be made. For some people in the movement, to choose between less than perfect options, even though they might positively affect the very lives of the poor and disinherited, was wrong.

In the winter of 1965 I took part in a confrontation on this issue. On one side were Bayard, Al Lowenstein, and myself; on the other, Jim Foreman, Ella Baker, and Ivanhoe Donaldson, all of whom had supported the "hard" line at Atlantic City. Foreman angrily charged that Bayard and Al, and particularly Al, had supported the compromise primarily because they wanted to win the Vice Presidential nomination for Hubert Humphrey. Both Bayard and Al then pointed out that they had not favored the compromise but were only for considering it as one option among many—and Foreman agreed that that was true. Such facts did not, however, impress the militants participating in the debate. For them, even to have considered the possibility of something less than total and complete victory—to argue on grounds of political practicality—was treasonous. As a result, a difference on tactics was turned into a bitter dispute over principles.

But it was not only the militants who were changing. In the fall of 1964 I went up to the Brotherhood to get my final briefing on a trip I was making the next day to Mississippi. When I walked across 125th Street to the railroad station on the East Side I discovered that whereas once I had felt so righteous and innocent and safe in the ghetto, now I was apprehensive and fearful. The Muslims and nationalists whom we had thought of as marginal and sectarian when we organized the rallies at the Hotel Theresa in the fifties had not organized Harlem. But it now was manifest that their angers and hatreds had expressed a much deeper truth about the people of that community than we outsiders knew.

In one sense, it was a relief to get to Mississippi. Morty Schiff, a friend from New York reform politics who was in charge of outfitting SNCC with a private radio network for protection against Klan and police vigilantes, met me at the airport. The bodies of the murdered SNCC activists Chaney and Goodman and Schwerner had only recently been discovered, and while I was in the state—the very model of a carpetbagging, atheistic, socialistic integrationist—the accused killers were arrested. So Morty and I drove very carefully through the white section of Jackson, fearful of being picked up by a racist policeman on a minor traffic charge. Only when we got to the restaurant in the ghetto where civil rights workers gathered did we feel we could relax. In New York I had been frightened of blacks, in Mississippi of whites.

The sense of security and community that I felt in that restaurant turned out to be illusory. The movement in Mississippi, I soon discovered, was filled with internal hatreds.

I went to talk to Charles Evers at the NAACP office and he told me how the supermilitant SNCC workers would come into an area, make a brave and dramatic stand, perhaps endure a beating by the police, and then leave. The local black population was then left to suffer the racist fury the militants had provoked. And Evers was bitter about the way in which the SNCC activists scandalized the black community with their life-styles and dress. After that conversation I went back to the SNCC office and was told that Evers was afraid, an Uncle Tom, a sellout. There were also tensions developing within SNCC itself: some of the blacks were upset at the casualness and arrogance of the Ivy League tourists who had taken up the black man's burden as a summer vacation project and had then returned to Harvard or Cornell.

On balance, Evers had much the better of the argument. To euphoric radicals, he and Aaron Henry and the other NAACP activists seemed moderate and much too accommodating. Yet they were the ones whose lives were committed to Mississippi; they were the ones who stayed and eventually prevailed in raising the political and economic level of the great mass of blacks. There were good and brave men and women in SNCC and they certainly succeeded in dramatizing the outrages in Mississippi, in part by their own willingness to suffer and even to die. But they were not there for the duration, they were not rooted in the daily lives of the people whom they romanticized.

I understood that point with particular clarity on the last day of that trip to Mississippi. I had driven from Jackson to

Biloxi on what seemed to be perpetually lonely highways with only sheriffs' cars on the road. I spoke at a little church in the black slum of Biloxi for the Freedom Democratic party. There were some fine SNCC workers there as well as one of the most stupid activists I have ever met. After my talk he carefully explained to the audience that the reason "we"—he was white—made such an impression at the Democratic convention was that "we" wore overalls rather than coats and ties. He went on in his apostrophe to sartorial radicalism for quite a while, apparently not noticing that almost every black man in the church that day wore a coat and tie and the two or three people who came in overalls had carefully put on white shirts and ties. These people were, after all, coming to a refuge from their workaday world and their "middle-class" clothes were an assertion of their dignity. That SNCC activist, on the other hand, was looking for a Social Force and ignoring people. He thought there was a mystical rural proletariat which would leap from poverty over the stage of mass consumption and arrive at the professed asceticism of the student Left in a single bound.

The debate within the movement was, however, decided for us from on high and everybody lost. In the winter and spring of 1965 Lyndon Johnson prepared the escalation of the war in Vietnam. That was to signal the end of the progress that the blacks and the poor had been making in the first half of the decade.

Strangely enough, that sad turning point coincided with a great victory for the freedom movement. In March, Martin Luther King was leading a campaign in Selma. There had been disputes even on the battle lines: the SNCC militants wanted to provoke violent confrontations while King and his allies were sincerely committed to nonviolent tactics. However, on the final day of the march from Selma to Montgomery the divisions abated and we were again a part of the beloved community. I flew down with friends from New York and we found ourselves in the early morning at a big field near a Catholic school. As we slowly began to move out, we passed through rutted, muddy little streets lined with broken-down houses. There were Negroes sitting on the front porches watching in disbelief as that vast assemblage of blacks and trade unionists and priests, bishops, rabbis, nuns, and students streamed by. Some looked on with tears running down their cheeks.

When we reached one of the main streets of Montgomery the scene was eerie. There were no citizens anywhere, only feder-alized guardsmen grimly lining our route through a ghost town, protecting our rights under a court order. At the state capitol all one could see were the Stars and Bars flying over the birthplace of the Confederacy. Finally we spotted an American flag off to the side. There were a few speeches but two songs caught the spirit of the day. We sang "Blowin' in the Wind," asking how many men must die before a man can be free. A little later on some tactical genius realized that the symbolism of the Confederate flags could be turned to our ad-vantage. We stood there and we sang the "Star-Spangled Ban-ner" and it welled up like a revolutionary anthem.

That was, I think, the last day of the civil rights movement which had revived in 1954.

VI

There were many activities after the Selma-Montgomery demonstration, of course. In June of 1965 I spoke at a South-ern Christian Leadership Conference educational meeting in Atlanta. Bayard was the organizer. Now the pressure from the militants within SCLC forced him to put on a black in every session in which a white had originally been scheduled to lead the discussion. And that fall there was a small pre-conference in Washington to help plan the White House Civil Rights Con-ference of 1966. Under the leadership of A. Philip Randolph and Bayard, and with brilliant technical help from Leon Key-serling, we had drafted and lobbied for a "Freedom Budget," which would provide genuine full employment for the black and white poor through social investments and which would also benefit the entire society. A truly bizarre—and perhaps prophetic—incident took place on the periphery of that gathering.

A White House aide told a few of us that President Johnson was worried because several of us—King, Rustin, Farmer, and myself—were also sponsors of a SANE march against the war in Vietnam.* Johnson was concerned, we were told, that we might utilize the conference as a platform to denounce his policies in Indochina and had even considered canceling the meeting. We had no intention of disrupting the event, yet the change in mood evidenced by Johnson's fear was of enormous significance. The civil rights coalition that had grown throughout the first five years of the decade was being torn apart by Vietnam. Still, I did go to a Texas buffet in the White House and Lyndon Johnson came around and shook all our hands and Aaron Henry came over to me and said, "Mike, we're eating barbecue in the White House."

We continued to fight for the Freedom Budget and promoted the alliance of blacks and whites on economic and social issues, but the war was destroying that alliance faster than we could hope to put it back together again. When King decided —quite rightly I believe—that he had to attack the unconscionable American course in Vietnam, the split deepened. I saw him for the last time a few months before his death. We met in New York to discuss the plans for the Poor People's March. Bayard, and I to a lesser degree, argued that the march had to focus on realizable demands. There could not

---

* During the hearings on the Watergate Scandal in the summer of 1973, I discovered that I had made another presidential list as a designated "enemy" of Richard Nixon's White House. I was proud of having been honored in this fashion and received a number of congratulatory letters and calls. On reflection, I am not amused. Whether my politics are right or wrong, they have always been open, straightforward and democratic. Nixon's people were trying to intimidate me for my opinions; presidential power was attacking the Bill of Rights.

be one more symbolic victory, we said; the movement desperately needed real gains. But the rising mood of nationalist anger was felt in the room and King could neither agree with our argument nor formulate an alternative to it.

Typically, though, he asked me to prepare the first draft of a manifesto for the march. To his death, Martin Luther King, Jr., was an integrationist who thought it natural to ask a white to write the first statement of the movement's purpose. He laughed when he asked me to take on the job and said, "You know, we didn't know we were poor until we read your book."

The next thing I knew I was sitting in front of a television set in New York and the program was interrupted to report the assassination of Martin Luther King, Jr. So we organized one more march. Bayard went down to Memphis and many of us followed in a jet chartered by Victor Gottbaum, the head of District Council 37 of the State, County and Municipal Employees. When King was killed he was helping the sanitationmen of Memphis to organize in that union. We marched through the silent, empty streets of that city and the only motion we saw or noise we heard came from the weapons carriers and tanks that were there to protect us. Coretta King spoke, so did Abernathy, and Jerry Wurf gave a moving address on behalf of the union. But King was dead and so was the movement.

Was it because of King's murder that the beloved community came to an end? In part. Had he lived, there would have been a commanding, towering figure speaking for integration and social justice. No matter how nasty everyone became toward everyone else, his presence would have saved the spirit of the movement. Yet, as I sensed at that last meeting with him, King was sorely tried at the time of his death. He felt, I think, that he was at a kind of impasse: he had to respond to the militants and break with some of the white liberals on the issue of the war, but both those steps would take him away from the nonviolent and integrationist values that were at the very center of his existence. In the speech he gave the night before he died, he said that, like Moses, he had seen the Promised Land but that he would not be able to lead his people into it. This remark has been widely interpreted as a premonition of death. I think it was the despairing cry of a man who did not know which way to turn.

The movement also died because the dream of a beloved community was, and had to be, an illusion. In a country profoundly suffused with economic, social, and psychological racism, it is possible to build a little island of love for a while; then the exigencies of struggle intervene, and one must choose from among competing bills, decide between politicians, deal with egos—and the community turns on itself. Some friends from Bayard's old cadre think that the division began at the moment of triumph of the March on Washington in August, 1963. At that point we had moved, in Bayard's famous phrase, from protest to politics. In protest there is the possibility of a beloved community; in politics there is not.

And then there was the war in Vietnam. If Lyndon Johnson had not escalated that tragedy in 1965, if the huge Presidential and Congressional majorities of 1964 had held together and been used to implement Freedom Budget programs, if the demands of black people had been partially met, then many things might have been different. As it was, Vietnam caused Johnson to miss the greatest opportunity in recent American history. There was a mood of good feeling in the early sixties that genuinely moved the conscience of white America. Had the Administration continued to put its energies into the struggle that attitude made possible, it might have been able to begin the end of the Civil War. It chose Vietnam instead. At the same time, anyone who took nonviolence seriously, as King did, could not help but be profoundly outraged by the carnage in Indochina. So a good number of the black activists, and most of their radical and liberal allies in the white middle class, went into increasingly bitter opposition to the government.

The two finest traditions of the American liberation move-ment had come into conflict with each other. The exigencies of building an interracial movement of the black and white workers on the basis of economic demands—Randolph's vision—suggested that one try to ignore the war, or at least not put it in the forefront of struggle. Peace activism would alienate a major section of the organized white labor move-ment, which was so crucial to that tactic. But the imperatives of even a strategic commitment to nonviolence—King's great contribution—required that anyone who spoke, or thought, in the name of Gandhi denounce the unconscionable war in Vietnam in no uncertain terms. The ideological synthesis and the political alliance that provided the basis for the great vic-tories of the early sixties were shattered.

I suppose I felt the change most poignantly in the spring of 1968. Martin King was dead and buried; Robert Kennedy was moving toward a rendezvous with his assassin in Los Angeles. I went down to Resurrection City in Washington, the makeshift town the Poor People's March had erected on the mall near the Lincoln Memorial where all the great demonstrations had taken place. They were running a "Poor People's University" there, which was as grandiosely named as many of the other activities in the camp. For Resurrection City was not the site of the brotherhood and sisterhood of the poor, but a place of tension and violence in which all the disintegrative forces loose in the lower depths of the society were tearing people apart.

After I spoke an angry—almost psychotic—black attacked me as if I were a Dixiecrat Senator who had come to Resur-rection City to reject his just demands. His harangue was long and incoherent and I listened quietly because I was afraid that he was going to jump me. Finally, his passion was spent and the meeting was over. I almost ran out of the camp and along the walk past the Lincoln Memorial, fleeing what seemed to me the shambles of the beloved community.

5. The New Left

The New Left of the 1960s flourished, at most, for five years. It was partly the creation of the mass media which, following the tradition of agents provocateurs in radical organizations, delighted in ultra-Leftism. It was a movement of the privileged, and often self-righteous, young which began with an excessive innocence of the Marxist past and ended by repeating the stalest and most outworn of Leftist clichés. It nominated a number of substitute "proletariats"—the youth, the blacks, the poor, the dispossessed—to play the role the working class had been assigned in Marxist theory, and it was wrong every time but refused to learn from the experience. When everything else had failed, the most frantic of the activists turned to nihilism and terror, blowing up some of their own number in the process.

In spite of this history the New Left was one of the most important, and hopeful, signs of the decade. In a burst of creative idealism it announced the entry into American life of a new political force, a conscience constituency based on unprecedented institutions of mass higher education. It asked fundamental questions about the system and legitimated the notion of radical alternatives for an entire generation. It was the precursor and inspiration of movements it sometimes opposed, like the campaigns of Eugene McCarthy and Robert Kennedy in 1968, and of George McGovern in 1972. It was a portent of basic changes in the American class structure, not simply a collegiate episode, and the trends to which it gave witness and the vision it so imperfectly articulated are going to be more relevant in 1980 than they were in 1965.

I was present at the birth of the New Left. I knew it as a social phenomenon and as a sad personal experience associated with my own middle-aging and some of my most spectacular stupidities.

I

Because of the date of my birth it was almost inevitable that I should have played a role in the formation of Students for a Democratic Society (SDS), the organization that became one of the focal points of the New Left.*

I was born in 1928 on the very eve of the Great Depression. Because of that economic cataclysm my generation was quite small; bad times make for low birth rates. But that demographic fact alone hardly explains the fate of my contemporaries. A generation, as Karl Mannheim has suggested, forms its social ideas for the first time at about seventeen years of age and that experience provides some basic themes that last for a lifetime. I turned seventeen in 1945, the year. of anti-fascist triumph and Roosevelt's death. The society at that time was still under the spell of New Deal emotions but within the next few years, between 1946 and 1948, it turned toward the Right under the impact of the Cold War. So I and my peers came to political consciousness on the cusp between periods of reform and reaction.

In 1948, for instance, Students for Democratic Action (SDA) was a mass organization with over 10,000 members, as were the Young Progressives of America (YPA), the youthful followers of Henry Wallace who were led, and manipulated, by a small, but quite effective, Communist cadre. The socialist students, though fewer in numbers than SDA or YPA, were

* In what follows I will focus almost exclusively on the white New Left. In Chapter 4 I touched on the other crucial component of the movement, the black militants of the Student Non-Violent Coordinating Committee.

enjoying their best years since the Depression had radicalized so many youth. By 1958 the Progressives did not exist, the organized liberal students were a remnant, and the socialists were the happy few I described in Chapter 3. With the emergence of Joseph McCarthy in 1950 as a national figure, a mood of repression and fear swept the campuses. As a result, my generation and the one that immediately followed it in the fifties were frightened in spirit as well as few in number.

I was atypical. I had become an activist in January, 1951, when I went to the Catholic Worker, at the very moment when many of my contemporaries were retreating from the struggle. Starting in 1955, I had begun to make those national speaking tours, some of which lasted more than two months. In that context, it was practically fated that I should meet the founding sons of the New Left in the late fifties. That encounter came about through no particular virtue of mine; just one rung above them on the generational ladder, I was one of the very few people with whom they could talk.

Demography and politics were interpenetrating in the case of those first New Leftists. They were the vanguard of the "baby boom" generation born after World War II. Indeed, one could chart some one-to-one correlations between that phenomenon, which began in 1945 when the returning veterans opted for early parenthood in surprising numbers, and the growth of SDS. The latter took place exactly when the first sons and daughters of the baby boom reached eighteen—and college—in 1963. Here again, it was not population itself, but population in a particular economic and social context, which was important. The huge post-1945 generation benefited from an incredible increase in the places available to students in the colleges and universities. It was the very first generation of what has been called the "knowledge economy." It also enjoyed the relative prosperity brought about by the policies of John F. Kennedy and Lyndon Johnson, the very liberals whom the radicals were to dismiss so contemptuously.

In the "Port Huron Statement," SDS's enormously influential manifesto of 1962, there was an awareness of some of these trends. "We are people of this generation," the statement begins, "bred in at least modest comfort, housed now in universities, looking uncomfortably to the world we inherit." Read carefully—and particularly with the understanding that these few phrases do not apply to any other major segment of a generation in history—it serves as a very accurate description of the social base of the New Left.

All these things are clear enough in retrospect. In the late fifties I was simply aware that there was a breath of wind rustling in the sails of American radicalism.

II

In the late fifties and early sixties the University of California at Berkeley was not only a hopeful place politically, but more than that, the Left was actually friendly.

There had been a furious struggle during the McCarthy period over a loyalty oath for faculty members, and there had been so stringent a ban on controversial speakers that Adlai Stevenson was once refused the right to appear on campus. But a brilliant and humane technocrat, Clark Kerr, helped resolve the crisis over the oath, and when he became president of the university he repealed the speaker ban. Kerr attracted outstanding educators to Berkeley and the social science faculty was dominated by serious theorists, most of whom had had a sophisticated Marxist background. Once, to the delight of the socialist students, a luminary of the sociology department who had been a Trotskyist in his youth was walking with Kerr when he met a trade unionist out of his past. The former comrade greeted the professor by the only name he knew, his party name (a pseudonym that, romantically or realistically, some in the movement adopted). Kerr, as befitted his cool sophistication, did not blink an eye.

The real ferment, of course, was not taking place in the faculty but among the students. A group of activists coalesced in the late fifties around an imaginative project: the creation of a student political party. For some time the Left had regarded student government as a sandbox in which the more ambitious conformists were allowed to play at democracy. With the formation of the new student party, Slate, the radicals at Berkeley had decided to utilize that façade as a framework for political education and perhaps even as a means to student power.

Practically all Leftist tendencies joined in this project. In considerable measure that unity was possible because of the collapse of the Communist party after the Khrushchev revelations about Stalin and the Hungarian Revolution and Russian counterrevolution of 1956. Before that, the Communists had successfully identified themselves with an indigenous tradition of working-class radicalism on the West Coast. They had seized the inheritance of the Wobblies and the Seattle General Strike of 1919 when frightened Americans looked with horror at what seemed to be a "Soviet"—a council of workers' deputies —in the state of Washington. In the San Francisco area the memories of the great strike of 1934, led by Harry Bridges, and the Oakland General Strike of 1946 were still very much alive. The International Longshoremen and Warehousemen's Union (ILWU), with many Communist or pro-Communist militants, was a serious political force that had once dominated the California CIO.

Then in 1956 American Communism was demoralized. For the next five years—until Fidel and Che provided an appropriately romantic and generous rationale for totalitarianism—the Communist issue that had divided and tormented the American Left since the Communists split from the Socialist party in 1919 was no longer central. Khrushchev had denounced his predecessor's crimes (but not his own) and had sent Russian tanks to shoot down revolutionary workers in the streets of Hungary almost on the very anniversary of the October Revolution of 1917. After that, no one wanted to defend Russia as the image of the future. So democratic socialists, red diaper babies from the ILWU, and unaffiliated mavericks of a dozen varieties worked together around Slate.

On my speaking tours I used to stay as long as I could in Berkeley, sleeping on the couch at Art and Anne Lipow's house. There on the edge of the Pacific a radical-Bohemian world existed that was very much like the one I had known at the University of Chicago in the late forties. At the Steppenwolf and the Blind Lemon there was an ambiance of folk music, Marxism, and sexual freedom, the Left-wing trinity of that period. Later, in the mid-sixties, the "street people" came to Telegraph Avenue over by the university, but they were much less literate and talkative than we had been; they were part of the Counterculture, which celebrated the value of non-logical communication and even violence. That scene later degenerated into the miseries of drugs, petty theft, and vandalism. In the late fifties, however, there was a friendly freemasonry of the Left.

We went to San Francisco's North Beach, too. Allen Ginsberg and the Beats had put that area on the cultural map, and the Co-Existence Bagel Shop was a standard stop on the American underground. The rites of Leftist nonconformity had a long history in the Bay area: there are references to Kenneth Rexroth in the revolutionary mural that decorates Coit Tower, the monument to San Francisco's firemen; Lawrence Ferlinghetti's City Lights Bookstore was the latest manifestation of that phenomenon; so were the bars, like Vesuvio's, where we drank when we came across the bay. It seemed obvious enough that the cultural rebellion in North Beach and the political beginnings at Berkeley were of a piece.

And yet there was a small cloud no larger than a man's hand on the Berkeley horizon. The collapse of the Communist myth had not simply discredited Joseph Stalin; it had undermined the very idea of socialist analysis as well. Those of us who were trying to build an organized socialist movement could work easily enough with the unaffiliated Slate activists, but they were impatient with our program and our agreements about practice often concealed differences with regard to theory. This was a portent of later developments within the New Left itself. Most of its founders, like the people in Slate at Berkeley, distrusted any ideology. Because my generation was so small and defeated, and because Communism, which had been wrongly identified as revolutionary Marxism, had been discredited, they did not have a vibrant sense of their links with the radical tradition. In the first period that was an enormous advantage; later on it turned out to be a source of bewilderment and disintegration. We didn't know that then; it was just a very good time to be in the East Bay.

The ideas being generated in Berkeley and elsewhere fertilized one another. One reason was the growing ease with which semi-affluent students could move around the country and learn from each other; another was the CIA.

The CIA's contribution to youthful rebellion occurred in 1959, the year in which the Communists, their youth fronts, and sympathizers were sponsoring a World Youth Festival. For their own reasons they had decided to venture out from behind the Iron Curtain and to stage the event for the first time in the West, in Vienna. The CIA, which, unknown to the public, had become a center of Cold War liberalism, began to finance an alternate American delegation to compete with the official group. They enlisted the aid of Gloria Steinem and others and proceeded to channel funds surreptitiously into the effort to build an anti-Communist group.

I stumbled on the CIA front in Los Angeles and immediately figured out that it was some kind of government operation. However, I naively and wrongly assumed that it was simply a matter of the State Department's encouraging some rich individuals and corporations to give financial aid to the American youth who wanted to go to Vienna to challenge the Communists. The CIA tricksters had meanwhile offered to help me get to the festival and I was in a quandary. Was it permissible for a socialist to accept a subsidy from an outfit being patronized by the State Department? (Had I dreamed that the

CIA was involved, there would have been no issue.) I took that question to the National Committee of the Young People's Socialist League and there was a long debate in which, inevitably, someone pointed out that Lenin had accepted railroad transportation from the Kaiser when he went from Switzerland to Russia in 1917. It was decided that I would tell the front group that I would accept an airline ticket from them only if I could go on my own, completely independent of their organization, and with the explicit understanding that I would attack American capitalism and foreign policy as vigorously as Communism. That did it. The offer of help was withdrawn forthwith and I paid my own way, having nothing to do with what turned out to be the CIA's dirty games.

The CIA's motives were as anti-Communist as its methods were despicable. But in its scandalous efforts to make young Americans the dupes of their own government it had helped legitimate youth politics. The festival was discussed on campuses around the nation and even the good young people who were taken in by the CIA spooks were changed by the experience of going to Vienna. My own trip had many personal consequences—it convinced me to go to Europe and live there for a year and it affected my attitude toward Communism. In Berlin on my way to Vienna I sat as a member of the Executive Committee of the International Union of Socialist Youth and camped out in Rehberge Park with young socialists from around the world. It was before the construction of the Berlin Wall and we spent a good part of every day roaming the streets of East Berlin, where I was repelled by a drab city with 1984 banners everywhere proclaiming "Work for Us Is a Joy, for We Work to Build Socialism." In Vienna I saw the festival organizers turn goons loose on dissidents. The night Paul Robeson sang, some young people who carried signs about the Hungarian Revolution were beaten. I myself had several tense moments. I went with a group of socialists and a carload of Viennese plainclothes police (the city administration was socialist) to distribute leaflets outside the festival center. We were followed and watched by strongarm squads organized by the local Communists, and even though we had official protection they managed to snatch and tear up our throwaways. On another occasion the Iraqi delegation discovered that I was talking to some of its members inside the compound and it was touch and go until I finally persuaded them that I had picketed against America's invasion of Lebanon and could not therefore be an imperialist agent.

In the stadium at one of the mass rallies the Russian delegation released "peace parachutes" when it entered; everyone had to rise, and the crowd chanted rhythmically, hypnotically, *Mir y Drujba, Paix et Amitié,* Peace and Friendship. It was my first totalitarian rally and it reminded me of the newsreels I had seen of Hitler at Nuremberg.

Back in the United States, student consciousness and rebellion continued to grow. At the University of Michigan a group of young people who were to become the founders of Students for a Democratic Society very deliberately modeled themselves on Slate when they created their own student political party around 1960. I had been coming into Ann Arbor for some time, staying at the house of a Japanese-American comrade, Lefty Yamada, who had been recruited into the movement in a detention camp during World War II. Tom Hayden was the editor of the *Michigan Daily* and, inevitably, we met. Hayden was (I use the past tense in speaking of Tom because, although he is very much alive, his style has changed considerably) one of the unlikeliest political leaders who ever became the guru of an intensely loyal following. Physically, he was unprepossessing, a nondescript youth of no great presence. His manner, which either prefigured or inspired the characteristic style of SDS leaders, was understated, unemotional, anti-heroic. Yet there clearly was an intense Leftist commitment burning inside Tom, who had, ironically, grown up in the parish of Father Charles Coughlin, the pro-fascist and anti-Semitic priest.

In the first period of our acquaintance I tried to win Hay-

den to socialism. He accepted much of my analysis, yet he
balked at the socialist idea itself. My analysis, he said, was too
bound up with dogma and obsolete, bookish controversies.
What radicalism needed was a fresh start, a rethinking of
perspectives that would avoid the old rhetoric, with its sectarian Europeanisms, and speak in the authentic vocabulary of
America. In this approach Hayden, like the Slate activists in
Berkeley, was expressing what was to become the dominant
philosophy of the New Left, simultaneously its strength and its
crucial weakness.

One reason for Hayden's agnosticism about theory was that
the imperatives of practice were so obvious. The civil rights
movement had surged forward with the sit-ins in the winter
and spring of 1960. That year, at the Ann Arbor conference
in support of the sit-ins, there were students from small Catholic colleges who had never had anything to do with the Left
but who now responded to the challenge of the movement in
the South. Also that spring students demonstrating at hearings
of the House Un-American Activities Committee in San Francisco were hosed down the steps of City Hall by the police.
For the next several years the issue of HUAC was second only
to civil rights among the activists. Fulton Lewis III had made
a "documentary" movie on the events in San Francisco called
Operation Abolition, whose thesis was that the anti-HUAC
movement was being directed by Communists who wanted to
abolish the Un-American Committee. Lewis showed the film
around the country, lecturing on the dangers of this newest
Red conspiracy.

I must have debated Lewis more than a dozen times in that
period: at Brooklyn College, Vassar, Drake, and Fairfield,
among other places. At the 1961 Congress of the National
Students Association in Madison, Wisconsin, the Right-wingers
demanded that Lewis be given the opportunity to present his
position to the delegates who were considering a resolution favoring abolishing HUAC. My friends from SDS were there as
the organizers of the Liberal Study Group, a sort of caucus of

the democratic Left. They persuaded the opponents of the committee that I was the best person to counter Lewis. A collection was taken to fly me to Madison—the small group of pro-Communists winced at having to pay the expenses of such a vocal anti-Communist—and the debate was held in a densely packed church.

During our previous encounters Lewis had always used the same speech, but I watched the movie each time, studied the script when HUAC published it, and constantly shifted my line of attack. At Madison Lewis was giving the more liberal version of his standard argument and suddenly a new incongruity flashed through my mind. In rebuttal I told the audience about it. Lewis had said that the demonstrators outside City Hall were good Americans fighting for a wrong cause. The conspiracy to abolish HUAC, he argued, was really only taking place inside the building where, he charged, the Communists were in control. The pickets outside were, he said, sincere if misguided. But, I reminded the students, when they saw the movie earlier they had heard Lewis' own voice, while the camera panned over those non-Communist good people outside City Hall, saying (I paraphrase, but accurately), "The Communist party had assembled its cadres to carry out Operation Abolition in San Francisco . . ." The audience roared; the debate was over.

Afterwards there was a sense of exhilarating comradeship among the SDSers, the socialists, and myself. Tom Hayden and Sandra Cason ("Casey") invited me to their wedding and members of the Liberal Study Group repaired to a victory party. NSA, we all knew, was about to repudiate the House committee decisively. The atmosphere then was something like that of the beloved community in the civil rights movement. The issues that concerned us—the emancipation of black America, the abolition of HUAC, the end of "in loco parentis" control of students on campus, the repeal of capital punishment—were all ethical questions. We did not have to make hard political choices or work out careful strategies. We were a crusade, and a rather happy one.

Less than a year after experiencing that fraternity and closeness at Madison, my stupidity was to pit me against those friends. I recall the experience, personally painful as it was and still is, because I think it illuminates the generation gap that bedeviled the New Left.

III

The crisis took place at the United Automobile Workers camp at Port Huron, Michigan, where SDS assembled in the summer of 1962 to adopt its famous Manifesto. The failure in communication was distinctly personal, a product of my own worst judgment. It was also generational and, perhaps, inevitable—though I must admit that my errors certainly exceeded the bounds of historic necessity.

There had been disagreements before the Port Huron meeting. In the spring of 1961 we all went down to the University of North Carolina at Chapel Hill. I had been going there to speak for some years at the invitation of Anne Queen, the director of the Young Women's Christian Association. A native of the Southern mountains who had worked her way through Berea College, Anne had most improbably made the YWCA a center of controversial and even radical discussion. At that meeting in 1961 there was a dispute between those who emphasized political struggle to realign the existing party system and those who looked toward the organization of groups outside of all the established institutions. Hayden was with the latter group, Steve Max, a good and hard-working militant, was with the former.

That dispute was to become the central axis of debate and of organizational splits in the late sixties but it was not at all that emotionally charged at Chapel Hill. In the year leading up to the Port Huron convention there was harmony and even euphoria. I worked closely with Hayden and Al Haber, a soft-spoken, scholarly activist, the son of a social democratic professor at Ann Arbor, and the paid functionary of SDS. The unspoken assumption among us was that in any dispute between SDS's parent body, the League for Industrial Democracy (LID), and the youth, I would, of course, side with the latter. It was a period of growing excitement and hope: one night I interrupted a civil rights rally at PS 41 in New York to present Tom Hayden who had just returned from jail in Albany, Georgia. And Hayden wrote an article in *Mademoiselle* in which he said that there were only three people over thirty whom his generation trusted: Normas Thomas, C. Wright Mills, and Michael Harrington. Shortly thereafter I forfeited that trust.

It was not at all clear when the SDS meeting took place at Port Huron that the organization was about to become the central force in the white Left. In 1962 there were only several hundred students in SDS. The Young People's Socialist League (YPSL) had a thousand members and, in conjunction with some pacifists, had built the Student Peace Union into an organization of 10,000, the largest youth movement since 1948. In February of 1962 the SPU had sponsored a protest against nuclear testing in front of the White House. Some 8,000 young people showed up; President Kennedy sent coffee to the pickets protesting his policies. But the YPSL was soon to destroy itself in the course of a fratricidal and super-theoretical faction fight that had a disintegrative effect on the SPU. In that particular context, the anti-ideology ideology of SDS looked most attractive and sensible.

At Port Huron we discussed night and day. There were two related issues that led to the most heated debates: Communism and American liberalism.

My anti-Communism was formed in the traditions of revolutionary anti-Stalinist Marxism. It was not simply a theory, but an emotion as well. I felt as one with those Left socialists and syndicalists in Spain whom Orwell described in *Homage to Catalonia* and I had actually learned the history of those struggles from the Spanish exiles with whom I worked in the Anti-Franco Committee. When the Hungarian Revolution took place in 1956, as I noted earlier, it utterly demoralized all the apologists for Russian totalitarianism, removing the Communist issue from its contentious place at the center of the American Left.

But the six years that separated Hungary from Port Huron defined the space of a new generation. When Tom Hayden and the other SDS activists became active in the late fifties and early sixties the American Communist party was a discredited remnant of a movement that had once dominated more than a third of the industrial unions in the United States. And in 1962 at Port Huron the recent, and disgraceful, Bay of Pigs invasion was much more alive than the memories of Hungary. The founders of SDS were in no way Communist, but they could not see why I attached so much importance to some of the formulations in the first draft of their Manifesto, particularly those that seemed to imply the United States was the prime source of evil in the Cold War.

So my notion of a progressive, Leftist anti-Communist made as much existential sense to them as a purple cow. For them, anti-Communism was *simply* the excuse American reactionaries used whenever they wanted to masquerade their own viciousness in some noble rhetoric. For me, anti-Communism had certainly fulfilled that reactionary function, as when the CIA made its sordid deal with the Batistallanos in the aborted invasion of Cuba, and as such it had to be fought vigorously. But a resolute struggle against reactionary anti-Communism, including a principled defense of the rights of Communists, required, in the name of democratic and socialist values, an equal struggle against Communist totalitarianism. My logic, I still think, was compelling. But the students at Port Huron had not shared the experiences that made this logic so vivid to me.

The argument over American liberalism was related to the issue of Communism. For Hayden and most of the delegates, all the liberals had capitulated to Joe McCarthy and had played the reactionary anti-Communist game. Therefore, one could not look to the standard agencies of social change—the workers in their unions or the middle class in ADA—but had to find a new point of departure. In that first period of SDS there was a tendency, deeply influenced by the writings of C. Wright Mills and the accomplishments of the Zengakuren in Japan, to see youth, and college youth in particular, as exactly such a new force.

The truth was complex in this debate. There had indeed been American liberals—far too many of them—who, sometimes out of fear or guilt about their past "softness" on Russia, had become genteel accomplices of the McCarthyites. But there had also been liberals and democratic radicals who had defended the rights of American Communists even as they rejected Communism. More to the point, if one dismissed the entire American labor movement and the liberal middle class, what hope was there of ever building a majority coalition that could transform the most powerful and imperial capitalist power in human history? Liberalism, I argued, was most certainly not an adequate answer to the problems of the time; that was why I was a socialist. But the liberals represented the mass Left wing of American politics and one had to identify with their humane values in order to help them go beyond their own present program.

Here again the generational differences were at work. I had lived through eight years of the Eisenhower Presidency. During a good part of that time I scorned those who worked in the liberal wing of the Democratic party and waited anxiously for the emergence of a revolutionary consciousness among the workers. Then as I emerged from the sectarian meeting halls and began to crisscross the country and to make contact with political reality, I began to change. In 1958 I had seen the tremendous vitality within the unions as they fought against "right-to-work" in Ohio, California, Washington and other states and played a decisive role in electing the most liberal Congress since the New Deal.

In many ways, the SDS leaders and I were moving in opposite directions and had intersected. They had begun as moderates, nonsocialists who took the formal promises of American democracy with innocent and deep seriousness. I had come from a Marxist tradition which understood that there was a basic antagonism between the American rhetoric of equality and the American reality of class injustice. They were becoming progressively more cynical; I, more hopeful. Precisely because they had not worked out a program but simply responded to situations, they could be fairly casual about embracing contradictions. They thought that Walter Reuther should give them UAW money and accepted it gladly when he did; but they also regarded Reuther as an establishmentarian trade unionist who had sold out the rank and file. They were in favor of political realignment but dismissed the liberals who were essential to it.

We argued into the middle of the night, sitting in the dining hall of the UAW center, drinking beer. To this day, I think that there was considerable substance to my main points. The SDS was indeed vague about its attitude toward Communism and its anti-liberalism made it impossible for it to project a realistic majority coalition for social change. Both these flaws were to contribute to the crackup of the New Left in the late sixties. I, however, treated the confused young idealists who made these understandable errors as if they were hardened intransigents. Then an accident made our failure of communication even worse. I had to leave the meeting before a decision was taken on the disputed parts of the "Port Huron Statement." I was told several days later that the convention had not made any changes in the draft. In fact, it had responded quite generously to my criticisms. But before I found that out, I committed myself, emotionally and politically, to attacking the SDS leaders—my friends and comrades.

The confrontation took place at a board meeting of the League for Industrial Democracy (LID). The LID dated back to the Debsian period in American socialism; it had been founded in 1905 by Upton Sinclair, Jack London, and Harry Laidler, and it became a meeting ground for trade unionists, socialists, and Fabian intellectuals. In the thirties Norman Thomas was prominently identified with the LID and so was John Dewey. It was also in that decade that the LID youth group, the Student League for Industrial Democracy, had been manipulated and captured by the Communists. That experience had intensified the anti-Communism of the aging leadership, which remained in 1962. So when they heard that their youth were once again going soft on the Russians, they reacted with alarm.

I was a godsend to the traditionalists on the LID board. I was relatively young (thirty-four) and had been very active in the anti-HUAC fight, so I could not be dismissed as a red-baiting old fogey. I therefore became the spokesman for taking harsh organizational measures against SDS: locking them out of their office, firing Al Haber, refusing to put Steve Max on the payroll even though he had been duly elected at Port Huron, and so on. To their eternal credit, people like Norman Thomas and Harold Taylor fought against me. Unfortunately, my position carried.

At the end of the summer I went with Norman Thomas to meet with the SDS leadership at the University of Ohio campus, where the National Students Association Congress was being held. I began to confess my errors and that smoothed over some of the hurts. But at that Columbus meeting I was aware that I had lost the confidence and trust of the young people. At the end of our tense reconciliation Casey Hayden said, "Well, I know now what it must have been like to be attacked by the Stalinists." She exaggerated—even in my worst moments I never descended to the vilification of opponents practiced by the Communists—but the thrust went home. After more than a decade of rebel activity I had sided with established elders against nonconformist youth. Why?

In part, the answer is unhistorical and circumstantial. I had become a minor guru for the SDSers and enjoyed the political and moral authority that status conferred. Then, when a question came up that was crucial to me but not too important in

their experience, they had rejected my advice. Suddenly I was
no longer the youthful maverick of the 1950s. There was a
new generation on the scene and I was threatened, not simply
by a political disagreement over Communism and liberalism,
but by my own middle-aging as well. So I fought back, stupidly and bureaucratically, as much out of wounded ego as
from ideological convictions. And then there was that unfortunate accident that made me wrongly think that nothing I
had said that night in the dining hall at Port Huron had had
any impact whatsoever.

Yet these are only mitigating factors. The conflict was, I
think, inevitable, and had I acted on the basis of better information, more maturity, and a greater understanding of the
differences at stake, that would only have postponed the day
of reckoning. We of the fifties Left were simply too weak to
serve as a point of departure for the New Left of the sixties. We
were pathetically few in number, the veterans of a beleaguered
holding operation. Their Christopher Columbus vision of
themselves as the first to discover the truths of radicalism was,
alas, a most logical deduction from their own experience and
our failures.

But if I am quite ready to acknowledge my personal fail-
ings in this unhappy history, I am not at all prepared to concede political error on all points in the dispute. SDS's rejection of my point of view was certainly understandable and
even fated but it was not necessarily right. By completely
turning away from liberalism and rejecting the accumulated
wisdom of the Left in all its previous tendencies, the New Left
did indeed emerge as a fresh and hopeful force on the American scene. But later on the failure to deal with program and
philosophy was to prove costly. In 1965 Jack Newfield wrote
in *The Prophetic Minority* that "the student groups today are
too de-centralized and anti-ideological to be captured by any
manipulative cadre." Yet within three years the Maoists of the
Progressive Labor party had won about half of SDS and had
driven the other half to ultra-Maoism and even terrorism. One

reason for that disastrous development was that SDS's Leftism had been defined so emotionally that it could not withstand the attack of a disciplined cadre. The other was that the organization had burned all of its bridges to the mainstream of American labor and liberalism. It therefore was not subjected to any of the constraints of real-world movements engaged in daily political struggles for concrete gains. It could, given the opportunity, devour itself in private.

IV

I spent 1963 in Europe. When I returned to New York I found the New Left growing and deeply involved in a search for a substitute proletariat.

The notion of a "proletariat" was first used by a romantic philosopher Franz Baader, in 1835, and referred to the impoverished masses who were being created by the emerging capitalist society. It was Marx, of course, who gave the term its decisive political definition: a working class driven by the very conditions of its existence to rebel against the system itself. In his first formulations of the theme, in the *Communist Manifesto,* Marx vastly oversimplified social reality and argued that capitalist society was rapidly polarizing into two classes, a gigantic proletariat and a tiny bourgeoisie. But even after he corrected that view and took notice of the growth of the new middle stratum, Marx always saw the workers as the key agency of social change. It was not just that they suffered exploitation—slaves, serfs, and others had been exploited throughout history—but that they did so in a unique way. They were herded together in huge factories and city slums and driven to form unions out of the day-to-day struggle for a crust of bread. They soon discovered that the state could annul the gains of any one class struggle and therefore formed political parties that aimed at changing the very class basis of government itself. So their revolution was not episodic, like the *jacqueries* of peasants, but an inexorable result of the reality of daily life; and since it sought control of the means of production which, for the first time in history, could provide plenty for all, this revolution could abolish the class distinctions and hatreds that scarcity had made inevitable.

There are many things that can be disputed about this vision, yet, for all its flaws, it is a rich, historically dense analysis of the perspective of the Left. The Western labor movement did not play the revolutionary role Marx had assigned it, but it was—and is—the most powerful single force for social change within capitalist society. In the early sixties this was not at all apparent to SDS (or for that matter to American intellectuals in general). They heard only the ritual affirmations of capitalism and stern denunciations of Communism from the trade unionists. They did not understand, or care about, labor's commitment to full employment legislation, national health care, tax reform, and the like. Later on the AFL-CIO support of the war in Vietnam and its rejection of a quota of jobs for blacks alienated the young radicals even more.

In part, this SDS hostility to the unions, despite its Leftist rhetoric, was related to the class composition of the new movement, which was white middle and upper middle class. In saying this I hardly want to suggest that one's social class at birth determines one's political views for a lifetime. By such a crude misreading of Marxism it could be proved that Marx himself, who grew up in the relatively comfortable Rhenish middle class, was incapable of ever becoming a Marxist. However, one reason that the class origins of SDS are important in this regard derives from another fact: these children of affluence were students during a decade in which the public investment in higher education rose faster than the Gross National Product. It was not simply that their mothers and fathers—and childhoods—had been privileged; it was also that their college years were handsomely subsidized.

It was, then, not an accident that some of the strongest SDS chapters were built at elite institutions like Harvard, Berkeley,

Ann Arbor, and Columbia. These students' isolation permitted a radical commitment to the "working class" that was combined with an ignorance of, and even a contempt for, actual workers. To a "revolutionary" who had been exempted from the daily struggle for existence, grubby questions about wages, hours, working conditions, and medical bills seemed petty. But if the unions, with their unideological concentration upon the immediate welfare of their members, were not the basic agency of social change, where in America was there a proletariat?

The history of SDS from 1962 at Port Huron to its effective dissolution in the summer of 1969 is the story of a search for a new proletariat. At first it was to be youth and/or students; then the blacks and the minorities; then the white poor in a populist alliance with the black poor. In every case, the SDS theorists identified a very real source of discontent. But in no case did they define a force, or even a coalition of forces, capable of transforming American society. As a result, they were unable to link their politics to any mass movement. They were forced in upon themselves where, in a radical frenzy that increased in direct proportion to their distance from the real world of social struggles; they conducted the class struggle against one another rather than against the American bourgeoisie.

In 1964, when I returned to the United States, this process of internal disintegration was in its early stages. That fall I spoke shortly before the election at Berkeley. The first big sit-ins of the Free Speech Movement had taken place when an old socialist comrade, Dick Roman, put himself in the path of a police car that was taking away a CORE organizer who had violated a disputed university rule. Lewis Feuer had been one of the most articulate faculty members in defending the students' point of view in the negotiations with Clark Kerr, just as he had been a major figure in the defense of the student charged with attacking a policeman during the anti-HUAC demonstrations of 1960. A thoughtful and decent human being, Feuer had been teaching at the University of Vermont when I first met him in 1951. Over the years at Berkeley I had come to know him as one of the professors most deeply and sincerely concerned with the emerging student movement.

When Lewis chaired a meeting at which I spoke in the fall of 1964 he told the audience that he would have been happier if, rather than campaigning for Lyndon Johnson as I was doing, I were running as a socialist for the Presidency. The audience, which included most of the campus activists in SDS, responded enthusiastically. That evening was one of the last of its kind. Within months the protests on campus had escalated and Feuer, who looked at political questions with the scrupulousness of a moralist, discovered that he could not go along with some of the more extreme demands. Then, in a rather typical and miserable fashion, the students began to berate him as a sellout, an agent of the administration. Lewis was, I think, deeply hurt, as well he might have been, and left Berkeley not too long afterward with bitter feelings toward the young people who had betrayed him. I have not agreed with some of the theories this mood produced in him; but I have always understood, and sympathized with, Lewis' feeling that he had been used.

I recount the incident because it illustrated an important trend: the growth of New Leftist intolerance and conformism, the beginning of the game of more-militant-than-thou which was to last for four years and drive some people to the ultimate proof of their "radicalism"—armed terror. In 1965, when Feuer's confrontation with his one-time allies took place, the war in Vietnam had been escalated and the hopes for reform, which were shared even by the SDS of 1964 ("Part of the Way with LBJ" was their slogan in the election), had been shattered. In February, 1964, I had talked to a cheering audience of about a thousand students at Berkeley about my hopes for Lyndon Johnson's war on poverty. A year and a half later, in the fall of 1965, any speaker who spoke kindly of Johnson would have found it difficult to hear himself above the catcalls.

Another sign of that growing alienation was a letter I received from Tom Hayden just after I came back to New York in 1964. Tom was, even after the bitterness of 1962, quite friendly and open and told me that he was moving away from the politics of realignment of the major parties, a goal we had once shared. He was looking, he said, for forces outside the Democratic party and outside the unions. That quest led him, and the majority of SDS which he then influenced, to try to organize on a community basis in the slums and ghettoes. The effort centered around the Economic Research and Action Project (in the inevitable acronym, ERAP).

The theory behind ERAP was compelling enough at first glance. The people in the slums and ghettoes, it was argued, are ripe for organization. They constitute—and I am not sure whether it was Gunnar Myrdal or Herbert Marcuse who first used the phrase—an "underclass" with a common lot and common grievances. So the radicals would go into those communities and become a catalyst by raising demands for jobs and/or a guaranteed income, and by fighting on local, neighborhood issues. In the process, they would also create a political—or revolutionary—base for themselves. More often than not these attempts at community organizing were inspired by Hayden's vision of a new populism and therefore sought to unite the black and white poor in a common front.

There were two main reasons why every single ERAP attempt failed. One had to do with the SDSers themselves, the other with the people they wanted to organize.

In the winter of 1965 I gave a speech at the University of Michigan and went over to the ERAP headquarters afterward for an informal discussion with the activists. Typically, Rennie Davis, one of the brightest of the ERAP group, was off on a trip to try to get foundation support for the revolution. I asked the other ERAP people whether or not they had made a lifelong commitment to community organizing. They assured me that they had. But how, I asked, are you going to survive? To marry? To have children? Can the poor possibly pay you poverty wages for your services? There were no answers to my questions.

In other words, these students were, as I wrote in the *New York Herald Tribune* about my visit to Ann Arbor, the new Narodniks, the newest manifestation of that student drive to "go to the people" which had asserted itself so strongly in nineteenth-century Russia. And, like the old Narodniks, they had no roots in the daily lives of the masses with whom they wanted to struggle. Like the SNCC activists in Mississippi, they could come into a community and help in the struggles and then they could, and did, leave. The people remained behind with their old miseries.

Secondly, ERAP romanticized the people. Slum dwellers are not forced into solidarity by the discipline of work and the antagonistic presence of a single boss (or foreman) in a factory. Their social existence is much more diffused, and they often prey upon one another rather than uniting in common battle. The oppression they experience is at least as demoralizing as it is radicalizing, which is why slums produce junkies and alcoholics as well as militants. They are not a proletariat.

There was, however, a theory which seemed to show that the failures at community organizing were only temporary. An impending economic catastrophe brought on by technological innovation was supposed to save the radical movement from its contradictions by throwing millions of workers out of work, thus making them open to Leftist appeals. A manifesto of the Ad Hoc Committee on the Triple Revolution was a seminal document for this point of view. It was drafted, in the main, by W. H. Ferry, then the vice president of the Center for the Study of Democratic Institutions in Santa Barbara, and it also drew upon some of the ideas of Robert Theobald, a radical market economist who believed that automation was destroying the traditional capitalist link between work and income. Consequently, Theobald said, the society would have to provide a guaranteed annual income in order to survive. I was a signatory of the final document; so were Gunnar Myrdal and Bayard Rustin.

The notion of a coming structural crisis in capitalist society rapidly became an article of faith for the New Left. If a huge

portion of the American work force was about to become obsolete, then radical ideas that had little appeal today might
win over disinherited masses tomorrow. In this perspective, the
poor were not to be raised up into the working class, as in the
liberal scenario; the working class was about to be pushed
down into poverty and would become revolutionary as a result. In the spring of 1965 Nat Hentoff, a journalist who reflected the most recent trends in the movement, proclaimed
the Guaranteed Annual Income as the basic demand of the
new radicalism.

The Triple Revolution analysis was wrong, a fact I can
hardly gloat over since I used a part of it in my book, *The
Accidental Century*. We had accurately identified a tendency of
the economy to produce more and more goods with fewer
workers because of accelerating technological innovation
since World War II. We had rightly rejected the complacent
Keynesian faith that some judicious fiscal planning would
allow the nation to cope with all of the resulting problems.
But we had wrongly and mechanistically assumed that the
trend would express itself only through mass unemployment.
Hundreds of thousands were, to be sure, driven out of the
labor market altogether and therefore deprived of the right to
be a jobless statistic (only those actively seeking work are
counted). And by 1972, Herbert Stein, Richard Nixon's chairman of the Council of Economic Advisors, had formally
abandoned the goal of reducing the jobless rate to 4 percent.
But in the sixties some job seekers were absorbed into the
army and war production for Vietnam, and still others were
sent to college. We had not realized that the public works programs we talked of might take the form of killing Vietnamese.

So the central themes of the New Left in 1964 and 1965
turned out to be illusions. The community organizers did not
find a new proletariat; the economy did not break down under
the impact of automation. Yet even if the New Left was
wrong in some of its crucial assumptions, it was still a hopeful
phenomenon. By 1966–1967 SDS had reached out to stu-

dents in nonelite Midwestern universities. I talked to new young radicals at the University of Indiana chapter who came from American Legion and even Klan homes. Indeed, I got along so well with these indigenous rebels that one of the sophisticated leaders of the group later explained to me that his recruits were just not well enough educated to see through a sellout like myself.

In other words, SDS developed within a growing constituency in America: the institutions of mass higher education. And if it did not articulate the demands of a new proletariat, it was a genuine portent of a new, and growing, political force.

V

Then came the escalation of the war in Vietnam, the decisive event of the decade. At first it was an enormous boon for SDS; later on, an indirect cause of its disintegration.

I had been actively opposed to American policy in Indochina since I first became aware of it. In 1953 and 1954 I took part in demonstrations and wrote articles denouncing the American financing of French imperialism there. During the Kennedy years, when most of the liberal community accepted the gradual increase in troop strength as a proper exercise in the containment of Communism, I was writing editorials in the Socialist party newspaper, *New America,* attacking the President for his support of Diem. In the spring of 1965 I wrote in *Partisan Review* that "escalation of the Vietnamese —or any other—crisis would not only end talk of the War on Poverty and the Great Society, but threaten World War III."

In that spring of 1965 I had been involved in the discussions about SDS's first anti-war march in Washington. I had urged them to make it clear that they were not acting as the champions of a Vietcong victory, but rather as opponents of American intervention and advocates of withdrawal and peace. Even if one did not share my hostility to Communist-led movements, I argued, one had to understand that the American peace activists could not fly the flag of an organization engaged in battle with American troops. A. J. Muste and Norman Thomas shared my concern. They and some other older veterans of the peace movement issued a statement on the eve of the SDS march asking that the students not become pro-Communist out of an overreaction to America's unconscionable policy. For reasons which I will detail in the next chapter, I was not a signatory though I certainly agreed with the main thrust of the statement.

This incident touched off a fierce debate over a nonissue: whether Communists should be "excluded" from the peace movement. I developed my own position in two long articles in *The Village Voice* during 1966, which provoked a storm of correspondence and criticism. The quarrel was over a nonissue because I, and those democratic Leftists who agreed with me, at no point proposed the "exclusion" of Communists, or anyone else, from the anti-war demonstrations. Let the entire membership of the Maoist Progressive Labor party join in the ranks, I said in the *Voice*. No one will ask them to leave or call the police. But, I also said, let the march be publicly and officially opposed to Maoism and support of the Vietnamese Communists as well as to reactionary militarism in Saigon. Then when someone waves a Vietcong flag and the press jumps at the opportunity to portray the entire demonstration in that image, there will be a clear basis for dissociating the majority of the marchers, who are not partisans of the Vietcong, from the tiny minority who are. I thought, and said at the time, that were I more cynical, I would have suspected that the Vietcong flag wavers had been planted by the FBI. Agents provocateurs have always been ultra-Leftist. I felt that any movement that appeared to be a fifth column for Communists doing battle with Americans would have no chance of winning the people of the country to the idea of withdrawal from Indochina.

In the fall of 1965 SANE sponsored a march against the

war. I successfully persuaded the organizers to have Dr. Spock direct his demands for peace not simply to Washington and Saigon, but to Hanoi as well, calling for a negotiated settlement. I sat at the Washington Monument listening with pride as Norman Thomas told the audience that he did not want to burn the American flag but to cleanse it of the defilement of the Indochina war. That, it seemed to me—and, more importantly, it was to seem to Eugene McCarthy and Robert Kennedy in the campaign of 1968—was the way to speak to the people.

Thomas' speech, however, was not the most influential one of the day. It was the address of Carl Oglesby, the new president of SDS, that stated themes that were to dominate the New Left for the next several years.

"We are here again to protest against a growing war," Oglesby said. "Since it is a very bad war, we acquire the habit of thinking that it must be caused by very bad men. But we only conceal reality, I think, to denounce on such grounds the menacing coalition of industrial or military power, or the ominous signs around us that heresy may no longer be permitted. We must simply observe, and quite plainly say, that this coalition, this blitzkrieg, and this demand for acquiescence are creatures, all of them, of a government that since 1932 had considered itself to be fundamentally *liberal*." Truman, Oglesby argued, was a "mainstream liberal," Ike a "moderate liberal," Kennedy a "flaming liberal."

At Port Huron in 1962 the SDSers were disenchanted with liberalism and determined to go beyond it. In Washington in 1965 Oglesby and his friends viewed liberalism as the enemy.

In fact, Eisenhower was not any kind of "liberal," but a conservative who reluctantly accepted the welfare state because he sadly learned that he could not dismantle it. John Kennedy, far from being a "flaming liberal," was a brilliant and charismatic pragmatist who never had much affinity for ideologists of any stripe. It was, to be sure, Kennedy's internationalism that had led him into the tragic escalation of the American presence in Indochina. But that was not a reason to reject all liberal internationalism. Indeed, when a mass anti-war movement did really begin to develop and affect American policy—above all, in the McCarthy and Kennedy campaigns of 1968—the overwhelming majority of the participants were people who called themselves liberals and opposed America's policy in Indochina for precisely that reason.*

Oglesby's perspective was eventually to isolate SDS and the New Left and become a major cause for the disintegration of the movement. But the anti-war activity that took place in the first period of growing opposition to America's Vietnam policy was extremely valuable and effective. In particular, the teach-ins were a mass educational movement that often provided the peace cadres with excellent factual analyses of the tragedy in Indochina. There is no question that these activities between 1965 and 1967 laid the foundations for the McCarthy and Kennedy campaigns in 1968, when the anti-war cause became a potent political factor in the very mainstream of American life. Thus if it is necessary to fault Oglesby's analysis, that is not to say that the militancy that it inspired was without effect.

But negatively, the escalation of the war was the cause of so extreme an alienation from American society of some of the young that it eventually turned them to a despairing terrorism. Coalition politics, the strategy of trying to build a new and progressive majority within the Democratic party, is "coalition with the marines," Staughton Lynd said in an influential article in 1965. Therefore, he argued, SDS, which had maintained ambiguous ties with the liberal and labor movements up to 1965, must strike out on its own. However, if the unions and the liberals and the democratic Leftists of my persuasion were all untrustworthy, or worse, from whence would salvation come? Lynd and Oglesby and company had effec-

---

* In 1971 a Yankelovich poll undertaken for the JDR III Fund even discovered that 51 percent of the students who identified themselves as New Leftists also called themselves "liberals"—as against 44 percent who called themselves "radicals."

tively "excluded" most of the people of the United States from their movement. To whom would they now turn?

To themselves. In a marvelously romantic vision of the April, 1965, march, Lynd wrote of how "it seemed that the great mass of people would simply flow on, through and over the marble buildings [of the government offices], that our forward movement was irresistibly strong, that even had some been shot or arrested nothing could have stopped that crowd from taking possession of its government. Perhaps next time we should keep going, occupying for a time the rooms from which orders issue and sending to the peoples of Vietnam and the Dominican Republic the profound apologies which are due; or quietly waiting on the Capitol steps until those who make policy for us, and who like ourselves are trapped by fear and pride, consent to enter into dialogue with us and with mankind."

This is middle-class putschism. Its motives are absolutely good and sincere—Lynd himself is a thoughtful man of decent values and considerable courage—but this proposal essentially urges the seizure of the government by a white, upper-middle-class elite which has nominated itself as the spokesman for mankind. As bad poems demonstrate, honest emotions do not justify everything done to express them. The anti-warriors like Lynd were often sincerely and understandably engaged in the making of fantasies.

Che Guevara, of all people, agreed with me. There was an improbable dinner for him in New York one night in the mid-sixties when he was attending a United Nations session. It was organized by Laura Berquist, then an editor at *Look,* who had become a friend of Che's when she reported from Cuba. It was held at the mansion of an old friend of Laura's, Bobo Rockefeller, but it was not an exercise in radical chic since the thirty or so guests were all radical activists, not rich dilettantes, and the bomb squad searched the premises during cocktails. The inevitable American Left-wing differences were aired in Guevara's presence: I. F. Stone gave a

pro-Fidel toast after dinner; I followed with a toast on behalf
of those of us who were not for Fidel but had fought against
the Bay of Pigs and sought a Cuban-American reconciliation. At one point a black militant enthusiastically asked
Guevara if he didn't agree that guerrilla tactics would work
in the United States. Che's face first expressed disbelief and
it seemed that he was on the verge of laughter. But he caught
himself and explained soberly why he did not think there was
a Sierra Maestra in America. Guevara's realism on this count,
alas, was not shared by the Leftists in this country who first
romanticized him and then turned him into a martyred revolutionary saint.

At the beginning of 1966 the LID and SDS severed a relationship that had become so tenuous that it was only a formal-
ity. From then on my personal contact with the group was
only episodic and I watched from the outside as some of my
worst fears were confirmed. As SDS moved—or perhaps it is
more precise to say, as it was forced—away from the mass
forces of social change and turned in upon itself, the revolutionary ideologues of Progressive Labor won more influence.
After all, Maoism makes sense if American society is totally
and utterly corrupt. Indeed, it becomes the ideological excuse
for a despairing pessimism by showing how all reforms must
necessarily be self-defeating and that only a vague revolutionary apocalypse can save the nation. Since the official leaders
of SDS had for so long operated on the basis of an emotional
commitment and had never worked out a program, they were
hard pressed to deal with this threat from the "Left." When the
Maoists got the upper hand at one National Council meeting,
the national office faction appeared at the next conference
and announced that they were the real, the genuine, revolutionary Maoists. The escalations of more-militant-than-thou
had taken over.

As the declarations of undying dedication to the American
proletariat became more shrill and insistent, the New Left
watched sullenly as tens of thousands of students flocked to
the banners of Kennedy and McCarthy in 1968. Those anti-

war campaigns were, after all, exercises in bourgeois illusion. Gradually the SDSers drew the logical conclusion from impossible premises: Americans could not help America, only an uncorrupted and Fanonist Third World could do that; and therefore it was the duty of American radicals to become an armed, terrorist fifth column of the international revolution.

When some members of the Weathermen faction of what remained of SDS accidentally blew up a townhouse on West Eleventh Street in Manhattan, they were apparently making anti-personnel bombs (so the survivors announced). They had decided that it was no longer enough to destroy buildings in order to shake up the system; now they must kill people. Indeed, one could find a grisly symbolism in the event. These revolutionary novices ended their own lives, not those of their alleged oppressors, and did so, not in a slum cellar, but in a rich man's house worth a quarter of a million dollars. It would be easy enough to take those contradictions for the epitaph of the New Left. It would be wrong.

The details of the history I have recounted are sad, yet there is hope concealed within them.

In the years before World War II the American college was the preserve of a tiny minority, the children of wealth or the rare and lucky offspring of workers and farmers whose parents could afford to let them go to a state university. As a result, college graduates were politically conservative.* Then with the GI Bill of Rights after World War II, and the explosion of higher education in the late fifties and the sixties, the colleges, in an unprecedented development, became mass institutions. Nearly half of the available age group is now enrolled in some form of higher education.

SDS was not "caused" by this phenomenon but it was inti-

* Documentation for most of the statements about political attitudes made in this analysis can be found in "College Generations—From the 1930s to the 1960s," by S. M. Lipset and Everett C. Ladd, Jr., in *The Public Interest,* Fall, 1971; and in *The Changing Values on Campus,* A Survey for the JDR III Fund by Daniel Yankelovich, Inc., Pocket Books, 1972.

mately associated with it. Its ranks never numbered more than a small percentage of the millions of college students, yet it was the militant and activist vanguard that articulated attitudes and values that extended to perhaps 40 percent of the college population. Surveys of the campus in 1971, *after* the collapse of the organized New Left, showed that distrust of the dominant corporate institutions of the society was widespread. The higher education constituency had, in short, been profoundly influenced by Left-wing views.

In one cynical conservative theory this is not too disturbing. Students, it is said, live in an unnatural, hermetic world. When they go out and encounter "life," that is, when they face the miserable and often unnecessary limitations of human existence, they will be beaten down like the rest of us and forget their youthful dreams of justice. This sour hypothesis, fortunately, is only partly true. The careful empirical analysis of Lipset and Ladd revealed that recent college generations have indeed moderated their views after entering the workaday world. But, and this is a crucial finding, this process was relative, and they remained more radical, even though they had been somewhat conservatized, than their predecessors. They were not lifelong militants, but they were affected positively by their youthful militancy all their lives.

Therefore, I see the New Left of the sixties, for all its failures, as a historic turning point in American life. It dramatically signals a new mass intelligentsia which has been won to some important Leftist ideas. There is every reason to believe that these millions will be relatively more radical than their fathers and mothers during their adult lives. And there is evidence—in the McCarthy and Kennedy campaigns of 1968 and the McGovern campaign of 1972—that this might well change the politics of the nation.

There are, to be sure, unhappy possibilities in these trends. The class position of these new radicals is privileged, even when they most vociferously identify with the poor, and they may—as they have at times—nominate themselves as an elite to save the incompetent masses from their own unfortunate stupidity. They could go on trying to imagine themselves as a new proletariat, a force that can by itself save the nation, but that idea, as the elections of 1972 showed so conclusively, is a delusion. Yet there is reason to hope. These rising generations of the Left could become part of a new majority movement to transform American society in the most basic way. Which of these tendencies will prevail is a question that is going to be settled through struggle within this constituency. Sadder and wiser than I was at Port Huron in 1962, I hope to take part in it.

6. Success

My nervous breakdown began at a Unitarian church in San Diego one Sunday evening in March, 1965.

I had been introduced and was about to give a speech on poverty in the United States, an utterly routine and satisfying experience for me. As I reached the podium I suddenly felt faint and had to grip the sides of the lectern in order to keep my balance. Then the sense of being on the very edge of losing consciousness became so intense that I had to sit down and explain to the audience that I was indisposed and could only go on if I were seated. I did finish, mainly by pressing my legs into the chair to distract myself with a little pain from what seemed to be the imminence of keeling over.

I cut the question period short and went back to my motel. By the time I reached the room I was sweating profusely and there were tremors in my back and chest. I wondered if I were having a heart attack. The next day I flew back to New York in a daze and went to bed. The doctor who came and examined me, like several others I went to see during the next few weeks, could find nothing physically wrong with me. But why, then, did I feel worse than ever before in my thirty-seven years?

In 1965 I was a modern, sophisticated, cosmopolitan man. I had read my Freud and lived in a New York world where the majority of my friends had been, or were being, psychoanalyzed. I could do a literate psychological gloss on the symbolism of a poem or a play or a movie, only I had never met my own id, at least not face to face. Now—and it was months before I realized this was the case—my unconscious had seized me by the scruff of the neck in a surge of pent-up destructive fury. It was, quite literally, an id, an "it," an alien thing that took over my life and dictated frenetically and imperiously to my rational, daylight self.

The immediate cause of the crackup was obvious enough and I fastened upon superficial factors to convince myself that it was only a passing incident. In the week before that San Diego speech I had been involved in an only slightly untypical, and quite insane, schedule. I arrived in Santa Barbara, California, from New York on a Sunday night, and for the next five mornings I participated in, or led, a seminar at the Center for the Study of Democratic Institutions. On Tuesday afternoon I lectured at the University of California at Santa Barbara; on Wednesday evening I spoke at a large meeting at Sacramento State College and drank well into the night with the socialists who had arranged the event; early Thursday morning I flew from Sacramento to Santa Barbara for the seminar, and that afternoon I drove down to Los Angeles where I addressed the staff at Los Angeles County Hospital.

On Saturday I drove again to Los Angeles and went to a party in the Bel Air section of the city. There I met writers and directors and actors, among them Edward G. Robinson, who had loomed so large in the films of my boyhood, and Daniel Taradash, the director of *From Here to Eternity*. Our hosts had an extraordinary collection of modern art on the walls and that was a fascinating source of conversation. There was also a message from my id. At first the floor of the house seemed to sway slightly under my feet, and I drank quickly to blot out that seasick sensation. So the next day, when I drove to San Diego, the accumulated fatigue of the week, and the aftereffects of the alcohol that had seen me through the night before, were obviously at work.

Thus there was good reason to think that a foolish pace had caused a minor upset. Shortly after I returned to New

York from San Diego I flew down to Montgomery, Alabama, for the last day of Martin Luther King, Jr.'s march from Selma. Although the mood was joyous and hopeful, there were tensions in the late afternoon when the National Guard was suddenly defederalized and we were left without protection in a hostile city. Indeed, our fears were justified; Viola Liuzzo, a Catholic activist and mother from Detroit, was murdered that night on the road from Montgomery to Selma. And at the airport A. Philip Randolph, with whom we were waiting, was stricken with what turned out to be a not too serious heart attack. The fact that I could cope with these grueling and disturbing events reinforced my optimistic belief that the sickness in San Diego had been caused by mere overwork.

I was wrong. In Montgomery, as I was to realize later, I had been acting in terms of an image of myself—a civil rights militant—that was clear and unambiguous to me. But as soon as I got back to New York I had to confront once again some powerful, and repressed, antagonisms within myself. These forces were to dominate my life for the next year or so and profoundly influence it for still another three years. Indeed, I can feel their effect to this day. I had encountered anxiety.

That does not mean, as it does in everyday speech, that I felt a sense of vague uneasiness. In psychoanalytic language anxiety describes a much more frightening outburst of the unconscious. There are fluctuations in the stress of everyday life and a person's mood varies with them. Sometimes, though, tensions and frustrations will accumulate until a seemingly trivial event will trigger an explosion: after a day of driving crowded freeways with a carful of whining children, a key jamming in the lock of the front door will send a parent into a rage. Now I lived constantly just an inch away from such a howl of psychic protest.

It is almost impossible to describe this kind of anxiety to someone who has never felt it. At the extreme, it confuses perception itself, and there is that sinking sensation of being on the verge of a dead faint I knew in San Diego. Or the commonplace street suddenly seems angled and awry as if reflected in the mirrors of a fun house and you clutch at a wall for support. On an errand of no importance, a motor races or someone jostles you slightly and the day goes to pieces. Or when sitting in a peaceful, quiet room in a favorite chair, a nameless queasiness suddenly wells out of the pit of your stomach and you recoil, your shoulder blades digging into the back of the chair.

When the crisis deepened, my wife and I went to her parents' home in Westchester County. I still thought that just a little rest and quiet was all I needed. But after a marvelously uneventful day I would walk into the post office and the mere fact that I was going to have to stand in line for a minute or two would seem so outrageous that I would flee in panic. That summer we took refuge in Santa Barbara, and the flight to the Coast, which I had made dozens of times, did not take so many hours but rather an infinity of minutes and seconds, each one a dangerous threat to my equilibrium. Even going to the Center and making an occasional comment in the discussions became an ordeal requiring prodigies of self-control.

What was it that had turned my life upside down? It was something more profound than, though related to and exacerbated by, my hectic pace. In April a friend guided me to her psychoanalyst, Elizabeth Thorne. For almost four years—during which the symptoms gradually, and then rapidly, decreased—I tried to understand what had happened to me.

To anticipate my conclusions, I was the victim of my own success, and the sudden access it offered to the fringes of power, the rewards of money, and the consolations of minor celebrity. My world had been transformed in an extraordinary number of ways in the period of a year or so and I could not, or would not, admit to myself what was happening. I pretended to be the person I had been; I refused to recognize who, or what, I was becoming. Eventually, all the turmoil and transition which my conscious self ignored could no longer be denied. If my rationality would not deal with it, then it would assert itself irrationally, as an "it" which took control of my "I."

In describing these things I do not pretend to outline a comprehensive analysis of them. I will purposely ignore the basic Freudian determinants, those decisive childhood relationships with mother and father that would be critical in a study of my intimate self but are irrelevant in a book that takes my personal experiences as fragments of a social history. So I focus not upon my character, but upon my "social character," upon the public causes of my private woes.*

In this, as in so many other things, I find that Karl Marx provides an excellent point of departure. In a brilliant insight into the collective psychology of the capitalist era Marx wrote in the *Communist Manifesto,* "The bourgeoisie cannot exist without constantly revolutionizing the instruments of production, the relationships of production, and thus all social relationships in general. In contrast, all previous ruling classes took the unchanging maintenance of the mode of production as the precondition of their existence. The constant transformation of production, the unbroken shattering of all social conditions, eternal insecurity and motion set the bourgeois epoch apart from all others."

In my generation this general law of capitalist insecurity took an unprecedented form. Because the economy increasingly depended on science and technology, there were dramatic changes in class structure. There was stagnation, even a relative loss of economic and social position, among manual workers and a remarkable growth in the openings for professionals and technicians. The sixties, the period of my crisis, was also the longest period of prosperity in American history, the result of the Kennedy-Johnson interventions into the economy.

All these tendencies converged to create a new social setting. The knowledge economy of computers, electronics

---

* A good summary definition and brief intellectual history of the concept of "social character" can be found in David Riesman's *Lonely Crowd.*

and high-paid technologists patronized intelligence as never before, and the growing constituency of the college-educated provided an audience for social critics, much as the middle class of Victorian England had for novelists. Prophets, and even false prophets, were honored in their own country. "Radical chic" and serious social concern developed together (a complexity which the scandalizers of "limousine liberals" must overlook if they are to maintain the purity of their outrage). Whatever the judgment of history upon these trends, I am sure of one thing: they had much to do with tearing me apart.

I

Success was thrust upon me. I didn't even hear about it until six or seven months after it happened.

I do not want to suggest for a moment that I was a humble man sought out by the lightning. I had, to be sure, disdained most of the conventional ladders of ambition. The years I spent writing poetry, traveling as an itinerant agitator, and finding the few dollars necessary for my support in the interstices of the affluent society were based on a rejection of bourgeois norms of aspiration. I had even preferred to hire out as a soda jerk or to work in a machine shop rather than to take an office job. The Bohemian-radical style, however, required no great courage for one who was young, healthy, and unmarried (it was, as a matter of fact, most enjoyable). And it was motivated at least as much by egotism as by a spirit of political, or aesthetic, self-sacrifice.

My contempt for the middle class derived more than a little from aristocratic pretensions. I had been in more than my share of slums and ghettoes and union halls during the fifties; I was viscerally angered by the system I rejected. But I also participated in a French tradition in which the literate anticapitalist looks down upon the vulgar tradesman. I had first encountered that attitude in *Partisan Review* and other little magazines in which avant-garde aesthetics combined with revolutionary politics. I, too, felt that it was demeaning to spend one's life making widgets, or speculating in widget stock, or writing contracts for widget transactions. There was, in short, an element—not the only, or decisive, one, but an element—of snobbism in my identification with the wretched of the earth.

In that perspective, I was too ambitious to want to waste my life in an unimaginative, bourgeois way. I wanted to play a role in movements that would change history and to write books that would last, and if that required that I be poor, so be it. As it turned out, I stumbled into a middle-class success. Like the Zen archer, I hit the target because I did not aim at it.

In December, 1958, when I returned to New York from my two-and-a-half-month trip across America I began to write the article on poverty in the United States which Anatole Shub had suggested to me. The article—"Our Fifty Million Poor"—appeared in *Commentary* in the summer of 1959 and caused a small stir. I received several letters from publishers asking me to follow it up with a book, and I filed them in the wastebasket because I had more important socialist work to do. But Herman Rosen, a socialist and economist, insisted that I had a moral duty to illuminate the reality that his profession ignored. And Emile Capouya, then an editor at Macmillan, offered me $500 just for signing a contract. It was, I thought at the time, an enormous sum of money.

I finished *The Other America* in 1961, and the book was published in March, 1962, to friendly, if modest, reviews. When the sale of the paperback rights and other royalties yielded about $1,500, I left for Paris on January 4, 1963. Six or so months before, my friend Dwight Macdonald had phoned. He was doing a review of the book for *The New Yorker* and wanted to ask a few questions. After we talked, I assumed that the book would receive one of those short notices in the back pages of the magazine, and I was annoyed that nothing had appeared by the time I departed for Europe.

Then one typically Parisian winter's day—gray, bone-chilling, and wet—I walked over to American Express to pick up my mail and found the tearsheets of Macdonald's review. It ran forty or so pages, longer than any review I had ever seen in the magazine, and was eventually reprinted as a pamphlet. I was delighted by the event but what I did not know was that my entire life had just turned a corner.

Macdonald's review of my book had the effect of a second publication date and made poverty a topic of conversation in the intellectual-political world of the Northeast corridor. The Kennedy Administration had been finding certain problems of unemployment more intractable than it had imagined. Then John Kennedy, who had been deeply moved by the suffering he had seen in West Virginia during the 1960 primary, asked Walter Heller, the chairman of his Council of Economic Advisors, if there were anything to these new theories about poverty. Heller told him that there was and gave him a copy of my book and some other material. Shortly thereafter Kennedy decided to make the abolition of poverty a major domestic goal. He had Robert Lampman, one of the few scholars who had taken an interest in the subject during the fifties, undertake an analysis of it for the Council of Economic Advisors.

I knew nothing of these things. It was only when my wife and I arrived in New York a few days before Christmas in 1963 that the fact of success suddenly began to dawn on me. There were calls from London from the British Broadcasting Corporation asking for my advice on a documentary on poverty; a trip to San Diego to speak for the Western Conference of Teamsters; an appearance on ABC network radio to do an instant appraisal of the poverty section of Lyndon Johnson's 1964 State of the Union Message; a call from Walter Reuther's office asking if I would be a keynote speaker at the founding meeting of the Citizens' Crusade Against Poverty. We were living at the time in a tiny seventy-five-dollar-a-month tenement apartment on an Italian working-class street in the South Village where the shower was a metal stall open to the ceiling just behind the kitchen and the bathroom was the size of a phone booth and warmed only by a plug-in heater. Our surroundings were the familiar and genteelly impoverished stuff of the past; the ringing phone was our link to a bewildering future.

One day in January, 1964, Paul Jacobs called. An ex-Trotskyist and union organizer, Jacobs is congenitally irreverent, serious, and puckish. I had met him when I was the organizational secretary of the Workers Defense League in 1953 and we had become good friends, working together on John Cogley's study of the blacklist in 1954 and 1955. Later Jacobs had become head of the Fund for the Republic's Trade Union Project and made me its utility writer, researcher, and conference summarizer. That had provided me with several thousand dollars of income a year and, more important, several transcontinental airline tickets a year which allowed me to agitate my way across the country in relative comfort.

Jacobs had just heard from Frank Mankiewicz. Lyndon Johnson had appointed Sargent Shriver to abolish poverty the day before and Shriver had turned to his Peace Corps associate, Mankiewicz, for help. (Frank was later to become an important advisor in the Presidential campaigns of Robert Kennedy and George McGovern.) Mankiewicz called Jacobs, Jacobs called me, and the next day we all got together for lunch in Washington. That lunch with Shriver, Mankiewicz, and Jacobs stretched out into two frantic weeks of sixteen- and eighteen-hour work days. The very first meeting was attended by Walter Heller, chairman of the Council of Economic Advisors; Willard Wirtz, the Secretary of Labor; Wilbur Cohen, the Under Secretary of Health, Education, and Welfare; Dick Goodwin of the White House Staff; Adam Yarmolinsky, a whiz kid for Robert McNamara at the Department of Defense; Richard Boone of the Department of Justice's Juvenile Delinquency Task Force; and others.

There was, I learned, a bitter struggle within the government over how to abolish poverty. Wirtz and his assistant, Daniel Patrick Moynihan, advocated a major emphasis on job generation and training; Heller, Cohen, and others wanted to put a community action program in the forefront of the new legislation. Shriver had the advantage of innocence. He had taken no position on these questions, and though well tutored in the facts of misery abroad, was relatively uninformed about the exact nature of poverty in America. This small task force was assembled in Shriver's Peace Corps office. In talking about the possibilities for new legislation, we also carried on a continuous seminar to educate Shriver, a quick-learning man, on the area of his new responsibilities. Jacobs remarked that "Sarge puts Benzedrine in the air-conditioning system." It was not unusual for Shriver to ask for a memo at ten in the evening, suggest that it be sent to his house by a White House car in the middle of the night, and schedule a breakfast meeting to discuss it with the exhausted author the next morning.

At the end of that two-week period we were finishing up Shriver's first presentation of a general strategy to Lyndon Johnson. Jacobs, Mankiewicz, and I dutifully wrote analyses in which the proposals stayed within the rather narrow political limits established by American society. But at the very end of the process the three of us decided to state what we really thought without any concern for the constraints of political possibility. We wrote that the abolition of poverty would require a basic change in how resources are allocated. That meant planned and massive social investments and therefore structural changes in the system. To our surprise, Shriver was delighted with our statement and incorporated a good part of it in his first report to Johnson. He returned from the meeting to tell us that the President had said (I paraphrase from memory) that if it took such innovations to complete the work begun by the New Deal, then we'd just have to make them. (Lyndon Johnson's best self, which was excellent, was to be a casualty of the war in Vietnam.)

It was all very heady and exciting to be arguing with Cabinet officers and indirectly presenting memos to the President.

But how could an anti-capitalist radical play a role within a capitalist government, i.e., in that institution Marx had described as the "executive committee of the bourgeoisie"? That was a difficult emotional issue for me, and my personal dilemmas reflected a much larger, and quite public, question.

Conventional pragmatists and ultra-Left ideologues would agree on what was happening to me. The pragmatists would say that I had become a socialist at twenty, which testified to the warmth of my heart, and that I was turning into a practical man at thirty-six, which demonstrated that I had a head. The ultra-Leftists would give a Marxist twist to this cynical thesis. They would say that I had been corrupted by the seductions of bourgeois status, and that in return for a pat on the head from the ruling class I was urging the people to accept a few crumbs rather than seizing the whole loaf, which was rightly theirs. The sophisticated sociologists of the fifties would describe my transition in terms taken from Max Weber. I had been following an ethic of ultimate ends, they would say, in which transcendental, and politically irrelevant, principles were crucial; I was now quite sensibly pursuing an ethic of responsibility in which one made difficult incremental choices and weighed the better against the bad in a finely calibrated balance, forgetting about the best which is, in any case, unattainable.

There is some truth to all these theories. The blazing revelations of youth, alas, are indeed dampened by the passage of time (at the University of Chicago I regarded a week without an intellectual epiphany—some new poet or novelist bursting upon me like a rocket—as a waste of time). Even a Promethean like Marx moved from the revolutionary simplifications of the *Communist Manifesto* to the much greater complexity of *Das Kapital* and the *Theories of Surplus Value*. And I would have been inhuman if I had not been flattered by the attention suddenly lavished upon me; as a result, my Marx did become somewhat more Weberian. But the whole truth of what happened to me—or, more importantly, what happens to any radical who seeks to actually influence the course of events in the most powerful capitalist society history has ever known— was more involved, more dialectical, than any of the platitudes about aging, corruption, and the ethic of responsibility.

Once the government had determined to do something about poverty, should I simply have said that its efforts were inevitably going to be inadequate and that in the not-so-long-run they might well benefit the rich more than the poor? That, it seemed (and seems) to me, would have been to turn my back on hungry, hopeless people who needed all the advocates they could find to push reform to its farthest limits. As it turned out, the war in Vietnam frustrated many of my hopes, a fact that was neither inevitable nor that predictable in early 1964. At the time I thought my function was to stay clear of bureaucratic involvement in the project, for that would have meant that I would have to loyally proclaim that this was the best of all possible wars against poverty. I could, however, be an independent supporter and critic who might help, or prod, federal officials into doing more for the poor.

The dilemmas I encountered are endemic to the socialist movement itself.

When I first became a socialist I accepted the revolutionary Marxist position as it derived from the Marx of the *Manifesto* and the Trotsky of the Fourth International. Any compromises with the bourgeoisie, I thought, would only retard the coming surge of radical working-class consciousness. We could work with the Reutherites in the CIO, making blocs with them against the boss, the Right-wingers in the union, and the Stalinists. But we held that Reuther was unconscionably soft on the capitalist politicians. Thus our cadres within the Reuther caucus would help the ranks to see that Reutherism was only a halfway house. When they understood that, they would form a labor party which itself would only be transitional to the emergence of a revolutionary workers' party.

In this analysis we shared the fatal flaw of Leon Trotsky's dying vision, even though we—I speak here collectively, not personally—had broken with Trotsky over the Russian Revolution. On the eve of World War II, a war he foresaw, Trotsky said that it was only the treachery of the Stalinists and the ineptitude of the Social Democratic leaders that was keeping the proletarians of the world from making a revolution. His own tiny Fourth International, he said, would lead millions at the end of a war that would necessarily disillusion the masses about their previous heroes. This would happen—and here Trotsky's profound Marxism veered back toward Hegel— because the Fourth International possessed the correct, the scientific, program. The war came as predicted, and so did the suffering and the bitterness of the people. The masses then turned to their old Stalinist and Social Democratic leaders and made them, not the Trotskyists, the beneficiaries of the postwar wave of militancy.

But then, something more than Trotsky's error was at work in my case: my crisis could be read as a minor psychological symptom of a major political problem in Marxism itself. The young Marx, like the mature Trotsky, had a somewhat apocalyptic vision of revolutionary change and he did not bother too much about the transition period between capitalism and socialism, which he presumed would be short and violent. But the mature Marx intimated, and his successors faced, a new situation—one in which the Left would win not power itself, but partial power. How, then, should radicals, who seek nothing less than a new civilization, act when they could preside over increments of power? Did they capitulate to the bourgeois order if they made it more tolerable for the people under circumstances where that was all that was possible? This dilemma has haunted European socialism (and Communism) for three-quarters of a century. I, unfortunately, acted it out inside my head. I came, I think, to the right conclusions but the emotional cost was high.

By 1960 I had begun to understand how wrong I had been to accept the simple, revolutionary scenario of the young Marx. The change began when I first made real contact with

workers and blacks and realized, among other things, that
the Reutherites were the genuine, and utterly sincere and militant, Left-wing of American society. It was furthered by an
intellectual process through which I came to realize that
Marx himself had abandoned, or revised, some of his earlier
polarizations (that speculation eventually led, in 1972, to
my book, *Socialism*). In 1961 I had to face up to the changes
in my thinking as I was writing *The Other America*.

The question was simple enough: Should my book on poverty argue for socialism? I decided that if I even mentioned
the word socialism, I would divert attention from the plight
of the poor, evoke all the misconceptions Americans had
about the term, and would then have to deal with the myths
the word had conjured up. Proposing a specifically socialist
solution would make it more difficult for the millions of trade
unionists, liberals, and men and women of good will to see
the reality of poverty. I felt (and feel) that the "other America" can be abolished prior to a revolutionary reconstruction
of American society. I thought (and think) that sophisticated
executives might realize they are losing more in the economic
underworld than they are gaining from tolerating it.

At the same time that I made this decision, I also decided
to write another book—which became *The Accidental
Century*—in which I would develop my socialist philosophy.
In the interim I would make it clear that one did not have to
be a socialist to be outraged by the existence of poverty in the
wealthiest society in human history, and that it would require
planning and social investments to deal with this scandal even
in a reformist way.

I came to these conclusions in 1960 and 1961 when I had
no idea that important men in Washington would be the least
interested in what I had to say. So when I got the opportunity
to work with powerful Democratic liberals in a struggle
against poverty in 1964 I had no principled hesitations about
accepting the invitation. But if my mind had rejected the en-
thusiastic simplifications of my radical youth, my heart had

not. One part of me was delighted to participate in a discussion that might make some change in the lot of a migrant worker stooping in a blazing field in California; another part still lived in spiritual blue jeans and believed, as my socialist comrades at Antioch College used to say, "If it's bourgy, it can't be good."

Then there was money. Not that my modest celebrity brought the riches that many, and particularly my detractors, imagined. The delayed recognition of *The Other America* meant that the greatest part of the book's sales were in the paperback edition, where the royalty was a little better than three cents a copy, rather than in hardcover, where a sale was worth twenty times that to me. But even if the checks were for thousands of dollars rather than the tens of thousands fantasized by my critics, it was more money than I had ever dreamed of seeing. At the same time, lecture fees began to climb from $300 an appearance to $1,000. I had reached the age of thirty-six managing to hold my income well below $5,000 in every year but one. Now I began to receive middle-class rewards. It was another devastating experience.

Here again, I had no problems of principle. Even when I was living at the Catholic Worker in voluntary poverty during 1951 and 1952, I had always said that it was not money, but the things you had to do to get it, that I rejected. And, as a Marxist, I had always objected to those radicals who pictured the good society as a place of Spartan asceticism. The bourgeoisie had, it seemed to me, developed a number of valuable things—among them democratic liberties, good food, clean airy rooms with fresh sheets—that were not evil in the least, only maldistributed.

My mind was clear on the issue; my emotions were not. In particular, I disliked being paid large sums for giving a speech. I felt that my ability to talk is a natural gift which I hold in trust for people who cannot speak for themselves, not a commodity to be offered for sale. I went to Norman Thomas to discuss this problem because I knew he had faced it in his own life. He advised me to speak for free whenever I could, but that where speakers were paid, I should ask for as much as William F. Buckley, Jr., or anyone else. It was not noble, he said, to voluntarily reduce one's fees on the commercial market, since it would not benefit mankind but only some promoter or other speaker. So I made a policy of giving at least two unpaid speeches for every paid one.

My personal conflict over speaking fees also touched upon an aspect of American culture in the sixties. With the exception of a few high-paying magazines like *Playboy*, free-lance writing is not well paid. An article for *The New York Times Magazine* in that period brought $400, but it might take weeks of work and research; a piece in *Commentary*, which took great intellectual effort, would yield even less; and my contributions to *Dissent* were normally voluntary offerings. Yet a single speech could bring in $1,000 (and cost the sponsor $1,500, since the agency took a cut of one third). Such a price was paid because a speaker could provide instant, painless enlightenment to an audience and would socialize with the organizers at dinner. So these talks became the main basis of my income and made it possible for me to donate most of my waking hours to the cause. Indeed, all wings of the American Left had leaders who survived because of this peculiar capitalist indulgence.

In Houston several years ago a nightmare came true. Before a talk the Rightists of Young Americans for Freedom distributed a leaflet attacking me politically. Then in the question period one of them asked me if I were going to contribute my $1,500 fee to the poor. I replied that I thought it detestable that the system should turn my gift into a commodity. I would work with all my might to create a society in which people would have the economic security that would permit them to share all their talents with their neighbors for the sheer joy of it. But to act as if that blessed day had already come, I went on, was to refuse to face reality. I would therefore take the fee for myself and use it so that I could spend even more time doing volunteer work in the struggle against the Young Americans for Freedom and other reactionary groups. The audience responded with a near ovation; I felt both intellectually persuaded by what I had said and a little cheap.

However, I could no longer look at the issue of money from the point of view of a vagabond social philosopher. Now I was married. My wife had been my salvation when the breakdown came. If she had not been prepared to share my anxieties—which turned me into an impossibly touchy person —I am not sure that I would have survived the experience as well as I did. She had hardly married me for my wealth: when we exchanged vows according to the unromantic rites of the Napoleonic code in Paris, I had a few dollars in my pocket, a torn plastic raincoat, and ten notebooks on the crises of our times. We lived for the next several months on wedding presents. Now both of us wanted children. A voluntary, Bohemian poverty for adults is one thing; an involuntary poverty imposed upon babies is something else.

What I encountered was the profoundly bourgeois character of the nuclear family. That institution—which I regard as reactionary and yet better than any other present system for the propagation and care of children—is based on the egotistic assumption that one's children should have at least as many opportunities as one has had, preferably more. It therefore provides an idealistic self-sacrificing rationale for greed, competitiveness, and the other Adam Smithian virtues. On the other hand, I had spent two years living the communal life and knew its limitations (significantly, Dorothy Day used to say that revolutionaries should not be married) and I could not accept the glorification of the extended family.

In a sense these difficulties with money were analogous to the political conflicts I felt in Washington when powerful men started to pay attention to what I said. In each case the problem was the same: Anyone who wants to change the system basically must still live within it and utilize its institutions, even if only to transform them. Even at the Catholic Worker, where we lived in voluntary poverty, we were dependent on the contributions of friends who made their money in a capitalist economy. So the Archimedean point on which every radical stands is a compromise. That is, I know, a necessity; it is also a contradiction.

That Sunday in San Diego in March, 1965, all these pressures and contradictions exploded within me. The itinerant radical agitator, the writer of articles with long titles for magazines of small circulation, the practitioner of a comfortable poverty on the margin of the affluent society, could not recognize the middle-aging participant in the discussions with men of power, who was married and received middle-class fees for giving anti-capitalist speeches. Thus the frantic schedule was not so much the cause of the breakdown as one of its symptoms. One way I dealt with the bewildering transformations of my life was to ignore them. By accepting every invitation to give a talk, by being casual and open to every demand, just like in the good old undemanding days, I could pretend to myself that I was still that other Michael Harrington who had lived in New York from 1949 to 1963. Eventually that masquerade, and the furious pace it required, could not go on any longer. I came unstuck.

Prosperity, as Emile Durkheim understood long ago, often offers its unhappy beneficiaries an embarrassment of choices, whereas during periods of hunger and economic depression the imperatives of life are simple and obvious. I was to learn to appreciate that truth, and many others, in the nearly four years of psychoanalysis that followed what had seemed at first to be only a fainting spell but which turned out to be, among other things, a fearful case of social vertigo.

II

Psychoanalysis is not a science. The discipline was founded by one of the most profound thinkers in Western history and it has carefully amassed an enormous amount of data and theory over the years. But compared to the practice of somatic medicine, it is an art.

I had become aware of this even before I was forced into therapy by my breakdown. In the several New York worlds in which I lived—Bohemian, radical, and intellectual—I was exceptional in that I was thirty-seven before I went into analysis. It was, and is, a sign of the times that emancipated and educated people, who think of themselves as a cultural vanguard, should be so beset by personal troubles. The Yahoo would take this as proof of the instability and untrustworthiness of a deracinated, privileged elite. That judgment is a reactionary half-lie and an unfortunate half-truth.

The social conquest of some of the more outrageous cruelties of existence, like high rates of infant mortality and starvation, has deprived men in the advanced societies of some of the most important and vicious certitudes of the past. It is not an accident that the crisis of religion, the institution that most profoundly articulated the ancient fears, should coincide with the partial liberation of some people from the dominion of nature's mysteries. My friends often had no money, but that was usually because of their choice of life-style rather than an economic given. Most were atheists or agnostics and could not take their woes to God or one of His priests. And they had matured in an intellectual milieu that took the Freudian revolution for granted. So the Yahoos are right to link social class and intellectual pretensions to a high incidence of psychoanalysis.

Where the Yahoos are tragically wrong is in the assumption that they themselves are sane and sound. There are convincing data showing that the incidence of neurosis and psychosis for all social classes, except the poor, is within the same general range. The poor tend to much higher rates of psychosis than any other class or stratum, because the life of poverty is a constant assault upon the psyche as well as the body. In that vast sector of American society that stretches from the working class well into the middle class there are tens of millions who suffer from the maladies Freud diagnosed and who do not know it. Their depressions and manias, their alcoholism and violence, their sullen resentments and bursts of vitality, are simply taken as "normal."

I certainly do not want to claim a moral superiority for the witting neurotics as opposed to the unwitting—for the mainly educated and upper class people who seek professional help as against the less advantaged who do not. I only insist that the pressures specific to these times weigh upon everyone, but that educated secularists are more likely to admit this fact and therefore are more likely to see analysts. However, Freud's early hope that self-awareness of neurosis would itself constitute a cure has not been vindicated. Therefore, the personality of the therapist is so much more important than the personality of the surgeon or the internist. The process of healing is shared and interpersonal unlike the use of a pill or a scalpel.

I had known these things years before I appeared at an analyst's office. In the early fifties a homosexual friend had decided that he desperately wanted to open himself up to the possibilities of heterosexual experience. He went to see several analysts who offered to help him to adjust to his homosexuality but proclaimed, on grounds of what they regarded as Freudian principle, that he could never change. Finally, he found a doctor who felt that it was at least possible that he could enjoy heterosexual sex, which is what happened. Other friends quit their analysis in disgust; still others seemed to turn it into a sustaining, and endless, neurotic experience.

I was fortunate. The friend and comrade who knew of my troubles had me call her analyst, Elizabeth Thorne. A born Midwesterner with a friendly, open manner, Thorne does not look like the extremely sophisticated New Yorker and psychoanalyst that she is. She is neither a doctrinaire Freudian nor a dabbler in therapeutic chic. A student of the late Theodore Reik and a doctor of psychology (as well as a lawyer), she is perhaps more at home in classic Freudian theory than many who become analysts via the medical school route. Yet she was not the least bit rigid in applying her categories. At the outset we talked face to face; then after a while I tried lying on the couch, which I did not find particularly helpful, so I sat up and that was that.

At no point was there a sudden blinding revelation, a tearful or a joyous moment when I dredged up some memory that illuminated my whole life. There was fairly often a sense of relief, of having gotten things off my chest, and there were even eerie instances when a discussion would provoke, and then release, a physical symptom. Still, with my layman's limitations, I am not at all sure exactly how my years of analysis relate to the Freudian theory that suffused them. That they were extremely valuable is beyond question; whether they had much to do with the classic models of personality, I am not sure.

There is no question that I did get to meet my unconscious and even to understand it a bit. Since I was dragged to the door of analysis by my id, I hardly had to speculate over whether it existed. It was the force that was dominating my life and the experience was about as subtle as being hit over the head with a brick. What I did learn was that I tended to convert repressed emotions into physical symptoms. By the end of the four years I realized that there was probably not a single part of my body which had not expressed some feelings that my mind would not recognize. In San Diego attitudes I had refused to confront rationally, because I found them dangerous, communicated themselves to me in the form of a feeling of faintness, chest pains, and profuse sweating.

Freud had dreamed that science would eventually discover the physiological basis of such neurotic (and, more importantly, psychotic) behavior. Yet now the very real possibility that this dream will come to pass fills me with a certain fear. The molecular biologists are not simply unraveling the genetic code, which programs so much of the general constitution of the individual; they are also discovering the chemical concomitants of human behavior. At present, they feel that the potential for controlling people through drugs or electronics is limited: existing moods and tendencies can be heightened or moderated, but a new personality cannot be fabricated. But the political potential of such power is frightening. It was Aldous Huxley's unique contribution that in writing *Brave New World* in the thirties when economic arguments rationalized dictatorship he understood that genetics and psychology had even more of a totalitarian potential.

At any rate, I had to rely on talk, not pills. It is extraordinary how much one can learn through rambling or, in grander rhetoric, through free association. The repressed material is often found in the conscious self, in disguised form. At times it seemed to me that Thorne, and the Freudians generally, took an aesthetic view of humanity in which every man and woman is a symbolist. More optimistic than Molière, one of whose characters suddenly realized that he had been speaking prose all his life, they see all of us as unconscious poets. If, with the aid of an analyst, you can actually listen to yourself, if you can hear your own words literally, i.e., if you take your symbolism seriously, then you can get some remarkable clues about your hidden self.

There was, for example, the experience of the door. The session would be over and I would be leaving. I would turn and say, "By the way, it's not important, but I just thought of something." Then I would relate an incident or feeling which, one millisecond before I spoke, seemed to be of no great significance but which, even as I heard my own voice, would be the most obvious and revealing statement, a synthesis of all that had gone before. At such moments, the existence of a subterranean self was no longer a hypothesis; it was a tangible fact.

The role of the doctor was to listen more carefully, more expertly, than the patient. Thorne did not affect the classic Freudian invisibility and impersonality. When things were going rotten for me, or well, she would empathize with my distress or happiness. She was extremely attentive and sensitive to nuance, interrupting me only to ask pertinent questions. In my arrogance I was certain that I was an interesting case, but I used to ask her if she had ever delved into someone's innermost self and discovered that it was boring. She said no, but I am not sure whether that is a tribute to mankind's variety or to her own fascination with the human personality.

We began on the non-Freudian immediate level of simply dealing with an immediate problem: how to give a speech or just walk down the street without being attacked by anxiety. There was little talk then of early childhood experiences and mother and father but rather a concentration on the next challenge. That process involved considerable discussion of changes that had taken place in my life and the puzzlement and resentment they had occasioned. But it also included a most mundane—and incredibly useful—concern with commonplace detail.

I would, with Thorne's help, try to anticipate every stage of a trip with meticulous imaginative precision. No aspect was too routine, including the cab ride or the question of whether or not I would have dinner with the organizers of the meeting. When I got to my destination, I would ask to see the hall in which I was going to speak, and I would stand behind the rostrum and try to get the feel of the place. Once, at Middlebury College I was rushed without warning into an old-fashioned and very high pulpit. The particular insecurity of this period of my life, plus a slight tendency toward acrophobia, made me cling to the lectern as if it were a life raft in a raging sea. Another time I discovered a few moments before I was to do a live telecast via satellite to England that my friends from BBC wanted me to stand at the edge of the platform of the New York State tower at the World's Fair. I had flatly refused, thereby almost precipitating an international media crisis, when my wife suggested that I sit in a chair. I did, and talked of leisure and civilization while holding on for dear life.

Sometimes I would even run through a crucial speech with

Thorne just to be sure that it did not contain any psychic booby traps. When, for instance, I would be dealing with the ultra-Leftist criticisms of my own point of view, there was always the possibility that the turbulent emotions associated with my relationship to SDS would be awakened. If I knew that in advance, if I could say to myself, now I am giving a speech and dealing with this problem politically and intellectually, I could avoid that surge of surprised feeling that might otherwise threaten my composure.

Through this procedure I also discovered the therapeutic value—and destructiveness—of liquor. When the crisis first hit, one of my reactions had been to drink to recover my sense of well-being, particularly if I went to a cocktail party where free-floating stimuli—the babble of voices, hostile people, friendly people, strange people—would be assaulting me from every direction. The simple, and disastrous, way to deal with that situation was to overdrink and I followed it often enough (not, however, to anything near the point of alcoholism). The problem is that liquor wears away the nerves and makes one even less capable of coping with the world the next morning. Norman Mailer is right: all artificial highs, induced by drugs or alcohol, must be paid back by the body, and if you accumulate too many such exhilarating debts, the result can be a breakdown.

But judicious use of a drink, I found out, was much more effective than any tranquilizer on the market. So I got into the habit of having a martini before I spoke. The first time I was scheduled to talk in the morning, my semi-Puritan attitudes (for some reason I have always felt that carousing is all right after sundown, but not before) were offended by the idea of drinking that early in the day. But my equilibrium was more important than my prejudices: I had a breakfast of tea, toast, and dry martini. Before another early speech, at Claremont College in California, I felt especially foolish as I furtively drank a bottled airline martini in a garden under the pretext that I was going over my notes.

During this time there must have been people who thought

that success had turned me from a convivial socializer into a withdrawn snob. They did not know the inner anguish which, for a year or so after San Diego, preceded my every public appearance, even going to a party or walking into a bar. Yet strangely, even in the worst moments of my breakdown, my ability to write was never in the least threatened. When I had retreated to my in-laws' house in Westchester and could hardly manage to walk down a street, I could still sit calmly at a typewriter and work happily. But then, writing is solitary, not social like a speech, and so many of the contradictions and fears that attended a talk were not present.

On the immediate, therapeutic level, my time with Elizabeth Thorne was invaluable. The knowledge that I acquired about how to deal with everyday stress and strain was a crucial factor in my recovering from the immediate effects of the breakdown. But what of the larger claims of psychoanalysis?

After almost four years of analysis, I am at a loss to give a straight answer. Toward the end of that experience when I was trying to sum it up in conversations with Thorne, I told her that I wondered if the worth of the discipline might not be totally independent of its theoretical foundations. The fact that I had been forced to take myself so very seriously, that I had sat and discussed my problems with a sensitive, intelligent, and trained person, were of obvious value. But did one then have to accept a model of the personality as a dynamic unity of id, ego, and superego? The unconscious existed, as I knew beyond a doubt, but did it really function within a matrix primarily determined by one's relationship to mother and father? It was clear that those childhood experiences were crucial, even decisive, and that few, if any, other people would ever have such an influence, as model or anti-model, as those early and most basic figures. But did that mean that the Freudian theory of the Oedipus complex is true?

Part of the problem is familiar to me from my studies in Marxism. Like Marx, Freud was a profoundly dialectical thinker, meaning that in his system any event can be interpreted in a contradictory way. One might imitate one's parents—or react against them. The assertion that the relationship with mother-figure and father-figure was crucial could not therefore be empirically verified since the same theory could be used to explain diametrically opposed courses of development. I had little doubt that Freud had asked the right questions but I am not sure that his answers were right —or that they were wrong. I am positive that my time with Thorne was well spent. I just don't know precisely why. I can't even say that the problems that led to my crisis have been resolved. I still feel ambiguous about money and power and success. There was no conversion experience, no moment of revelation when I became a new person and decided to go back to a life of voluntary poverty or forward to a guiltless hedonism. The contradictions of my time and place and personality continue to war inside my head, only now I am more aware of them, and though they still bedevil me, they don't assert themselves in that gibberish of the id, in fainting spells and free-floating fear.

One thing, however, is certain: psychoanalysis as I have undergone it cannot possibly help the millions of people who desperately need aid. That, of course, has been recognized by the best Freudians for some time, yet I think the point worth stressing. It is not just that the cost of an analysis is so high, although this is obviously a factor. It should be possible to socialize psychoanalysis along with the rest of medicine, even though some Freudians of strict obedience would be upset that the patient was thus being deprived of the pain of paying (which they view as a necessary token of commitment).

More pertinently, psychoanalysis is an artistocratic, perhaps even an ascetic, discipline. It requires a sense of self, a dedication that often does not exist among those most in need of therapy. It demands a kind of patience and perseverance usually found only among those most permeated by the Protestant ethic; a belief that present pleasures should be deferred in the name of a more enjoyable future. So I do not think that psychoanalysis, even if freely available and in the revised form in which I encountered it, could become a technique accessible to the great mass of people.

There have been many attempts to overcome these limitations. Therapy has been divorced from any attempts to seek after basic causes; there have been innovations in group therapy and psychodrama; and various encounter and insight movements have tried to deal with the problems of entire ballrooms of people at the same time. My impression is that none of these experiments has been totally successful and that some —particularly encounter groups in which leaders have little formal training—can be positively harmful. I do know that as the culture becomes less religious and more secular—a trend not only compatible with, but perhaps productive of, a revival of superficial religiosity—more and more people are going to become aware that they need help.

And yet, the events of the summer of 1972 surrounding the nomination—and deposing—of Senator Thomas Eagleton of Missouri as Vice Presidential candidate of the Democratic party made me realize how woefully uneducated the great mass of Americans still are in this area. That sad incident also forced me to face up to a considerable ambiguity.

I had attended high school for a while with Tom Eagleton's older brother Mark, and I used to see the future Senator, a friend of my Uncle Dave's, at the private midnight mass which Father Dismas Clark said for the Fitzgibbon family and friends on Christmas Eve. Then in the fall of 1971 I participated in a Washington symposium on mental retardation sponsored by the Joseph P. Kennedy, Jr., Foundation. The various speakers dined at a number of homes in the capital on the final night of that program and I spent several pleasant hours at the Eagletons', reminiscing about St. Louis and talking politics.

So I was quite happy when I watched on television as Tom Eagleton got the Vice Presidential nomination. I knew of his excellent record, and I had been impressed by his forthright position in favor of Bangladesh when I talked to him at his home. And I suppose I felt a certain amount of pride that a St. Louisan should have been picked for the second spot on the ticket. When a few weeks later Eagleton revealed that he had been treated for depression and undergone shock therapy, I suspected that the worst was coming and it did. A significant number of Americans still thought that to have a breakdown is a sign of insanity or grave mental defectiveness. A reporter even cruelly badgered Eagleton about the simple human fact that he sweated under the hot lights of a television studio.

The Yahoos were, in short, still very much in control. After all the years of public education, a major percentage of the American people, perhaps a majority, still equated an emotional crisis precipitated by overwork with madness. The political wisdom of the way in which Senator McGovern handled the issue—and of Eagleton's own failure to volunteer the information about his past problems—will be debated for years to come. But one thing is certain. For all the triumph of Freudian categories in popular speech and the mass media, an almost primitive fear of psychic turmoil is still widespread. My heart went out to Eagleton.

My mind did not. I have no idea whether my experience was anything like his, but I do know how devastating it is when a healthy, active person is literally run into the ground and must turn in desperation for professional help. That breakdown must be understood as an aberration of the emotions, not of the mind, as a psychological overload that has nothing to do with the individual's basic mental capacities. At no point had I been "crazy"; neither, as far as one can tell from newspaper stories, had Eagleton. Yet, for all my sympathy for him, I do not think that someone who has undergone that kind of crisis—and I most specifically analogize it to my own—should be subjected to the kind of pressures that weigh upon a President, or his possible successor, in a nuclear age. The nation cannot take that kind of risk. The point is not merely speculative. As Secretary of Defense, James Forrestal suffered a much more serious breakdown than Eagleton or I, hallucinated about an invasion of Florida, and killed himself. What if he had been President?

In my own case, things began to look up after the difficult years of 1965 and 1966. But it was not until 1970—five years after that evening in San Diego—that I could casually accept an invitation to give a speech and make it without careful prior calculations and a drink. And to this very day, every time I approach a podium I rehearse the excuse that I had prepared during 1965 and 1966: I am sorry, ladies and gentlemen, but that bug I have been battling these last days seems to have reached me and I can't go on. I never had to do that, not even in the worst period; but the possibility that I might, even now that the breakdown is long since past, is never that far from my mind. Perhaps that is why I am so ambivalent about the Eagleton affair.

These are times of permanent insecurity, as Marx understood. Or perhaps the more precise formulation which fits my own case—and I suspect Tom Eagleton's and a good many others of whom we will never hear—is Durkheim's. Prosperity and accomplishment can be, as that great French sociologist understood, more menacing than failure and despair for they are not as straightforward. I had been caught up, against my will, in the surge of upward mobility that followed World War II, and that is a difficult fate for a man who originally wanted to be a poet. An outsider, a Marxist, I had been patronized by the newly created, and quite affluent, audience for social criticism. Eventually, I was even accused of being insufficiently apocalyptic about the doom that was soon to destroy the pampered radicalism of some of my readers. And so in this strange twilight of the bourgeois era I had my attack of social vertigo.

7. The Tightrope

In October, 1972, I resigned from the national co-Chairmanship of the Socialist party. The immediate reason was my conviction that the party was giving de facto support to Richard Nixon. The more profound cause was a split in our socialist cadre which, though it involved only a handful of people, sharply focused the political conflicts of American society in the sixties.

The issue came to a head at the meeting of the party's National Committee that October. There were three positions presented with regard to the candidacy of George McGovern: no statement of Socialist preference for any candidate; a backhanded endorsement of McGovern which essentially condemned him with faint praise; a forthright assertion that McGovern was not only clearly superior to Richard Nixon but had also introduced crucial questions, like the taxation of unearned income, into the political process. It soon became obvious that there was no real difference between the proponents of neutrality and those who reluctantly came out for McGovern; both detested the candidate and his movement. They disagreed only about how public they should make their disgust.

I listened in stunned amazement as an old friend and comrade announced that she hoped Nixon would smash McGovern. She had joined the movement in the fifties and had been questioned by the FBI about her activities when she was in her late teens. She had worked in the civil rights movement for years and had been a volunteer in Mississippi at a time when that required great personal courage. What astonished me most of all was that she thought she was being true to her Marxist principles when she concluded that a Republican victory in 1972 was in the interest of the American workers, the minorities, and socialism itself.

At first glance, the idea of a Marxist case for Richard Nixon is so bizarre as to be irrelevant to anyone but students of political pathology. Yet our party's seemingly sectarian history may well help to illuminate some of the great public debates of the period. We fought over the same questions that preoccupied major social movements a thousand times more important than we. Because we were small and on the margin of power, we theorized and wrote large the policy conflicts that swirled about us. As James Ring Adams wrote of my resignation in the *Wall Street Journal,* "This event looks more and more like a turning point in the recent history of the moderate American left." Adams assigned such importance to a relatively modest happening because he thought it revealed deep-seated trends in the labor and liberal movements.

I have a personal problem in treating the breakup of our socialist cadre as a symbolic moment of the 1960s. After I had finished the first draft of this chapter, Max Shachtman, a central figure in it, died. One of the crucial questions in my analysis is how Shachtman, a lifelong revolutionary Marxist, could have temporized over, and given effective support to, the most senseless war in the nation's history. With his death, I wondered if I should not give up working on an assessment that would necessarily be critical of his final years.

And even during those last years, when we hardly spoke to one another and were engaged in bitter struggle, I never lost my respect and affection for Max. My book *Socialism* appeared in May, 1972, when the faction fight was raging and yet I wrote in the Acknowledgments that "I am permanently and deeply indebted to Max Shachtman, who first introduced me to the vision of democratic Marxism and whose theory of bureaucratic collectivism is so important to my analysis." And beyond that political and intellectual debt, there was Max's personality: that warm, vibrant, utterly serious man who nevertheless sometimes laughed until he cried.

I decided to violate the principle of *de mortuis, nil nisi bonum,* for two reasons. First, Shachtman was a public man who had only contempt for those who, like the Trotskyists, turned a departed leader into an icon. He arrived at his attitude on the war as an honorable man, as a socialist, and as an idealist. He defied the police when he became a Communist militant in the twenties, braved the libels and physical assaults of the Stalinists when he became a Trotskyist, stood up against Trotsky himself on the issue of the Soviet Union, and disregarded comfortable Leftist verities in the name of what he took to be a more difficult truth about Vietnam. That he was tragically in error on that last count does not change the facts.

Second, and more important, I want to correct the mythology of the anti-war movement in which I proudly participated. Some of the understandably outraged foes of the abomination in Vietnam have depicted it as a simple battle between the forces of peace and justice on the one side and the war criminals and their political accomplices on the other. It was much more cruelly subtle than that, a tragedy in the Hegelian sense of the term, a conflict of goods as well as of good and evil. Perhaps I can personalize the ethical complexities of the sixties by talking of good and decent comrades, like Max Shachtman, many of whom had proved their dedication in clashes more bitter than I have ever known, and who, on the basis of excellent principles, were fundamentally wrong.

I

In 1964 and 1965 it seemed to us socialists that our dream of a political realignment in America was about to come true.

We focused our energies on building a new League for Industrial Democracy (LID). The sixties, we thought, were going to be a time of renewed reform, the first such period since the New Deal. In that perspective, the LID was supposed to become a center for discussion and debate where trade unionists, blacks, and intellectuals could meet and analyze events and programs. Our basic analysis followed from our conception of coalition politics. There was no one group —not the unions, the poor, the intellectuals, nor the middle-class liberals and radicals—which could transform American society on its own. There was a convergence of economic self-interest for the white working class and the impoverished minorities, since both stood to gain from full employment achieved through planned social investments. In the confluence of these mass movements, the more affluent advocates of social change would find millions whose idealism was intensely practical and politically dynamic. The LID, as we saw it, was to be located at the intersection of these various constituencies.

We started by broadening our contacts with the labor movement. Walter Reuther and Jack Conway, then head of the Industrial Union Department of the AFL-CIO, began to help us; we were in touch with I. W. Abel, the new president of the Steelworkers, and with Lane Kirkland, then George Meany's right-hand man, now the secretary-treasurer of the AFL-CIO. We were perfectly aware that most Left theorists had written off Meany and his friends as conservatives and that some even regarded Reuther as too moderate. But we had determined to be truly radical: to involve ourselves with the leaders elected by the American workers themselves, rather than with those imaginary figures who should have been leading a revolutionary proletariat that did not exist. We had followed, or been involved in, too many fights in the labor movement to be ignorant of the dangers to socialist principles in making alliances with the trade union bureaucracy. Some of us had been sued for hundreds of thousands of dollars by Harry Bridges of the

West Coast Longshoremen's Union because of our support for some rebellious rank and file members. And one of our best people, Herman Benson, was becoming the most articulate, and active, champion of union democracy in America. But even though we understood the problems and the risks, we felt that to seek to preserve our purity in righteous isolation from the real labor movement was even worse than to risk cooperation.

We also turned toward new allies among the intellectuals. Irving Howe and several members of the editorial board of *Dissent* joined the LID board; so did some brilliant younger academics like S. M. Miller of New York University and Herbert Gans of Columbia. Bayard Rustin was, of course, with us and still working closely with Martin Luther King, Jr. Norman Hill, who also came on the board, was one of the national leaders in a revived CORE. It seemed to us that our hopes for a new period of social creativity were realistic. History was finally moving our way.

But we had hardly started to act upon our new perspective when the war in Vietnam began to escalate. In the first phase of increasing American involvement in 1965 it was taken for granted among us that we were all with the peace movement and against Lyndon Johnson's intervention. We had, after all, spoken and demonstrated against American support of the French in Indochina in 1953 and 1954. As editor of the Socialist party newspaper, *New America,* I had argued against Kennedy's increases in troop strength in 1961 and 1962 on the grounds that reactionary anti-Communists, no matter how great the military aid they received, could never become an alternative to Communists who had won the leadership of a genuine popular movement for national liberation.

I went to SANE's anti-war rally in the fall of 1965 and listened with pride and affection as Norman Thomas told the throng at the Washington Monument that he did not want to burn the American flag but rather to cleanse it of the stains of Vietnam. That, it seemed to me, precisely defined the task of the peace movement. It could never reach out to the great mass of the American people if it appeared as a partisan of military victory for the other side. And it could genuinely identify with those democratic, anti-imperialist aspects of the American heritage that were being betrayed by the government in Southeast Asia.

It was because of such feelings that I played a role in an incident that was to bear upon the future of the anti-war effort. I had talked with the leaders of the march and then drafted a text, which Dr. Benjamin Spock read that day, in which he called upon the North Vietnamese as well as the South Vietnamese to put an end to the bloodshed. As time went on, many activists—including Spock himself, I think—were to regard my attitude as much too soft on Washington.

In 1966 the escalations became even more massive and the first open signs of disagreement appeared in our socialist cadre. Over the next four years our internal debate was to touch upon some of the crucial political themes of the decade: the relationship between war and morality; the question of anti-Communism; the evaluation of the new social strata that formed the basis of the peace movement; the assessment of the official AFL-CIO position on Vietnam. Although we did not know it in 1966, our high hopes for America had just been shattered in Southeast Asia.

One of the first confrontations within our group took place at a community room in Penn South, the housing development put up by the Garment Workers Union where Bayard and a number of our people lived. On my side were Irving Howe, Emanuel Geltman, and Stanley Plastrik, editors of *Dissent* who had been Shachtmanites in their youth but had broken with Max during the Korean war. Ironically, they had differed with him then because they thought that he too nearly equated the evils in capitalist democracy and Communist totalitarianism, refusing to see the superiority of American democracy. But they had remained principled critics of American society throughout the fifties—and defenders of the rights of Communists. Now there was a reversal of that argument. Shachtman was sympathetic to Johnson's policy; the *Dissent* editors were hostile to it.

The meeting rapidly became quite tense. Shachtman launched into a vigorous Marxist attack on pacifism and the moralistic approach to politics.* For Max, condemning the Vietnam war primarily on the grounds that it was immoral was an exercise in phrasemongering which one could expect of students and professors who had no sense of political movements. Of course, he said, the war is horrible and the killing should be stopped as soon as possible; of course the United States is involved with dictators, scoundrels, and knaves; of course the bombing should cease. But the hard question, he continued, is the political basis on which the nation acts. Would there be unilateral withdrawal of American troops leading to a Communist victory? A coalition government? Concessions from the North Vietnamese as well as from the South Vietnamese?

There was, I thought, real substance in this line of reasoning. In the peace movement one did indeed encounter an emotional, simplistic revulsion against the war that ignored all the difficult and complex questions it posed. Shachtman, I am sure, agreed with me that we never should have gone into Indochina in support of the French in the first place. Indeed, he had been one of the few Americans who had said that quite clearly when our indirect intervention began in 1946 and 1947. He was also right to charge that some idealistic antiwar activists were operating on a righteous indignation which is no substitute for politics.

But still, Shachtman was wrong. The *Dissent* editors and I were not motivated by pacifist absolutism or sentimentality. We had made a political analysis of America's self-defeating policy of aligning itself with reactionary anti-Communists. Then

---

* When I recount disputes in this chapter, I do not pretend to remember literally conversations that took place some years ago, or even to paraphrase them. I do think I am accurate about their basic content.

(and I am not sure how explicit we were about this on that particular evening but it was a basic point) Shachtman's approach tended to reduce Marxism to a kind of pragmatism without ideals. By overreacting to the simplistic moralizing in the peace movement, he had come perilously close to eliminating morality from the socialist vision altogether. In that case, what distinguished Shachtman's refusal to oppose the war from the position taken by Hubert Humphrey and other liberals who were the decent, unwilling agents of calamity?

In order to make this error, Shachtman had had to neglect a brilliant lesson in Marxism which he himself had presented to the American public. In the thirties the *New International*, a Trotskyist journal under Max's editorship, had published an exchange between Leon Trotsky and John Dewey. One of the points at issue was the relationship of means and ends; the charge made against Marxism—or at least against its Leninist variant—was that it taught that any means were justified by a good end. Trotsky had quite convincingly argued that the means and ends cannot be separated, that the means become the end. Therefore a socialist revolution, which sought to make men the masters of their own destiny, might have to use force, but it could not possibly reach its goal by the systematic use of deceit within the working class.

Marx himself had made a similar point in his writings about British imperialism in India. He regarded British brutality in the subcontinent as the unwitting instrument of historic change in that it broke through the reactionary, institutionalized torpor of Indian life. At the same time, he condemned the British actions as barbaric and opposed them by trying to find revolutionary alternatives to them. Marx refused, then, to turn morality into a shrewd adaptation to power, even when that power was accomplishing, albeit brutally, certain necessary tasks. It was Stalinism that formulated the proposition that anything done by the leaders of the proletariat, including the most savage attacks on the proletariat itself, is licit and even good. As Trotsky—and Shachtman—had so well understood, a thousand Stalinist speeches about the mobility of the goals being pursued did not change the real ends which were implicit in the totalitarian means being employed.

Shachtman had rightly helped us realize that in the America of the sixties we could only help transform unconscionable arrangements of power by participating in real, and sometimes ambiguous, struggles. We had, thank God, left that proud isolation in which we waited for a messianic revolutionary rising that was never to come. But our new practicality had led some of our comrades, Max among them, to a pragmatism about the most important moral issue of the decade. If, I thought, we accepted Max's methodology, then our Marxian and socialist tradition was nothing more than a sophisticated rationale for tactics that politicians, blissfully unaware of the dialectic, had been using for years. There was a point at which, after taking into account all the historical circumstances, one had to say of America's role in Vietnam what Marx had said of the British rule in India: it was wrong and barbarous.

Another source of disagreement among us—one which also tore the liberal-labor coalition apart—concerned the domestic consequences of the war.

The landslide of 1964 had elected the most liberal Congress within a generation. With an activist President still under the spell of his New Deal youth, the stage was set for the most hopeful period of reform since the days of Franklin Roosevelt. The middle-class activists in the peace movement often ignored these very weighty domestic considerations just as they refused to take into account the political intricacies of an American withdrawal from Indochina. But if these socially privileged anti-warriors saw only the moral issue of Vietnam, and ignored its other aspects, Shachtman and his associates turned that error upside down.

The crucial failure involved the issue of "guns or butter."

The Freedom Budget, a comprehensive and carefully documented plan for full employment through social investments, had emerged from our work at the preparatory sessions of the White House Conference on Civil Rights in the fall of 1965. A. Philip Randolph presented it, Shachtman named it; Leon Keyserling, the chairman of the Council of Economic Advisors under President Truman, did most of the technical work, and Bayard coordinated the entire effort. The budget itself was unveiled in 1966 during the period of escalating war. So the question was posed: Could one separate the struggle for jobs for all from the issue of Vietnam? In our socialist cadre we all agreed that we wanted hawks and doves to unite on domestic programs. The position of George Meany and the ALF-CIO Executive Council on the war was, I thought, wrong. But that did not change the fact that Meany and the Federation were the most politically powerful and committed forces fighting for national health insurance, full employment, tax reform, public housing, and the other social investments crucial to the Freedom Budget. It was, I believed, intolerable to tell a hungry, miserable family in an urban ghetto that it must wait upon the success of an anti-war movement primarily composed of the well-fed before it could enjoy a decent meal.

That was a simple enough attitude. The more complex issues concerned one's assessment of the relationship between guns and butter and the tactics that followed from it. It was indeed true, as Bayard and Keyserling and others argued, that America was rich enough to afford both guns and butter. But was it politically possible simultaneously to give a top priority to both the tragedy in Indochina and the fight for a decent America? I thought not and feel that history has proved my case. When the war took over in Washington in 1965, the talent, the passion, the political power that had been mobilized for the fight against poverty were diverted to Vietnam.

In his State of the Union message in January, 1964, Lyndon Johnson hardly mentioned Communism or the Cold War, a fact that disconcerted some Right-wingers. When I went to Washington to work on the Shriver task force in February, 1964, and throughout that year, the war on poverty was an exciting issue, attracting some of the best minds in the capital. Shriver's phone rang incessantly as federal bureaucrats, unionists, religious leaders, blacks, intellectuals, and everyone else tried to get into the new act. There was a buoyant, hopeful spirit abroad in the land. By the fall of 1965 a nervous Lyndon Johnson was scanning the guest list at a White House conference to see which of the participants had also endorsed SANE's demonstration against his war policies. It is certainly true that there were difficulties in the social programs that had nothing to do with Vietnam. But the decisive fact of the mid-decade was that the political and emotional priorities of the Government changed. Domestic reconstruction was no longer central; Southeast Asia was.

Lyndon Johnson himself corroborated this analysis. The American intervention in Vietnam was an undeclared Presidential war. Since the Administration was always glimpsing light at the end of the tunnel, the assumption was that the government could soon get on with the social programs if only the anti-war hotheads would refrain from destroying the 1964 electoral coalition. So Johnson did not ask for taxes to finance his military policies—which was his own tacit admission that he thought the nation was unwilling to vote for both guns and butter (it was also the most important single cause of the galloping inflation of the late sixties and early seventies).

Shachtman and his co-thinkers brought those Johnsonian politics into our tight little world. They predicted the demise of Vietnam as an issue every year for six or seven years; they tried to ignore the war and concentrate on domestic questions on which all of us still agreed; they refused to recognize that guns-and-butter, though an economic possibility, was a political and psychological impossibility. The man most trapped within this argument was Bayard Rustin.

Nothing could ever diminish my affection and admiration for Bayard. However much I might disagree with him on an issue, he remains the bravest man I have ever known, and certainly one of the most dedicated and committed militants. He had spent a lifetime in the pacifist movement when Vietnam escalated and out of courageous principle had gone to prison during World War II in opposition to what I believe was a just war. His past predisposed him to join with the peace activists. At the same time, his work with King, his leadership in the 1963 March on Washington, and his imaginative and tireless activity on behalf of an alliance between black and white working people had finally given him the chance to influence the struggle against poverty. If he joined the anti-war militants, his own career would hardly suffer; he had been a functionary in pacifist organizations for years. But, he believed, the hopes and possibilities he saw for black Americans, and other poor and deprived people, would be ended.

I think Bayard made the wrong decision: to subordinate his anti-war convictions to what he became convinced were the imperatives of domestic coalition politics. He was wrong because this position presumed that the social programs could succeed while the war raged, and because it ignored one agony in order to deal with another. It was wrong, and it was understandable. It was his love of justice in America that led Bayard to ignore monstrous injustice in Indochina. Martin King made the other, the right, decision. With the knowledge that he was imperiling, if not destroying, his access to the White House, King became an outspoken critic of the war. But to say that Bayard was wrong in his choice is hardly to condemn him. T. S. Eliot once said that the greatest treason "was to do the right thing for the wrong reason." How, then, does one judge a man like Bayard, who did the wrong thing for the right reason?

II

The issue of Communism divided us, too.

I remember how surprised I was at Max's candor one day in the mid-sixties. He, Irving Howe, Tom Kahn and I were chatting in the LID office. Shachtman began to talk about the

Trotskyist attitude toward Communism in the thirties. It was, he said, at the very center of our thinking. We were really more passionately concerned about a switch in political line in Russia, or among the American Communists, than about the great battles taking place in our own country. For us, he went on, the Russian question was decisive and that obsession sometimes warped our judgment.

It was a remarkably candid admission, although it somewhat understated the problem by focusing exclusively on the thirties. In the last years of that decade—and of Trotsky's life—Shachtman had come into conflict with his mentor, as I recounted in Chapter 3. Shachtman had developed the Marxist theory that Communism—Stalinism, we would have said—represented a new form of class society in which a bureaucratic class owns the state, which owns the means of production. In practical terms, those of us who held Shachtman's position therefore regarded Communist movements as potential totalitarian ruling classes. That their militants were often utterly committed, brave, and as sincere in their socialist convictions as we were only compounded the tragedy. The peasants who soldiered in the great capitalist revolutions of the seventeenth to the nineteenth centuries had, after all, died valiantly to bring their bourgeois enemies to power. That decent Communists would unwittingly serve an oppressor of the working class was a similarly cruel irony.

All of us shared this analysis; as far as I know, we still do. We had opposed French colonialism in Indochina after World War II even though we were perfectly aware that the national liberation movement had been taken over by the Communists. We were particularly conscious of that fact because there had been a thriving mass Trotskyist movement in Indochina in the thirties—one of the few that existed anywhere in the world—and it had bested the Stalinists in open political competition on several occasions. That was one of the reasons why Ho Chi Minh murdered the Trotskyist revolutionaries as soon as he had the opportunity. Our knowledge of that grim history made it impossible for us to believe that Ho was simply a gentle, lovable "uncle." We realized that he was both a genuine, and very effective, leader of the masses, whose confidence he had won, and a product of Stalinism.

None of us had any illusions about the kind of government a Vietcong victory might bring. We knew that Ho and his comrades had killed thousands of peasants during forced collectivization in North Vietnam during the fifties (a fact they themselves had confessed), and though the historic enmity of the Indochinese and the Chinese made it likely that there would be "Titoist" characteristics in any Communist regime in that country, we expected that a bureaucratic collectivist state would result in the South if the Communists prevailed. We were hardly indifferent to that prospect. It meant that the people would be expertly and efficiently exploited so as to produce a surplus for modernization. That course might provide a basis for the industrialization of the country under the leadership of a new, totalitarian class. It was most certainly not socialism.

And yet we opposed the French until their expulsion in 1954 and the American policy of support to the Diem regime after that. Why? It was Shachtman, strange to say, who persuaded me on this point. There was, he argued, a symbiotic relationship between Stalinism in the Third World and the reactionary militarist regimes it usually fought. The reactionaries, particularly if they had massive American aid, recruited people to the Communist banner by making Communism seem the legitimate expression of the mass desire for national freedom and social justice. Therefore it was utterly self-defeating, among other things, to support an Emperor Bao Dai or a Diem as a lesser evil to the Communists, since the Bao Dais, Diems, and the corrupt ruling classes they led were the prime source of Communist strength.

Moreover—and on this point we followed an old socialist tradition—we believed that foreign oppression would only postpone the day of reckoning between the indigenous Left and Right. When, for example, we had supported the Algerian nationalists against the French, we were quite critical of the National Liberation Front and understood that it was an unstable coalition of bourgeois politicians, Communists, Trotskyists, and local chiefs. But even though we suspected that the French dictatorship would be succeeded by an Algerian dictatorship, we felt that the issue of freedom could only be posed in an independent Algeria.

Our anti-Communism did not, as some revisionist historians have argued, relentlessly push us into support of reactionaries backed by the United States. However, sometime in the mid-sixties Shachtman changed his mind. How could a man who had resolutely fought the limited American intervention in Indochina under both Eisenhower and Kennedy come to critically support Johnson's massive war? Max had opposed his country's policies when that put him in conflict with the established liberal wisdom about collective security. Now he critically supported those same policies, which put him at odds with a growing liberal consensus based to some extent on his own previous arguments. Why?

In posing this question I do not suggest that Max had decided that the war had been right in the first place, or that he had any sympathy for the military government in Saigon. He understood perfectly that we never should have gone into Vietnam in the first place and he yearned for a democratic— and anti-Communist—alternative to the dictators America relied upon. But in the last analysis he had decided that he would—reluctantly, perhaps—back American power in that country because it provided a shield behind which the democratic revolution could organize itself. Shachtman and his followers always saw much more of a democratic opposition in Vietnam than almost anyone else; therefore, they increasingly alienated themselves from the American peace movement until finally they stood outside it, as bitter critics.

The key to that transition, I suspect, might have been a kind of despair. When Shachtman broke with Trotsky in 1939 he still held to the basic Trotskyist premise that there was a mass alternative to both Stalinism and capitalism. For a while it was possible to think that Third World neutralism might play that role; also, the Hungarian and Polish rebellions in 1956 were under the aegis of revolutionaries who wanted to push forward from Stalinism to socialism, not backward to capitalism. Still, there was not—there is not—a single power that incarnates the socialist ideal, and it is difficult for a man to dedicate himself to a possibility that will probably not be realized in this century—if indeed, ever.

If socialism had thus become, at best, problematic, and Stalinism was on the march in Indochina, who then would effectively fight for democracy? An exchange between Shachtman and Leon Trotsky during their dispute in the late thirties illuminates this point. Trotsky had refused to accept Max's thesis that the Soviet bureaucracy represented a new class. But the Russian revolutionary refused to dismiss that possibility. He wrote, ". . . if the world proletariat should actually prove incapable of fulfilling the mission placed upon it by the course of development, nothing else would remain except only to recognize that the socialist program, based on the internal contradictions of capitalist society, ended as a Utopia. It is self-evident that a new 'minimum' program would be required—for the defense of the interests of the slaves of the totalitarian bureaucratic society." It was typical of the implacable Marxist that, even though he could imagine the failure of socialism, Trotsky could not for a moment think of giving up the struggle for the oppressed, only of changing its perspectives and tactics.

I wonder if something like Trotsky's logic was at work with Shachtman in the sixties. A tough-minded and rigorous thinker who had only contempt for socialist sentimentality, he would never have consoled himself with the old outworn slogans. Perhaps Vietnam forced him to a conclusion he hated: that his previous hopes for a "third camp" independent of both capitalism and Communism were an illusion. If that indeed was the case, then he might have reluctantly decided—in that same spirit that animated Trotsky and his willingness to carry on the fight, even if only in the interests of the slaves and without the hope of socialism—that he must brave the opposition of some of his former associates and the scorn of the liberal establishment and critically back America as a lesser evil in Vietnam.

Indeed, if one were asked to choose in the abstract between the reactionary policies of bourgeois democratic America and those of totalitarian Communism, the former are infinitely preferable, for they are much less destructive of freedom and human dignity. In Spain and Greece, and even in South Vietnam, there is a greater possibility that the underground opposition will survive as an organized force than in Russia, China, or North Vietnam. French imperialism never knew how to kill the Trotskyist revolutionaries in Indochina; Ho Chi Minh did. Our despots tend to be corrupt and inefficient; theirs are honest and murderously effective.

In posing the choice in that way (and Max signed a statement that did precisely that, although I would certainly not hold him to all of its rather sloppy formulations), Shachtman forgot one of his own most profound insights: abstract comparison of bourgeois democracy and totalitarian Communism cannot be transposed into a Vietnamese context precisely because American power in such a situation is not an alternative, but an incitement, to Communism. The United States made memorable contributions to the victory of Mao by supporting Chiang, to Cuba's going Communist by backing Batista, and to the creation of a bureaucratic collectivist state in North Vietnam by aiding French colonialism and the Emperor Bao Dai. It staved off the consequences of its own politics in South Vietnam only by "saving" the Vietnamese through a cruel, indecisive war that killed hundreds of thousands of them and rendered millions homeless.

The possible triumph of Communism in Vietnam, I said to Shachtman and his friends, was therefore a lesser evil to a war that certainly could have no progressive result. That did not mean that I rejoiced at the possibility of a Communist state in

the South. I denounced such a state in the peace movement at
every turn, and it was not always a popular thing to say to the
more fervid of the simplifiers. But in Hungary in 1956, where
there was a working-class socialist revolution, we had not advocated armed American intervention against the Soviet imperialist attack because that would probably have led to World
War III, a much greater calamity than a totalitarian dictatorship. Moreover, I felt—as I had learned so well from Shachtman in the McCarthy days when it was the liberal wisdom to
regard Communist power as a seamless monolith—that life
would go on in Indochina even after a Communist victory
and that the class character of Communism would eventually
provoke a new resistance there.

Communism played a critical role in our dispute. The esti-
mate of the peace movement and the new social strata upon
which it was based did too.

III

The anti-war activists of the sixties were overwhelmingly
white and middle class. Many of them were unconcerned
about the domestic political consequences of their actions and
were even contemptuous of that majority of Americans who
supported the war. There was a profoundly elitist tendency in
the movement that Shachtman and his friends denounced as
dilettantish and collegiate. Moreover, there was a vocal, and
regularly televised, fringe of confrontationists, exhibitionists,
and Vietcong flag wavers who could plausibly be dismissed as
freakish, or sinister, or both.

But in their derogatory comparison of this movement with
the trade unionists, my comrades failed to notice two of its
historic aspects. First, the anti-war young were right: Vietnam
was not only an immoral conflict, it was counterproductive
from all points of view, including that of progressive anti-
Communism. Secondly, the new strata of the issue-oriented
and college-educated who provided the mass base for this phenomenon were, and are, extremely important to the creation

of a new majority for change in this country. They most certainly do not have the stability of the trade unionists, that stubborn commitment to action which is born out of a struggle for one's daily bread. But then, no other class (with the exception of the most class-conscious group in America, the very rich) has that working-class cohesion.

An illuminating analogy to the young people in the peace movement in the sixties is found in Marx's concept of the petty bourgeoisie. That stratum, based upon small property, feared the bourgeoisie, which threatened to crush its small-scale competitors, as well as the working class, which threatened the abolition of private property altogether. In Marx's analysis (and there is much history to corroborate it) the petty bourgeoisie vacillated, turning now toward the party of order, and even toward fascism, and then toward the party of change, and even toward socialism. Because of their equivocations "petty bourgeois" became one of the most vicious epithets one could hurl at a socialist opponent. As a result, not a few radicals forgot a crucial point: Marxists were always determined to win the petty bourgeoisie to the cause of the revolution.

In a sense, all that is ancient history. The class of small property owners has not played a very important role in corporate and oligopolistic capitalism for some time now (although they certainly made their contribution to Hitler's triumph as recently as 1933). Moreover, the young people attracted to the peace movement were hardly shopkeepers, present or future. But like the petty bourgeoisie, they were an intermediate and ambiguous stratum. Their parents' background, which was middle class, and their own economic future as professionals or technicians often disposed them to look down on working people; their membership in the first generation of mass higher education, their participation in what John Kenneth Galbraith dubbed "the educational-scientific estate," often made them programmatic in politics and open to proposals for planned social investments that come from the Left. Since their organizations were not built upon the imperious necessities of making a living, they were episodic, subject to great fits of enthusiasm and depression. Their most characteristic form of expression was the mass demonstration, a combination crusade and picnic, and yet the education which these militants had received made them particularly adept at registering voters, canvassing, and other traditional political arts.

The internal contradictions of that peace movement were clear. The anti-warriors had a tremendous potential for good and some very powerful tendencies toward self-righteousness; they were enormously energetic and they periodically collapsed into lethargy. Shachtman and his associates saw only the negatives; I was determined to build upon the positives.

If anything, I underestimated the strength of these new forces. In *Toward a Democratic Left,* which was completed in the fall of 1967, I described a "new class" in the knowledge economy, but I was certain that Lyndon Johnson would be renominated. So even when I heard Joe Rauh present the case for an independent candidacy at a Negotiations Now meeting in Washington, I was not really persuaded. Curt Gans called me sometime after that and told me that he and Al Lowenstein were looking for a candidate for the Dump Johnson movement. Although I was convinced that Johnson and his policy had to be challenged in the primaries, I was just as sure that the effort would fail.

When Eugene McCarthy announced for the Presidency I supported him in an article in *Commentary* and in some speeches, but I was not at all hopeful of success and was in fact quite critical of the middle-class character of the campaign. So when Robert Kennedy declared right after the New Hampshire primary, I decided to support him. He, much more than McCarthy, could speak to the blacks and the working people; he might be able to build a mass coalition. Yet even then, I did not think he could win. Now I think otherwise. As I look back on the sixties, he was the man who actually could have changed the course of American history.

I met Robert Kennedy only once, but the moment was poignant. I had scheduled a lecture at Butler University in Indianapolis long before the Indiana primary became the first battleground for Kennedy and McCarthy. Before I left, I had called Arthur Schlesinger to tell him that I wanted to work for Kennedy, and at a press conference before my speech I had stated my preference for Kennedy on local television. That night, after I had finished at Butler, I went to a restaurant to meet Dick Goodwin, whom I had known since the anti-poverty task force of 1964. Kennedy was with him; so was the astronaut John Glenn.

"Mike gave you a good endorsement today, Senator," Goodwin said by way of introduction. Kennedy thanked me and then Goodwin added, "He said he couldn't back Rockefeller because he won't spend $150 billion on the cities." "My God," Kennedy replied with a smile, "you didn't say that I would, did you?" Goodwin then suggested that we formed a perfect team—Kennedy could go around the state with Glenn, one of his more conservative supporters, on one side and me on the other. Then we talked seriously, primarily about why so many New York reformers hated Kennedy, a phenomenon that troubled and puzzled him. He told me with a sort of hurt disbelief how a peace activist in San Francisco had spit in his face and called him a fascist.

We talked for an hour or so and then started walking down a chilly and empty street toward Kennedy's hotel at about 12:30 at night. Kennedy asked me if I would campaign for him in California, and I agreed. Suddenly an aging black man ran up and said, "You're Robert Kennedy, aren't you? My wife's sitting back in the car and she wants to meet you." Kennedy pulled his lapels against his face to ward off the cold, and trotted down the deserted avenue to shake one more hand for the day.

In California I reported in to Frank Mankiewicz at the Ambassador Hotel and was immediately dispatched for several days of duty at cocktail parties and colleges around the state. The contradictions of the peace movement were painfully obvious to me as I shuttled from Los Angeles to San Francisco and back. I defended Kennedy from the charge of being too conservative at a luxurious Beverly Hills home. At Berkeley, where I spoke from the steps of Sproul Hall, some young radicals in the crowd—perhaps the one who had spit in Kennedy's face was among them—catcalled as if I were speaking on behalf of the candidate of the Far Right. The prospect of a successful mainstream movement that would win real workers and blacks to the cause of peace and social change was not written in their sectarian scenarios and, in any event, a victory of the Left would destroy their righteous isolation.

There were other, more hopeful, moments in that brief California swing. At Los Angeles State I spoke at a rally with Cesar Chavez, that luminous apostle of nonviolence among the migrants, and John Lewis, one of the first leaders of the Student Nonviolent Coordinating Committee. Even though it was clear that we were reaching out to the people—the Chicanos knew Kennedy as the one Senator who had supported their union in its most difficult hours and who had come to break bread with Cesar Chavez when he ended a fast—I still thought we were going to lose. Kennedy, it seemed to me, would rally the most effective opposition to the war; he could not, I felt, win the Presidency. The day of his funeral, I understood that I had been wrong.

No one who traveled on that funeral train from New York to Washington will ever forget the emotion of that day. As we emerged from the tunnel on the New Jersey side of the river, we saw the first of that endless line of people who were to stand alongside the track in grieving respect. There were isolated figures; sometimes a veteran standing at salute; groups of nuns and schoolchildren; and everywhere, the black and the poor. I could not look out the window very often, because every time I did, I began to cry. The sorrowing faces along the way were a mirror of my own feelings. At Baltimore the station was packed and as we moved slowly toward it along an embankment, you could look down the streets of the ghetto and see the people standing and staring.

Inside the train the atmosphere was like many Irish wakes I have known. The genius of that macabre institution is to ritualize social relationships so as to distract the living from the intolerable fact of death. Some people drank; others chatted about politics. Ethel Kennedy and Edward Kennedy walked the length of that train and shook hands with every person on it. Daniel Patrick Moynihan, Adam Yarmolinsky, Frank Mankiewicz and I were talking and Pat said that, by God, all we really do well is to bury our dead. Then he said, look at this train, there is a government riding on it. And indeed, among the politicians, old and new, the intellectuals and the trade unionists, the blacks and the Chicanos on the train was the administration of Robert Kennedy that was never going to be.

Perhaps, as David Halberstam suggested at the end of his moving book on that campaign, it took Robert Kennedy's death to make the people realize how much they needed him. I think that was part of the emotion of that day, but not all of it. As the brother of the slain President, Robert Kennedy had touched millions; as the one white politician of stature who could communicate his passionate concern for blacks and Chicanos and the minorities, he had built up a new constituency; as the man who would have stopped the Vietnam war, he would have won the McCarthy activists to his banner in a general election campaign. He could reach out to Polish-American workers in Gary—and to the blacks, whom they feared. He was the one leader in America who could have led the nation out of the morass into which Vietnam had plunged it.

IV

Robert Kennedy might have united the quarreling factions of the Democratic party behind his candidacy in 1968. But with his death, the potential Democratic coalition disintegrated, and as a result Richard Nixon was twice elected President of the United States. During and after these events we socialists debated a critical question: What are the social forces which can be brought together in a majority coalition that will offer a progressive alternative to Nixon? At the center of our discussion was the issue of the American working class.

For years most intellectuals and scholars in this country were wrong about the working class and we—those of us in the socialist cadre who opposed the war and those who did not—were right. I put the matter with such arrogance because it is important to understand how Max Shachtman and his friends concluded that educated and affluent thinkers are so blinded by class prejudice that they cannot be trusted on any issue, including Vietnam. The "end of ideology" theorists of the late fifties and early sixties had argued that the Gross National Product had become so large that it was no longer necessary for antagonistic classes to struggle over its distribution. Now, they said, all groups could advance together. In a popular form this thesis was the philosophy of Lyndon Johnson's Great Society. Henry Ford and Walter Reuther, Martin Luther King, Jr., and moderate Dixiecrats were supposed to cooperate for the greater glory and prosperity of all. The class struggle was over.

Ironically, some conservative Republicans were taken in by all this talk (which reinforced their deepest misconceptions) and they insisted in the Landrum-Griffin law of 1959 that the rank and file be given the legal right to overrule their union leaders. In that way, these anti-unionists thought, the inherent conservatism of the average worker would act as a check upon the radical tendencies of the labor bureaucrat. The ranks immediately proceeded to use these new rights to reject the contracts their leaders had negotiated for them and to demand more money and better working conditions. Then, in the mid-sixties, the Vietnam-induced inflation wiped out wage gains and labor had to engage in bitter struggles simply to maintain a living standard it thought it had already won.

Intellectuals began to notice the existence of workers as a social class with its own institutions and attitudes. At the same time, the New Left was reaching the high point of its influence on campus and was turning from a nonideological radicalism to a vulgar Marxism mixed with more than a little middle-class petulance. Many sons and daughters of the upper middle class now began to argue for an alliance of workers and students. The working class to which the New Leftists referred —far to the Left of the union leadership, incipiently radical, proletarian according to the rubric of the *Communist Manifesto*—did not exist. Even so, their fascination with the subject was one more factor in making the society conscious that some kind of working class did in fact exist.

Within our socialist cadre, our conceptions of the working class did not derive from the events and intellectual fads of the sixties but from a much more general, more solidly based, Marxian perspective. Throughout the fifties we had rightly insisted that the typical worker, though not poor, was systematically deprived of enough income for a decent life. Moreover, we said that working in a factory, or behind the wheel of a truck, was a qualitatively different experience from life in the executive suite or even at the bank teller's window. Therefore there were class institutions, the trade unions, and class political organizations like COPE for mobilizing the labor vote.

In the fifties we developed this essentially accurate, somewhat romantic—and in the world of that period, lonely—analysis of the working class. We thought that the ranks of the labor movement were going to be radicalized. In the course of our evolution during the late fifties and the sixties, we had developed ties with a broad range of unionists, Meanyites as well as Reutherites. It was a point of pride with us that we did not look to the working class as it should be (i.e., as we wanted it to be), but as it actually was. In doing so, we risked our socialist souls, but then, taking risks is a normal hazard for any serious Leftist.

So when Hubert Humphrey emerged as the only real alternative to Richard Nixon in 1968, all of us backed him. Some did so with enthusiasm because they essentially shared Meany's support of the Johnson Administration, including its Vietnam policy. Others, like myself, did so because we understood that Humphrey, despite his association with America's tragic policy in Southeast Asia, was infinitely preferable to Richard Nixon. In this, what separated me from the McCarthy activists with whom I had worked was precisely our class analysis of American politics. For them, Humphrey's labor support was a mark against him. Was he not being backed by partisans of the war? For me, it was a major factor in his favor. It meant that his commitment to full employment, his racial policies, his Supreme Court nominations would be fundamentally better than Nixon's and that his foreign policy could not be worse.

Since I considered both labor and the peace movement essential to a progressive coalition, I spoke out for Humphrey during the campaign. It was not a particularly fashionable thing to do among the affluent Left. One night I spoke at a rally at the Palace Theatre for Paul O'Dwyer, the McCarthy partisan who had won the Democratic nomination for Senator. O'Dwyer had not yet made his endorsement of Humphrey and there was quite a bit of baiting of the Vice President. When I said that everyone should vote for Humphrey, I was not booed, but there was an air of shocked disbelief in the audience. At another rally at Manhattan Center veterans of the McCarthy and Kennedy campaigns did speak out for Humphrey—Arthur Schlesinger, Jr., and John Kenneth Galbraith among them. While Galbraith was at the podium two "crazies" came down the aisle, stark naked, and presented him with a pig's head on a platter.

This was an extreme case of the malaise among a fair number in the new peace constituency: the idea that "doing one's own thing" was somehow truly radical. What was important to those crazies was the salvation of their own souls on their own terms (preferably on stage). Politics was the decor of their personal drama, and if they were genuinely horrified by the war in Vietnam, their own psyches still came first. Waving a Vietcong flag at a demonstration or disrupting a peace rally—they never tried out their theatrics on less tolerant groups, like the American Legion—would certainly provoke their parents, and that was the essential liberation. That the very same actions might harden their fellow citizens in support of the war was of secondary importance.

Max Shachtman could, and did, point to such incidents as sound proof for his contemptuous dismissal of the entire McCarthy movement. (In fact, the crazies, like the ultra-Leftists in SDS, had been sullen and disappointed when peace became a serious issue through the McCarthy and Kennedy candidacies.) But despite the elitist tendencies in the broad McCarthy constituency, there was also a ready sympathy for the poor, the minorities, the unorganized workers. I felt that that tendency could be deepened, that the convergence of the labor movement and the new issue-oriented stratum was both possible and necessary.

While the McCarthy forces were acting ambiguously during the 1968 general election campaign, the unions were behaving with an exemplary commitment. Though all of the polls told them that Humphrey did not have a chance, they mobilized the workers and challenged the Wallaceites in the shop by arguing that a worker's class interest in Humphrey, i.e., in his job, was more important than any alleged racial interest in Wallace. The result was a remarkable corroboration of the theory that there is a politically conscious working class in America. For it was labor, and labor almost alone, which very nearly made Hubert Humphrey President of the United States in 1968.

Yet it was not as simple as Max—and I—thought. Humphrey received 42 percent of the vote and Nixon 43 percent, but Wallace took over 13 percent, i.e., twice the proportion of Eugene Debs' best year, and four times Norman Thomas' finest showing. We wrongly said to ourselves that we had almost won when in fact the right-of-center vote (Nixon plus Wallace) was about 57 percent as against Humphrey's 42 percent. In other words, the 1972 landslide for Nixon meant that the conservative vote had increased by only 4 percent as compared to 1968. I do not think that Max and his friends understood this complexity. On the basis of 1968, they assumed that labor was a near majority in the United States and they could therefore afford to indulge their opposition to the "New Politics" constituency of McCarthy, Kennedy, and McGovern. In fact, 1968 proved that labor cannot win alone; 1972 showed that the New Politics cannot win alone; and 1976 might prove that together they can carry the nation.

Shachtman and his co-thinkers could plausibly claim that they were being utterly Marxist in lining up more and more uncritically with George Meany. After all, they were proving their loyalty to the existing working class (for they confused the working class with the AFL-CIO and the AFL-CIO with Meany). In this judgment, as in the debate over socialism and morality, there was a dangerous tendency toward a pseudo-Marxist positivism. In France, for instance, Max's logic would have dictated support for the Communist party, the dominant working-class tendency; in Argentina, it would be a rationale for Peronism.

Meany has made enormous strides in his social thinking and has played a progressive role within the merged labor movement. He came from the relatively conservative milieu of the New York building trades, and yet he was a central figure in making the AFL-CIO more political and more concerned with planned social investments. That was no small accomplishment. But there are other tendencies in the movement, too. Walter Reuther was the most obvious example, but there are still others. In the summer of 1972 I went to a Labor for Peace meeting in St. Louis. It was held in a Teamster auditorium and attended by leaders from the Auto Workers; Amalgamated Clothing Workers; State, County and Municipal Employees; the American Federation of Teachers; the Butcher

Workmen; the West Coast Longshoremen; and other major unions.

Shachtman and company did not see these things. Instead they invented a new radical sin: they had become Right-wing sectarians. They employed a Bolshevik style and a purist Marxism in order to side with the forces in the center and right of the labor movement and to ignore the appearance of a new mass constituency with socialist inclinations. The sad climax came at that meeting of the National Committee of the Socialist party in the fall of 1972 when I heard "Marxist" arguments for Nixon.

Did this mean, to use American radicalism's most favored curse, that Max and his followers had "sold out"? Not at all. They were moved, I am convinced, by the most sincere and idealistic considerations. They had, after all, maintained extremely unpopular ideas in the face of government harassment. They could not be bought for money—only for love. And yet, they did pay a price for their commitment. For a series of involved reasons the labor movement normally tends to be rather monolithic. As Gus Tyler put it quite succintly in his *Labor Revolution,* ". . . unions, by their very nature, are easily affected by the virus of bureaucratic rule. Unions tend to be monosocial (like a parish church); to be combative (like an army); to be administrative (like a governmental agency); to be market-oriented (like a business). Taken together, these traits form a strong natural bent in established unions toward the 'one-party' system."

The ideal way for a socialist to relate to such a reality—in the fifties Max and the rest of us would have said the *only* way—is as the elected representative of the rank and file. Then there is no necessity to curry favor with the leadership, to adapt his program, to speak carefully and even deviously. That, however, has been an impossible perspective to maintain in recent years and a man or woman can keep his integrity and independence as a staff member of a union. But when an individual, or a group, assumes the function of being ideologists and political spokesmen for a labor leadership, they must submerge their personal differences, at least in public, and follow the official line at every point. That can be much more corrupting than simply taking money for it involves self-censorship. For instance, *New America,* the Socialist party newspaper edited from 1968 on by one of Max's closest associates, hardly reacted to the epochal struggle of the miners for internal union democracy. It responded to the brutal slaying of the rebel leader, Jock Yablonski, and his wife and daughter primarily in terms of how that tragedy might be used by the foes of labor. Joe Rauh, one of the most honest and decent men in American politics and the lawyer and advisor for the insurgent miners, was heartsick over that article—as well he might have been.

My friends had turned themselves into a fanatically anti-Communist clique of people with staff jobs in unions and related institutions. After the 1972 elections they were instrumental in setting up the Coalition for a Democratic Majority, an organization which argues that the Democrats can win in 1976 by driving the McGovern constituency out of the party. But the real corruption was not careerist or opportunist, it was political and ideological. Socialism was programmatically reduced to the immediate demands of the American labor movement; morality became a sophisticated adaptation to tactical necessity; the socialist function of practical prophecy was dismissed as dilettantish. All this was done by people with the best socialist will in the world. They were not scoundrels who were bought and paid for. That is why they are tragic.

In October, 1972, I resigned my co-chairmanship of the Socialist party. It was an unhappy moment for me personally since it meant breaking with comrades with whom I had worked for twenty years—with whom I had shared the isolation and fraternity of that loft on Fourteenth Street during the McCarthy period. I simply found it impossible to pretend any solidarity with people who, in the name of "Marxism," were helping Richard Nixon. My act was also a small symbolic expression of a larger antagonism, which pitted a section of the labor movement against the McGovern activists and their union allies (of whom, fortunately, there were a good number) in the election of 1972. Shortly after I resigned, Max Shachtman, to whom I am so profoundly indebted despite our differences, died.

What conclusion does one draw from this sad little history? Many radicals would, I am sure, say that it all goes to prove that when a socialist mixes in capitalist politics, he is selling out and has taken the first step down the slippery slope that leads to conservatism. Nonsense. The vocation of a radical in America in the last portion of the twentieth century is to walk a perilous tightrope. He must be true to the socialist vision of a new society and constantly develop and extend its content; and he must bring that vision into contact with the actual movements fighting not to transform the system, but to gain some little increment of dignity or even just a piece of bread.

If the radical becomes totally obsessed with his vision, he will fall off that tightrope into a righteous irrelevance; if he adapts too well to the movement he hopes to inspire, he will fall into a pragmatic irrelevance. His task is to balance vision and practicality, to fight not simply for the next step, but for the next step in a voyage of ten thousand miles. It is a precarious life and, alas, I think that some of my good comrades fell from that tightrope.

8. The Wager

Were I to calculate coldly, the message on my fragments of the century would be easy enough to decipher: my dreams for a socialist society of brotherhood and justice are a delusion.

As I said at the outset, this book, and my life and times thus far, describe a vicious circle. They begin in the time of Cold War and anti-libertarian repression, proceed through the somnolence of the Eisenhower years, and climax in the schizophrenic decade of the sixties. Now that we are once again in a period of reaction it would be easy to conclude that the notion that men and women can take command of their own history is preposterous, given the botch they have made of America during the last twenty or so years.

I do not come to that conclusion. I still seek the radical and democratic transformation not only of the United States, but of the world. In part, I base myself on people I have known and analyses I have read; in part, I am making an act of faith. But then, even the cynics and the utopia baiters are, though it would embarrass them to recognize it, men of faith. The great fact of these times is that we are in the midst of a transition to a new civilization and no one knows how it will turn out, only that it will be unlike anything that has gone before. None of us living this unprecedented transformation will survive to its completion. All of us who speak of tomorrow, including the naysayers and the pragmatists, are forced to be visionaries.

In what follows I will assert that the future may yet be humanely created but I will also present the contrary evidence, for my point of view is in tension. It is in full knowledge of my fears that I wager the rest of my life on hope.

I

Let me begin with a contradiction. A cultural revolution is taking place within a conservative economy and society and the upheaval is thus often perverse and anomalous. As a result, some say that all change is necessarily disillusioning.

The death of God is a case in point. In the Marxist anticipation, God was supposed to die so that Man could take his place. Until the modern era the supernatural had been the only explanation for a world people could neither understand nor control. But as men began to reshape nature—and, above all, as they turned it to human purposes in a socialist order of their own choosing—they would no longer need such myths.

It is characteristic of this century that a part of this prophecy was fulfilled, but under conditions which the prophets could never imagine. God died, but not under socialism. He disappeared in the midst of a powerful but decadent late capitalism which had rationalized everything except the system as a whole and therefore produced magnificently calibrated crises. So the new demons were more frightening than the thunder and lightning that awed the primitives because they were the bewildering consequences of human genius itself. It is bad enough to be an exile in God's world; it is worse to be a stranger in a world which you yourself have made. I know this as a trend and as an experience.

One morning during the summer of 1972, on Long Island, I was awakened and went out to find a frenzied mother, a neighbor who had just moved in next door, standing in the light rain. She told me that she was afraid that one of her babies, a twin, had died and asked that I go and make sure. So I walked into a still house and peered into one crib, where Lucas Rooney was sleeping peacefully, and then into the other crib, where I discovered Kevin Rooney dead. He had been the victim of sudden infant death syndrome, or "crib death," a disease that kills innocents in the first year of their life for no reason that science has been able to ascertain.

That scene would have moved anyone in any age, and I will never forget Kevin Rooney, or his brother, Lucas, who survived. There was, however, an aspect to that tragedy which was specific to these times. In 1910 one hundred children died out of every thousand born; in 1971, nineteen out of every thousand. The death of a baby was once a common occurrence, known to almost every family (my mother's and father's among them). Now that infant mortality is much rarer, "crib death" is all the more outrageous precisely because we can do nothing about it even with our miraculous medicine. And tomorrow if a way is found to prevent this syndrome, and only five children die out of a thousand, their deaths will become even more intolerable.

Marx thought that socialist man could learn to live with such tragedies. Master of external reality in his daily life, he would be a stoic atheist when confronted with the inevitable limitations of existence. Socialism, it was said, would raise human suffering from a fate to a tragedy.

We, of course, do not have socialism. Instead, there has been a partial, and mainly negative, mutation of the psyche. The old and superstitious restraints have indeed been banished— and with them the old consolations. Yet because our powers perplex us rather than make us confident, we have not built a naturalistic culture. We are, in the midst of our unprecedented and increasingly social achievements, lonely; the death of a baby becomes all but unbearable.

Birth and death have become problematic; so has copulation.

In the Greenwich Village of my young manhood, our rebellion against conventional morality was, as I noted earlier, moralistic. We were not engaged in aimless rutting but living according to the precepts of a strict anti-code. Just as the avant-garde artists had the philistines to remind them precisely how not to paint, we had prudes who helped define our emancipation. We were not as guilt-ridden as that most straightlaced of dandies, Charles Baudelaire, who declared that it was the sense of sin that distinguished the coupling of

men and women from that of animals. But even our briefest
encounters were, among other things, a choice, an affirmation
of values.

Though some of us did not know it, we thereby participated in a historic tradition. In the eighteenth century the assault of the aristocratic French libertines upon the mores of
the time was a precursor of the Revolution. The Marquis de
Sade, freed from the Bastille on July 14th, was not simply a
pornographer but a philosopher who counterposed a de-
mented eros to both God and tyrants. He was, as Albert
Camus understood, one of the heirs of Voltaire. But if the
Revolution seemed at first to be the instrument of a new morality, the bourgeoisie quickly acquired a stake in the status
quo and marriage became a central institution for the preser-
vation of private property and public decency. So capitalist
society became hypocritically puritanical with its double
standard for men and women and—even in Victorian England—its vast underworld of prostitution.

This was one historic source of that united front of political
and sexual radicalism that I described in Chapter 2. "Bourgeois" applied to a lying ethic and a vulgar aesthetic as well as
to a system of economic relations. In its first stage, the
Russian Revolution seemed to fulfill the socialist hopes that
the oppression of human sensuousness would be overthrown
along with the old order. As late as 1929, *Under the Banner
of Marxism,* an official journal of the Communist International, published Wilhelm Reich's "Dialectical Materialism and
Psychoanalysis," a study in "sex-pol" which defined the revolution as a sexual, as well as a social, liberation.

But Stalin's counterrevolution triumphed in Russia and
abolished the avant-garde legislation on marriage, divorce,
and abortion. The dictator needed large families and, above
all, discipline. Reich, that eccentric genius of the Freudian
Left, was expelled from the Communist movement (even as he
had previously been ostracized from the orthodox analytic
movement).

In Russia, then, the sexual revolution was expropriated

along with the other conquests of October, 1917; in the West, it was coopted. Up until the sixties bourgeois society maintained its official piety about God and Sex, but having effectively given up belief in the former, it had no real basis for limiting the latter. Thus the hallowed rules seemed to self-destruct (and certainly the collapse of Catholic dogmatism had much to do with the moment). At the National Students Association congress in 1961 the struggle was raised against the doctrine of *in loco parentis,* the rationale for supervision of the social and sexual lives of students by college administrations. We thought it was going to be a long and bitter battle. The opposition collapsed within five years.

This did not happen, however, according to the Marxist scenario. It was not part of a great movement that transformed economic structures as well as inhibitions. So instead of a new morality there was the *Playboy* philosophy. In a series of long articles in the most successful magazine of the post-war period, Hugh Hefner, its creator, made a radical, and generally excellent, case for civil liberties and the right of the individual to pursue sexuality wherever it might lead. This was asserted not in terms of some new and loving ideal of human conduct, but in the name of an acquisitive, egotistic, and utterly bourgeois ethic. Indeed, Hefner can be understood as a sort of erotic Horatio Alger. And just as that mythic entrepreneur required passive workers to cooperate in the fulfillment of his genius, so *Playboy* libertarianism demanded the wholesome, available nudes who were the secret of the magazine's success. The old values were living in sin with the new freedom.

Bertrand Russell made a much more perceptive analysis of what was happening than Hefner. In a discussion of marriage and morals in the twenties (which was cited against him in the antediluvian year of 1940, when he was denied a teaching post at City College for saying that intercourse outside of marriage could be licit), he talked of new trends. With the separation of sex and reproduction, Russell said, many important gains were being made. But there was also the very real possibility of the trivialization of sexual relations and, as a result, of all human relations. One consequence, he argued, was that people might come to care less about the future now that libido was no longer bound up with the survival of the race.

It is, of course, most difficult to assess one's own times, but I think that Russell's profound fears, rather than Hefner's shallow hopes, are being accomplished in this age. There are statistical data showing that a revolution in sexual conduct is indeed taking place (although studies indicate that the way we talked about the subject changed first and that behavior only caught up with candor sometime in the sixties). There is no indication, however, that it is having that emancipatory effect predicted by the Freudian—and Marxist—Left. The cultural revolution has been subverted by the conservative society in which it is taking place.

Or am I too gentle with my own hopes? Up until now I have been making a most optimistic assumption: if only the social revolution had taken place in the economy, then the changes in the superstructure—in our heads—would have been much more ennobling. A warm and loving society would have made possible warm and loving relationships. But is the problem the incomplete and contradictory transformation, of libertarian wine in bourgeois bottles, or is it deeper than that, a matter of the impossibility of creating a naturalistic and godless culture?

I have at times speculated about the role of ritual in a socialist society. Was it only a transient limitation of pre-socialist mankind that people wanted an outward sign of inner grace —a sacrament, be it religious or secular? That is the function of liturgies and flags and anthems, all of which speak to the God-seeker in us, that desire for a palpable purpose larger than we are. The religious, and repressive, view of sexuality with its insistence upon the higher meaning of pleasure provided that. But will these yearnings for a mysterious wholeness disappear in a rational world? Is it true, as the "Internationale" sings, that "We want no supreme saviours, no God, no Caesar, no Tribune"?

I do not know. What I do know is that creating a socialist culture is a much more difficult task than building a socialist economy. It can no longer be asserted that once the material base is transformed, then so, too, will be the inner man. It is not as simple as that, as I have learned from living in the midst of a cultural revolution in a conservative society. So I am awed by the audacity of what I still propose: a new civilization. For if the confusions and contradictions of the past decade or so have proved anything, it is that we need not simply economic planning and social allocations of our wondrous powers, but new values, new ways of living and loving.

II

Let me be more concrete, starting with a despairing experience that helps define my generation: watching a city dying.

On a hot summer's day in St. Louis in 1969 I was in a limousine with some relatives, returning from the cemetery where we had buried Aunt Agnes. Uncle Dave decided that, for old times' sake, we would go past the house on Bartmar Street which had been the center of the Fitzgibbon family from the 1920s until the early fifties. That street had once been part of a white middle-class neighborhood of big, three-story homes with leisurely porches and ample yards, like the one in which my grandfather grew his prize roses. Now it had become a black ghetto and the houses were disintegrating rapidly; some were already deserted. Everything seemed broken, burned, decayed; it looked like a devastated area in a war zone.

In Manhattan one does not see such physical ruin, yet the change during the more than twenty years I have lived here is just as unmistakable. The New York I discovered with all the passion of a convert is not the New York I live in now. It is not simply that builders seem to dismantle old Manhattan every morning and construct it anew by evening, although frantic architectural change is certainly part of the phenomenon. More than that, the population, the mood, the very spirit of the city have been altered beyond recognition. In 1950, when I began to frequent the White Horse Tavern on the West Side of Greenwich Village, I lived on the Lower East Side between Avenues C and D. Of a spring night, at two or three o'clock, I would leave the Horse and walk across the Village, pass through the Ukrainian community around First Avenue, cross Tompkins Square Park with its once-elegant town houses, and arrive in the streets of the Jewish ghetto. Sometimes as I came down Avenue C near dawn the merchants would be setting up their fruit and vegetable stalls. In that walk across Manhattan Island in the middle of the night I never once felt fear.

Living in New York in those days was to participate in an unobtrusive arrogance. I formulated that superiority complex one evening in 1950, sitting in the balcony of the Loew's Sheridan movie theatre (it has since, of course, been razed). I was watching *On the Town,* a musical that celebrates Manhattan, and I suddenly realized that New York was the only city in the United States that did not need a booster organization. People in Chicago or San Francisco always told you how many poets and painters and fine restaurants their town had. In New York we simply assumed that we were the best —in baseball as well as intellect, in brashness and in subtlety, in everything—and it would have been unseemly to remark upon such an obvious fact.

Manhattan was, as E. B. White wrote in that period, the one place in America where you never knew whom you might meet, or see, next. The Saturday when standard changed to daylight time in the spring of 1950 and cut the drinking time by one hour at the San Remo, a group of us simply walked up to Dylan Thomas, whom we did not know, and suggested a party. He invited us to his own party and I went off into the night excited that I was about to spend time with one of the finest living poets. To my great chagrin, Thomas did not discuss prosody with us but seduced the hostess with lightning speed and slipped into a bedroom instead. Still, one never knew when there would be a brush with fame, or even with genius.

Most of what I have just said about New York is, of

course, the prejudiced nostalgia of a privileged middle-class white. For the social peace of the city in those days was attributable, in part at least, to the silent suffering of people who did not bother their fellow citizens about the intolerable. And yet the mood I describe seemed to extend to all classes and races. We all knew—even if the psychic income was no substitute for food and medicine—that we were the best.

In the spring of 1968 I went back to that block where I had lived on the Lower East Side. A photographer for *Fortune* wanted a moody background picture for an article on my book *Toward a Democratic Left*. On Fifth Street the orthodox Jewish students with their black hats, their long coats, and their hair curled at the temples in a *payess* were gone; in their places were blacks and Puerto Ricans. The tenements had, like those houses on Bartmar in St. Louis, begun to rot of their own weight and the sidewalks exuded violence and hostility. I was now a bit apprehensive in the broad daylight on a street I used to walk without concern at three in the morning.

My experience was not isolated. For some years now the writers and intellectuals I know have not gathered in smug communion to describe the wonders of our city. We trade stories instead on how brutish and fearful life is becoming and how the streets are filthy with the droppings of myriad dogs. In the apartment where I am now writing there are metal shutters on the windows and doors, and the insurance company would not write a policy unless I agreed to install a burglar alarm. The taxis have bullet-proof partitions between the driver and the rider and armed guards stand outside most large buildings.

Where did they go, the St. Louis of my childhood and the New York of 1949? It is not just that I have grown older and a bit tired. When the mayor of Boston toured the devastated Brownsville section of Brooklyn in 1971, he said that the social ruin which he saw about him was "the first tangible sign of the collapse of our civilization." That portentous perception is not wide of the mark. Why?

The answer given by more and more intellectuals in the 1970s is neo-conservative: the spectacular failures of our various programs of the sixties, they say, simply prove that government planning and intervention cannot accomplish intelligent reform, much less a socialist transformation. But, in fact, the dying of the cities proves that Washington can indeed act effectively to implement its intentions. Our policies worked. The real problem is that they were tragically wrong, containing a hidden agenda for the destruction of the great cities.

The federal government underwrote and encouraged the most anti-social possibilities of our technology. By and large, the character of the gigantic shift in American population during the post-war period—and the urban death agony which was one of its results—was determined by a set of disastrous incentives created in Washington. If these policies were mad from the point of view of society as a whole, they made a great deal of sense to the corporate powers whose private interests were thereby socialized.

Agricultural subsidies, the Joint Economic Committee estimated in 1972, cost the public about $10 billion a year ($5.2 billion in direct outlays, $4.2 billion in increased consumer prices). Most of that money goes, of course, to rich and corporate farmers, and it has, among other things, permitted them to mechanize at twice the rate of factories since World War II. Over the years tens of billions in subsidies have helped drive poor, miserably educated people off the land and into the central cities. In the South a high proportion of these displaced persons from the rural economy have been black. And though the government spent money lavishly to maintain the living standard of those who were doing the dispossessing, it did practically nothing for the dispossessed.

In 1969 the then mayor of Atlanta, Ivan Allen, understood the effects of this process if not the cause. "We are the victims," Allen said at a White House meeting, "of the migration of twenty million people—all poor and most Negro." To which he should have added: and all forced or induced to migrate by federal policies. Richard Nixon himself intimated that incredible truth even though he did not state it in so many words. In a 1969 memo the new President wrote, "The American national government has responded to urban concerns in a haphazard, fragmented and often woefully shortsighted manner (as when the great agricultural migration from the South was allowed to take place with no adjustment or relocation arrangements whatever)." Only reality is more fantastic than Nixon's definition of it, for the migrations did not "take place" but were the inevitable consequence of federal programs that followed commercial priorities, i.e., gave to the rich rather than to the poor.

While the government was thus encouraging this migration of poor and unschooled people to the big cities, it was also subsidizing the exodus of the middle class out of those same cities. In 1972 alone there was more than $12 billion in "tax expenditures" for primarily middle-class and rich homeowners (this took the form of two deductions—for the interest on mortgage payments and for property taxes—and from the fact that Internal Revenue does not count the rental value of owner-occupied housing as income). That was well over twelve times the amount spent on low-income housing—but it was handed out discreetly, without any of the stigma associated with the official, and public, charity for the poor. Moreover, the main program designed to help those at the bottom of the economy—Section 235 of the Housing Code which provided federal subsidies for home ownership by the poverty-stricken—was used by unscrupulous speculators to sell substandard housing at inflated prices. Then—and here is part of the key to what happened to Bartmar Avenue in St. Louis—when the poor were unable to keep rickety, shoddy houses from falling down, they were accused of racial character deficiencies. The actual culprits were the Department of Housing and Urban Development and the private real estate industry.

Federal policies, in short, helped transform the class and racial composition of the great cities in a way that made them helpless to deal with a crisis subsidized by Washington.

In New York City that meant a vast increase in the number of those whom society had made desperate as well as an equally vast exodus of more stable families. For the average citizen, the most obvious feature of this process was an increase in the number of the impoverished minorities. In 1960, 14 percent of New York City was black; in 1970, 21 percent. Much of this growth in the Negro population came from the South, or from among the Southern-born, i.e., from those who usually were woefully unprepared to compete in a sophisticated urban labor market. At the same time, the income received by working people in general in New York, and by menial workers in particular, was inadequate and, in the lower reaches, utterly so. So there was a quantum leap in the welfare rolls.

The white man in the street was not aware of the complicated, and often perverse, federal forces behind these developments. For him, all his problems were simply the result of a flood of blacks and Puerto Ricans whom he regarded, more likely than not, as lazy welfare cheats. The minorities, on the other hand, were aware of how excruciatingly slow their progress was; they were also more terrified by crime in the streets than any other group (they suffered from it more than anyone else). Then the plague of heroin addiction spread among the young. Have-nots fought with have-littles. The city became increasingly hostile and antagonistic and the optimism in its soul was destroyed.

I do not for a moment want to suggest that it would have been simple to avoid this catastrophe—this is not the case at all—but I do want to stress that there was a hidden federal policy at work. Most of the government programs, from agriculture through housing to highways, had the consequence (sometimes unintended) of constantly socializing on behalf of the rich rather than the poor, of worsening (sometimes even creating) crises which the government then deplored. We did indeed act massively and audaciously—but thoughtlessly and in the wrong direction.

Another and related reason for the dying of New York City

is much more difficult to describe. It grows out of a completely justified revolt against oppression.

There was social peace in New York in 1949 in part because many blacks were not fighting against the unconscionable conditions under which they were forced to live. When I first started going to Harlem as a civil rights activist in the mid-fifties, I could roam the streets of that community, not because I was greeted as a brother in the struggle, but because I was a white man. Many Negroes protested that officials allowed more open crime—vice, narcotics, gambling—in their neighborhoods than in white areas, but their complaints had little effect. So the white outsider, even the one who came with open arms, was "protected" by the deference, and even fear, accorded to the color of his skin.

The frustrations and miseries of ghetto life were almost exclusively turned inward, expressed in street gangs, then in heroin addiction, and perpetually in violence. The relative quiet and safety I enjoyed in the Village and the Lower East Side were partly due to the fact that destructiveness had been quarantined in one section of the city. But then a number of developments intersected. Martin Luther King, Jr., led the heroic and nonviolent battle against racist laws and in the process desanctified white authority in general. A sense of relative deprivation grew as television vividly reported to slumdwellers on the affluent society from which they were excluded. At the same time, there was a psychic transformation among blacks and they no longer deferred to the Man. These tendencies asserted themselves precisely at a time of considerable migration from the backwoods South.

These various trends were not a fate. If the war in Vietnam had not diverted America from its most urgent domestic priorities, if there had been real and tangible gains for the civil rights movement, then most of the new militancy would have found constructive channels. In Montgomery, Alabama, during the boycott led by King in 1955, there were no sermons against crime, but it declined among blacks anyway. The lives of the people had been made more meaningful by the boycott; they had achieved a dignity that was incompatible with some of the old patterns of behavior.

In the sixties the opposite effect occurred. After all the lofty rhetoric of the first half of the decade—the media had proclaimed nothing less than a revolution and a Southern-born President had said, "We shall overcome"—there came the failures and betrayals of the war and the concomitant retreat from social commitment. The courageous then dug in for the long struggle; others went back to the privacy of careers or the self-immolation of drink and drugs; while still others turned to individualistic violence. The last were not the snipers and guerrillas; they were the furies of a blind and unpolitical rage.

Many good and sincere people looked upon this debacle and were dismayed. We did so much, they said to themselves, and it has come to naught. Therefore, they concluded, we must aspire less. These were the liberal conservatives of the 1970s.

III

The liberal conservatives were once liberals (or even radicals) who supported the social programs of Kennedy and Johnson. They believed the rhetoric of those efforts and did not notice that, along with some quite valuable increments of reform, the government was still operating primarily on the basis of anti-social—which is to say, private and corporate—priorities. Then the war in Vietnam subverted even the modest gains that had been made. Viewing the patent failure of programs but ignoring the fact that they had been designed so they could not succeed, the disappointed liberalism of some turned into a new conservatism.

An Englishman, Michael Oakeshott, had arrived at such conclusions a generation earlier than the neo-conservatives and became their guru. He wrote in 1962 that "innovating is an activity which generates not only the 'improvement' sought, but a new and complex situation of which this is only one of the components. The total change is always more extensive than the change designed; and the whole of what is entailed can neither be foreseen nor circumscribed. Thus, whenever there is innovation there is the certainty that change will be greater than was intended, that there will be loss as well as gain, and that the loss and the gain will not be equally distributed among the people affected; there is the chance that the benefits derived will be greater than those which were designed; and there is the risk that they will be offset by changes for the worse."

This analysis seemed to offer a profound explanation of what went wrong in the sixties and Oakeshott's attitude was adopted, in one form or another, by thinkers who wrote for magazines like *The Public Interest* and *Commentary*. Nathan Glazer's article, "The Limits of Social Policy," * provides an excellent framework for a brief look at this mood.

Glazer's article had quite an impact on the American intellectual community and, according to the testimony of Daniel Patrick Moynihan, was also read with sympathy by the President of the United States. How is it that a social critic who regarded himself as a moderate radical in 1960 is on the same wavelength as a reactionary Republican President a little more than ten years later? Glazer has an honorable record as an opponent of the Vietnam war (I remember him as one of the faculty members who helped me when I campaigned for Robert Kennedy in California in 1968) and he has long fought racism, poverty, and the other disorders of domestic American society. It is because I credit his *bona fides* that I take him so seriously.

Two factors played an important role in this transformation. Glazer was "deradicalized" because he saw the confrontationist Left of the sixties as intolerant, anti-libertarian, and basically destructive of the values upon which universities are built. That was more certainly true of that fringe of ultras who, when the horror of Vietnam burst upon the American consciousness, momentarily assumed an exaggerated impor-

* *Commentary*, September, 1971.

tance. But it did not, and does not, apply to that mass constituency which rallied to McCarthy, Robert Kennedy, and McGovern. But if one wrongly assumes that the nihilistic fringe of the sixties Left was representative of the Left itself, then Glazer's reaction is quite logical.

Secondly, Glazer is reacting against the era of the sixties. "Social policy," he writes, "is an effort to deal with the breakdown of traditional ways of handling distress." That, in itself, is an extraordinarily conservative definition. It would be much more accurate to say that social policy today is an effort to deal with unprecedented forms of distress caused by a technological revolution about which tradition knows nothing. "In its efforts to deal with the breakdown of these traditional structures, however," Glazer continues, "social policy tends to encourage their further weakening." Therefore: ". . . some important part of the solutions to our social problems lies in the traditional practices and traditional restraints." But how can one make the astounding assumption that traditional practices and restraints are still viable in the late twentieth century?

Our lack of knowledge, Glazer further argues, profoundly limits what we can do. He cites the failure of our housing program as one example that offers an excellent case for the theory that we have failed because we tried to do too much.

In 1949 Senator Robert Taft, the leading Republican conservative of his generation, concluded that the private housing market would not meet the needs of the poor. As a consistent and principled champion of free enterprise he therefore decided that this was one of those exceptional areas that demanded a public market. Taft became a sponsor of the Taft-Ellender-Wagner Housing Act of 1949. At that time he spoke of the necessity of building 810,000 units of low-cost housing in five years. As of 1973, those 810,000 units have not yet been built. That is hardly a case of excessive innovation.

In 1967 the Johnson Administration announced the New Towns in Towns program, a scheme designed to utilize surplus federal land in the central cities to alleviate the housing problems of the poor. There was the usual fanfare associated with the plans of the Great Society, and the innocent bystander, or even the academic professional, might have mistakenly thought that something was being done. As of 1972 that program had achieved the construction of less than 300 units of housing, i.e., less than a medium-sized private developer would have accomplished in the same period.

In 1968 there was another historic statement of intent. The language of the 1949 Act was repeated in the 1968 Housing and Urban Development law. This was done without embarrassment even though it constituted an official admission of one generation of failure and one generation of inaction. The country was then told that the government would insist on the creation of 26 million new units of housing—2.6 million for low-income people—within the next ten years. When the Nixon Administration took office, George Romney, perhaps its most conscientious and socially concerned Cabinet member, resolved to redeem the broken promises. There was much talk about technological innovation in "Operation Breakthrough." It produced little beyond the press releases, while the reality of Section 235 of the Housing Code subsidized private speculators to sell shoddy homes to the poor.

By 1973, the Nixon Administration announced that it was stopping all housing subsidy programs—the nation was running a 45 percent deficit on the 1968 goals—and the *Wall Street Journal* editorialized about the need to let market forces take over in this area. In the *Journal's* perspective, the central cities should be allowed to rot to the point where land became so cheap that businessmen would once again want to buy or rent it. There was no comment on what would happen in the interim to the millions condemned to suffer in the slums until supply and demand achieved their providential equilibrium. Like Nassau Senior, who wanted the Irish to starve in appropriate numbers to make laissez-faire work during the potato famine of the 1840's, the *Journal* did not concern itself with that human problem.

It may well be that we do not know enough about building

decent housing. Certainly the housing projects in the United States have been a failure. But even if that is true (and the fact that Europeans have built excellent new cities shows that it need not be), the actual reason for the American failure was not, as Glazer suggests, the humbling limits of our social knowledge. It was the fact that the government announced great programs but actually did very little, and that its basic priorities in this area as in every other were private and profit-oriented.

Daniel Patrick Moynihan, an associate of Glazer's, made a fine summary of the real problem in his book, *The Politics of the Guaranteed Annual Income*. He wrote of the sixties that "the social reforms of the mid-decade had been oversold, and, with the coming of the war, underfinanced to the degree that seeming failure could be ascribed almost to intent." Therefore, it is necessary to turn our new conventional—and conservative—wisdom upside down. We failed in the sixties not because we did too much, but because we did too little. Moreover, if we had acted radically, we could have simplified problems rather than making them more complex. The cautious policy of running job-training programs without providing work for the relatively few people lucky enough to enter them vitiated the effort; a decisive policy which would have guaranteed a job to every able-bodied citizen would not have failed.

Because they believe the Great Society's myth about itself, confusing promise with performance, Glazer and his friends advise caution and timidity and look backward. Glazer writes, "Ultimately we are not kept healthy, I believe, by new scientific knowledge or more effective curses or even better-organized medical care services. We are kept healthy by certain patterns of life." That is not true. The most traditionalist and family-centered places on the globe are, as a rule, the least healthy; the most modern—and deracinated—are the most healthy. But even if there were some validity in Glazer's romantic theory, the fact is that we cannot go back to the organic order of things.

The planet is collectivizing itself everywhere: in America, Russia, China, the Third World. The question is not, therefore, Will the future be collectivist? It is, rather, Can the collectivist future be made humane and democratic and libertarian? There is no choice but to be as revolutionary as the revolution that is already taking place. I do not thereby argue for some inevitable wave of the future. Perhaps human history will turn out to have been tragic; perhaps man will lose. But that issue is not yet settled and as long as it is in doubt one must struggle to make the prodigies of our hand and brain free us rather than enslave us.

I know these things in my head. I have seen them in a traffic jam on the Long Island Expressway. That breakdown is the work of cooperative genius: the serried automobiles from Detroit and Japan and Germany are products of a technology without frontiers, bringing thousands of people close together on an intricate system of high-speed roads overlooked by towering apartment buildings. The scene is utterly anti-social. The individuals, the families, are cooped up in the privacy of their cars, plugged into distant music, competing sometimes viciously with horns and curses for tiny little advantages of space and position, sometimes moving more slowly than the horses their grandparents rode. Our ingenious helplessness, our massed loneliness, are there to see. They are the quintessence of that socialization without solidarity (the phrase is Max Adler's) that is the all-too-possible future. Socialism is problematic, even difficult to imagine; it is also the only humane alternative.

The neo-conservatives speak as if the revolution of these times will moderate itself if only we are more humble. That is nonsense. It will then only proceed behind our chastened backs toward its worst variant. These thinkers have not listened to the century in which they live. They often provide shrewd and informed insights into particular issues and they usefully deflate the pretenses of the Left. All they miss is the most important happening of the age—a revolution that is inevitable in everything except its outcome.

IV

It was a cold day in New York City in late February, 1973. The caucus which I had led within the Socialist party—and which had been defeated in two conventions—had just held a conference. Trade unionists and intellectuals and students had discussed, with remarkable spirit, what to do after the political debacle of the 1972 Presidential campaign. Now the socialists among us were going to talk about our own perspectives.

We gathered on a Sunday morning at a seedy, decayed West Side hotel which, by the looks of it, certainly housed welfare recipients. Outside was the province of junkies and muggers and the fearful middle class. A black woman, thin and blank-eyed, surely an addict and probably a prostitute, leaned against the wall near the door. Our meeting room was shabby but it must have recently been used for a party or a reception because half-torn white streamers were hanging from the ceiling. We were a handful of people, perhaps eighty in all, the defeated remnant of a defeated remnant.

There was a lengthy discussion and gradually, imperceptibly, everyone recognized the mutual desire to make yet another new departure and to build a new socialist organization. The debate ended, the consensus emerged. I made a motion that we work toward a founding conference in the fall, and it passed unanimously. People milled around and suddenly a circle formed and some comrades began to sing the "Internationale."

That is how the revolution goes forward sometimes, in such ridiculous settings, sometimes among just a few people. The transformations of this century are not merely a matter of historic events; there is no day on which history will leap from necessity to freedom. There is rather a molecular process, composed of millions and even billions of personal decisions, whereby men and women assert their will to take control of their own destiny. "When the Communist artisans come together," Marx wrote in the 1840s, "at first theory and propaganda are their purpose. But at the same time they acquire a new need, the need for society, and what appears as means becomes end." Our tiny group in that West Side hotel was only a beginning, and most likely an insignificant one in the perspective of the twenty-first century. But if we do not begin, who will?

I do not romanticize, even though there is now a Pascalian cast to my Marxism. I am excruciatingly aware of the socialist failures of the past and of our woeful inadequacies in the present. But precisely because the social classes wearing their economic masks did not act exactly as they were supposed to and the struggle therefore became more complex and ambiguous than Marx ever imagined, the individual decision has become more important. That is not to say that the socialist ideal is merely a matter of private wish. Socialism is today the dream of the majority of mankind, even, as Hungary and Poland in 1956 and Czechoslovakia in 1968 show, of those who have been oppressed by imposters speaking its name. And yet, after more than a century, it is still beginning, a task to be accomplished, not a destiny to be awaited.

No one knows how the history we are living is going to turn out. All that is now possible in the midst of this unprecedented transition is to try to piece together our fragments. The ideal is, as George Lukacs once stated it, to understand the present as history, as the future in the process of becoming. That is what I have tried to do in this book, to see the massive trends in my experience, to learn from my experience about the trends. And yet, ultimately, we can only intuit the patterns. We can say that as long as it is even possible that these fragments can be assembled in a new wholeness, that these disintegrations can be made into the preparation for a new synthesis, then we must wager our lives on that possibility. Precluded from ever knowing whether we were right or wrong, we must begin the fight again, even if in a seedy room in a decaying hotel.